S-77 Law $5 95   F

S0-AGA-933

Israel & LaFave 2d Ed.

Editorial and Advisory Board

NUTSHELL SERIES

JESSE H. CHOPER
Professor of Law
University of California, Berkeley

DAVID P. CURRIE
Professor of Law
University of Chicago

YALE KAMISAR
Professor of Law
University of Michigan

ROBERT E. KEETON
Professor of Law
Harvard University

RICHARD C. MAXWELL
Professor of Law
University of California, Los Angeles

MICHAEL I. SOVERN
Dean and Professor of Law
Columbia University

CHARLES ALAN WRIGHT
Professor of Law
University of Texas

II

CRIMINAL PROCEDURE IN A NUTSHELL

CONSTITUTIONAL LIMITATIONS

By

JEROLD H. ISRAEL
Professor of Law, University of Michigan

WAYNE R. LaFAVE
Professor of Law, University of Illinois

Second Edition

ST. PAUL, MINN.

WEST PUBLISHING CO.

1975

COPYRIGHT © 1971 ISRAEL and LaFAVE

COPYRIGHT © 1975
By
JEROLD H. ISRAEL
and
WAYNE R. LaFAVE
All rights reserved

Library of Congress Catalog Card Number: 75–14986

Israel & LaFave Const.Cr.Proc.2d Ed.

PREFACE

This brief text is intended primarily for use by law students during their study of the ever-expanding field of criminal procedure. In preparing these materials, we have attempted to set forth as succinctly and clearly as possible an analysis of difficult problems of major current significance. In doing so, however, we have not waivered from our firm conviction—which we believe is manifested in our casebook on *Modern Criminal Procedure* (with Professor Yale Kamisar)—that there is no substitute for in-depth study of the basic sources: the leading cases in the field, and the critical and extended analysis of the cases to be found in the legal literature. Rather, we have undertaken this work on the assumption that the diligent student might also profit from a less cluttered look at some of the principal problems in the field. On the basis of our own experience with students and that reported to us by other teachers of criminal procedure, we believe this assumption is valid—that at some point it is useful for the student to examine only the forest and not the trees.

This is not a text on criminal procedure, but rather about *constitutional* criminal procedure. As anyone who has followed the work of the Supreme Court in recent years well knows, we have about reached the point—to borrow Judge Henry Friendly's phrase—where we may view "the Bill of Rights as a code of criminal procedure." Whatever one may think of this significant development, it is apparent that most of the difficult problem areas in the field of criminal procedure are now constitutional in dimension. The "constitutionalized" parts of the criminal justice process can be subjected to analysis in a book of this kind, while the others cannot because of the infinite variations in local practice.

In Chapter One of this book, we have attempted to trace this development whereby the Bill of Rights has attained foremost importance in criminal procedure, and there we have enumerated the many different procedural steps which are now subject to constitutional limitations. At this point, we have again found it necessary to be selective in our treatment, and thus only some of these steps are discussed in more detail in following chapters. We have limited ourselves to the "most pervasive right" to counsel and the various rights which the suspect possesses vis-à-vis the police (including a discussion of the scope of the exclusionary rule sanction used to protect those rights), on the ground that these are the areas in which a student in a basic criminal procedure course is likely to desire some supplementary reading. We conclude with a chapter on habeas corpus, the means by which the above rights are so often vindicated, because we have found that this increasingly intricate subject is a particularly troublesome one for law students.

For the sake of brevity and ease in reading this text, we have departed from the traditional citation style for cases. Where it would not be ambiguous, we have used abbreviations for the name of the governmental unit in the case name (e. g., U.S., N.Y.), and also have shortened the oft-used Commonwealth, People, and State to C., P., and S., respectively. We have cited only the official reporter for Supreme Court decisions, and only the regional reporters for state cases. As to the latter, the court of decision is indicated in parentheses with the date; only the state is indicated when the case was decided by the highest court in that state. Previous discussion of the same case is noted by a page reference within parentheses, and all such citations refer to the pages of this text. Traditional introductory signals ("see", "see, e. g.", and "accord") have been omitted where the case supports the text either through direct ruling, dicta, or the decision's general treatment of a particular issue.

Space limitations have also caused us to cite only leading, recent, and other illustrative cases. This, we again emphasize, should not be taken to mean that secondary sources—books, law re-

view articles, commission reports, and the like—
cannot be of considerable use to the student.
Those secondary materials which we have found
most challenging and helpful are cited in *Modern
Criminal Procedure.*

This text includes cases decided by the United
States Supreme Court through June 30, 1975, the
conclusion of the October 1974 Term.

J. H. I.
W. R. L.

July, 1975

OUTLINE

CHAPTER 2. ARREST, SEARCH AND SEIZURE

CHAPTER 3. WIRETAPPING, ELECTRONIC EAVESDROPPING, AND THE USE OF SECRET AGENTS

OUTLINE

§ 27. The Meaning of Miranda—Continued

CHAPTER 5. LINEUPS AND OTHER PRE-TRIAL IDENTIFICATION PROCEDURES

CHAPTER 6. APPLICATION OF THE EXCLUSIONARY RULE

OUTLINE

CHAPTER 7. RIGHT TO COUNSEL

OUTLINE

CHAPTER 8. RAISING CONSTITUTIONAL CLAIMS

OUTLINE

TABLE OF CASES

[Where a case is discussed continuously on several consecutive pages, only the initial page of discussion is cited. Where a case is discussed at several points in the book, the page reference marking the primary discussion is italicized. Cases titled Commonwealth v., People v., State v., United States v., are listed under the name of the other party.]

A

TABLE OF CASES

TABLE OF CASES

C

TABLE OF CASES

TABLE OF CASES

TABLE OF CASES

TABLE OF CASES

G

TABLE OF CASES

TABLE OF CASES

XXX

TABLE OF CASES

I

J

TABLE OF CASES

K

L

TABLE OF CASES

M

TABLE OF CASES

TABLE OF CASES

P

Q

R

S

TABLE OF CASES

TABLE OF CASES

T

TABLE OF CASES

TABLE OF CASES

TABLE OF CASES

†

CONSTITUTIONAL—CRIMINAL PROCEDURE

CHAPTER 1

THE CONSTITUTIONALIZATION OF CRIMINAL PROCEDURE

---

1. INTRODUCTION

The criminal law "revolution." Few, if any, areas of the law have undergone such significant revision over the last fifteen years as has criminal procedure. Indeed, the change in criminal procedure has been so rapid and far reaching that some commentators have characterized it as a legal "revolution" (although others prefer to view it as merely "accentuated evolution"). The United States Supreme Court has been a primary initiator of this "revolution". Almost every Supreme Court term since 1960 has been marked by several major decisions in the constitutional-criminal procedure area, and many of the significant changes in criminal procedure during this period can be traced to those decisions.

The Constitution and criminal procedure. The significant role of the Supreme Court in the development of criminal procedure is a product, in part, of the special emphasis upon criminal procedure in the United States Constitution. Of 23 separate rights noted in the first eight Amendments, 12 concern criminal procedure. The Fourth Amendment guarantees the right of the people to be secure against unreasonable searches and seizures and prohibits the issuance of warrants unless certain conditions are met. The Fifth Amendment requires prosecution by grand jury indictment for violation of all infamous crimes (excepting certain military prosecutions) and prohibits placing a person "twice in jeopardy" or compelling him to be a "witness against himself." The Sixth Amendment lists several rights that apply "in all criminal prosecutions"— the right to a speedy and public trial by an impartial jury of the state and district in which the crime was committed, notice of the "nature and cause of the accusation," confrontation of opposing witnesses, compulsory process for obtaining favorable witnesses, and the assistance of counsel. The Eighth adds a prohibition against requiring excessive bail. Finally, aside from these "specific guarantees," the Fifth Amendment's general prohibition against the "deprivat[ion] of life, liberty or property without due process of law" also encompasses criminal procedure.

Of course, these provisions are not self-defining. The impact of the Constitution upon criminal procedure depends in the end upon the Supreme Court's basic approach in applying these provisions. Interpreted narrowly, the constitutional guarantees would have a minimal effect on criminal procedure; they would govern only limited aspects of the total process and impose restrictions of minor significance in those areas. Interpreted broadly, and supported by various rules and remedies designed to effect their implementation, these guarantees could provide a comprehensive code that governs almost every aspect of criminal procedure. Current constitutional interpretation lies somewhere between these extremes. Several areas of criminal procedure remain largely untouched by Supreme Court decisions, and many others have been subjected to restrictions of limited scope. In other areas, however, the Court's decisions have established comprehensive sets of principles governing every major aspect of procedure.

The decisions of the past fifteen years, although not pointing entirely in one direction, generally have moved towards promoting further "constitutionalization" of criminal procedure. The pace of this movement has, of course, varied with the composition of the Court. The Court of the middle and late 1960's tended to push faster and further towards extensive constitution-

alization than the Court of the early and middle
1970's. The trend has been persistent, however,
throughout the entire period. Admittedly, some
recent decisions have narrowly construed limitations suggested in earlier decisions, and individual
justices have noted a willingness to consider overruling a few of those earlier decisions. Yet, taken
as a whole, the recent decisions still evidence a
movement toward further constitutionalization,
and they offer little to suggest that an overall
shift in approach is likely to occur in the near
future.

The movement towards further constitutionalization has been reflected primarily in two doc-
trinal trends—(1) the expanded application of
the Bill of Rights guarantees to the states via the
Fourteenth Amendment, and (2) the expansion of
the scope of those provisions both as to area of
procedure regulated and degree of regulation.
The sections that follow seek to explore, in a general fashion, the development of both of these
trends.

2. APPLICATION OF BILL OF RIGHTS GUARANTEES TO THE STATES

Introduction. The first 10 Amendments were
enacted as limitations solely upon the federal government. *Barron v. Baltimore,* 7 Pet. 243
(1833). The adoption of the Fourteenth Amend-

ment in 1868, however, significantly extended federal constitutional controls over the action of state governments. That Amendment provides, *inter alia,* that no state may "deprive any person of life, liberty and property without due process of law." From the outset, the Supreme Court has been troubled by the relation of the Fourteenth Amendment limitation upon the states to the Bill of Right's limitations upon the federal government. At least four separate views of the appropriate relationship between the respective Amendments have been advanced by various members of the Court. These views have been debated at length, usually in concurring and dissenting opinions, over the years. Among the most notable discussions are those found in *Adamson v. Cal.,* 332 U.S. 46 (1947); *Pointer v. Texas,* 380 U.S. 400 (1965); and *Duncan v. La.,* 391 U.S. 145 (1968).

A. BASIC INTERPRETATIONS

Fundamental rights interpretation. The "fundamental rights interpretation" of the Fourteenth Amendment finds no necessary relationship between the content of the Fourteenth Amendment and the guarantees of the Bill of Rights. The Fourteenth Amendment due process clause is viewed as incorporating "traditional notions" of due process, described quite generally as those principles "implicit in the concept of ordered liberty." *Palko v. Conn.*, 302 U.S. 319 (1937). As applied to procedure, this view of due process requires that the state afford the defendant "that fundamental fairness essential to the very concept of justice." *Lisenba v. Cal.*, 314 U.S. 219, 236 (1941). While a state violation of a procedural right noted in the Bill of Rights is viewed as a likely indicator that fundamental fairness has been denied, it is not necessarily conclusive.

Supporters of this view argue that, while some of the Bill of Rights guarantees may truly reflect that process needed to achieve fundamental fairness, others may reflect only the "restricted views of Eighteenth Century England regarding the best method for the ascertainment of facts." *Adamson v. Cal.*, supra (Frankfurter, J., con.). Moreover, even those guarantees that encompass fundamental rights may not do so in every aspect of the guarantee. For example, the Fifth Amendment double jeopardy clause prohibits the Federal government from retrying a previously acquitted defendant both where the government's justification for seeking a retrial lies only in its interest in gaining a second chance to prove guilt and where its justification is based on a trial error that tainted the jury verdict. Several authorities suggest, however, that the double jeopardy retrial prohibition is essential to basic fairness only in the former situation, since the government there has had a fair opportunity to present its case. Proceeding from the independent perspective of the Fourteenth Amendment, a court could readily rely upon this analysis to find that the retrial prohibition ordinarily is fundamental (and therefore applicable to the states) only if there were no error in the first trial. Even then, the final determination would be made in terms of the retrial presented in the particular case before the court. Though state retrials of acquitted defendants generally would not violate fundamental rights where based upon trial errors, exercise of such retrial authority in a particular case, taking into consideration the "totality of the circumstances" (e. g., whether the prosecution "invited" the trial error), could constitute a denial of due process.

Just as the fundamental rights interpretation does not require Fourteenth Amendment incorporation of the specific guarantees of the first eight Amendments, neither does it limit the Fourteenth Amendment by the scope of those guarantees. The emphasis is upon basic fairness, not upon compliance with the Bill of Rights, and a state procedure may violate due process even though its operation is not contrary to any of the specific guarantees in the first eight Amendments. Thus, a justice following the fundamental rights interpretation could hold unconstitutional the employment of television in the courtroom even though he believed that practice was not contrary to the defendant's right to an impartial jury (Sixth Amendment) or public trial (Sixth Amendment). The crucial question would be whether the practice, as applied in the particular case, was potentially so prejudicial as to have "infringed [defendant's] fundamental right to a fair trial assured by the Due Process Clause of the Fourteenth Amendment." *Estes v. Texas,* 381 U.S. 532 (1965) (Harlan, J., con.). (In this respect, the fundamental rights interpretation also has a bearing on federal cases since a similar fair trial requirement, extending beyond the specific guarantees, may also be derived from the due process clause of the Fifth Amendment).

Judicial critics of the fundamental rights approach contend that it promotes a largely ad hoc, personal application of the Fourteenth Amendment. They argue that general standards such as "fundamental fairness" grant a basically "unconfined power" to the judiciary that is contrary to the basic premise of a written constitution. *Duncan v. La.,* supra (Black, J., con.). Justices supporting the fundamental rights interpretation reply that its application is not basically subjective, but rests upon a pervasive consensus of society that can be determined independently of the justice's personal views. In determining whether a particular procedural right has been traditionally recognized as an essential ingredient of fairness, the Court can look to various "objective" factors, such as the significance attached to the right by the framers of the Constitution, the subsequent treatment of the right in state courts and legislatures, and the significance attached to the right in other countries with similar jurisprudential traditions. Although these factors do not provide a mathematical calculus for application of the Fourteenth Amendment, proponents of the fundamental rights interpretation argue that they supply as much objectivity as any other standard for interpreting that Amendment. Moreover, they argue, the fundamental rights interpretation is consistent with the history and language of the Fourteenth Amendment, as viewed in light of the traditional interpretation of the Fifth Amendment due process clause. *Adamson v. Cal.,* supra (Frankfurter, J., con.).

"Total incorporation" and "total incorporation plus." Several justices over the years have argued that the Fourteenth Amendment should be viewed as "incorporating" the entire Bill of Rights. Although never commanding majority support, this interpretation has had considerable influence in shaping the selective incorporation interpretation (discussed infra), which became a dominant force in the 1960's. Exponents of total incorporation contend that the intent of the framers of the Fourteenth Amendment was to make the first eight Amendments applicable to the states.

[*9*]

They also note that this view of the Fourteenth Amendment avoids much of the subjectivity inherent in a fundamental rights approach by confining the justices to the specific language of the Bill of Rights.

Exponents have disagreed, however, as to the extent of the confinement imposed by the total incorporation interpretation. Justice Black rejected the view that the Fourteenth Amendment encompassed "fundamental rights" that are not noted in the particular guarantees of the Bill of Rights. He also rejected the contention that the Fifth Amendment due process clause encompassed various fundamental rights not included in the other Bill of Rights provisions; he viewed that clause as requiring only that the "government * * * proceed according to the law of the land." *In re Winship*, 397 U.S. 358 (1970) (dis.). But other justices favoring total incorporation have argued that the Fourteenth Amendment due process clause (and apparently its Fifth Amendment counterpart) encompass various unenumerated rights, procedural and substantive, that are essential to "fairness" and "individual liberty." See *Adamson v. Cal.*, supra (Murphy, J., dis.); *Poe v. Ullman*, 367 U.S. 497 (1961) (Douglas, J., dis.). Their position has sometimes been described as "incorporation plus," since it views the Fourteenth Amendment as encompassing all of the specific guarantees of the Bill of Rights plus any

[*10*]

additional rights that may be viewed as basic to society under a fundamental rights analysis.

Critics of both total incorporation interpretations contend that these interpretations have support neither in the legislative history nor the language of the Fourteenth Amendment. They suggest that Congress would have clearly stated that the Bill of Rights was applicable to the states if that had been its intent. The critics of incorporationist theory also reject the contention that incorporation avoids much of the subjectivity inherent in the fundamental rights approach. Even under the more limited approach of Justice Black, they note, the focus of judicial inquiry often is shifted from the flexible concept of "fundamental rights" to equally flexible terms in the specific Amendments. Terms like "probable cause," "unreasonable search," and "speedy and public trial" are hardly self-defining and will be interpreted in light of the same contemporary notions of fairness that must be considered in applying a fundamental rights standard. Moreover, restricting the Court to the specific provisions of the Bill of Rights "leads inevitably to a warped construction of [the] specific provisions * * * to bring within their scope conduct clearly condemned by due process but not easily fitting into the pigeon holes of the specific provisions." *Adamson v. Cal.,* supra (Frankfurter, J., con.).

Finally, the critics also contend that the full application of the Bill of Rights would impose an undue burden on the states and "deprive [them] of opportunity for reforms in legal process designed for extending the area of freedom." Id. In large part, this argument reflects a disagreement over the "significance" of specific provisions in the Bill of Rights, but it also rests on the premise that problems of administering criminal justice at the state level make inappropriate procedures that may be readily accepted at the federal level. Thus, it is suggested that the requirement of indictment by grand jury would impose a far greater burden on states, particularly those that are largely rural, than upon the federal government.

Selective incorporation. The selective incorporation doctrine combines aspects of both the "fundamental rights" and "total incorporation" interpretations of the Fourteenth Amendment. Selective incorporation accepts the basic premise of the fundamental rights interpretation that the Fourteenth Amendment encompasses all rights, substantive and procedural, that are "of the very essence of the scheme of ordered liberty." *Cohen v. Hurley*, 366 U.S. 117 (1961) (Brennan, J., dis.). It recognizes that not all rights enumerated in the Bill of Rights are necessarily fundamental, and that other rights may be fundamental even though not within the specific guarantees of the

Bill of Rights. In determining whether an enumerated right is fundamental, however, a Justice following the selective incorporation doctrine would look at the total right guaranteed by the individual Amendment, not merely the element of that right before the Court nor the application of that right in the particular case. Once it is decided that a particular guarantee within the first eight Amendments is fundamental, that guarantee is incorporated into the Fourteenth Amendment "whole and intact" and is enforced against the states in every case according to the same standards applied to the federal government. There is, as one Justice has put it, "coextensive coverage" under the Fourteenth Amendment and the Bill of Rights provision. See *Johnson v. La.,* 406 U.S. 356 (1972) (Douglas, J., dis.).

Proponents of selective incorporation argue that the traditional fundamental rights interpretation errs in stressing the "totality of circumstances" in the particular case. Evaluation of the fundamental nature of a right in terms of the "factual circumstances surrounding each individual case" is "extremely subjective and excessively discretionary." Limiting a decision to only one aspect of the particular right presents the same difficulties; "only impermissible subjective judgments can explain stopping short of the incorporation of the full sweep of the specific [provision] being absorbed [into the Fourteenth

Amendment]." Moreover, proponents argue, an ad hoc determination of the fundamental nature of each element of a basic guarantee will only injure federalism by "requiring the [Supreme] Court to intervene in the state judicial process with considerable lack of predictability and with a consequent likelihood of considerable friction." *Pointer v. Texas,* supra (Goldberg, J., con.).

Critics have attacked selective incorporation as an artificial compromise between the fundamental rights and total incorporation doctrines that is not consistent with the logic or historical support of either. *Duncan v. La.,* supra (Harlan, J., dis.). Proponents of total incorporation contend that selective incorporation is equally inconsistent with the historical purpose of the Fourteenth Amendment and imports the same element of subjectivity as the fundamental rights doctrine. Proponents of fundamental rights also attack the historical basis for selective incorporation, noting that there is absolutely no legislative history supporting a "half-way house" between the traditional view of due process and the total incorporation thesis. Selective incorporation is also criticized as adopting the standard of the fundamental rights analysis, but departing from its basic premise— that the fundamental nature of a particular safeguard must be determined apart from its enumeration in the Bill of Rights. Certainly, the critics argue, aside from that enumeration, there is no reason to assume that the whole body of rules developed in interpreting the separate provisions of the Fourth, Fifth, or Sixth Amendments are equally essential to ordered liberty. Moreover, where the court's concern is primarily with procedural fairness, it must necessarily view the entire state trial process applied in the particular case, for the significance of a procedural right denied by the state often cannot be evaluated fully without considering what other aspects of procedure were made available by the state. These critics also contend that selective incorporation fails to make allowance for the special burdens involved in anministering criminal justice at the state level. Insistence upon a single standard regulating both state and federal administration, they predict, will result in the end either in imposing an unrealistic "constitutional straight jacket" upon the states or a relaxation of standards as applied to both federal and state officials in order to meet the special problems of the state. *Baldwin v. N. Y.,* 399 U.S. 66 (1970) (Harlan, J., dis.).

B. HISTORICAL AND CURRENT DEVELOPMENT

Developments prior to 1960. The relationship between the Fourteenth Amendment and the Bill of Rights was first considered by the Supreme Court in the criminal procedure context in *Hurta-*

do v. Cal., 110 U.S. 516 (1884). The Court there held that the Fourteenth Amendment did not encompass the Fifth Amendment guarantee that all infamous crimes be prosecuted by grand jury indictment. The majority opinion reached this conclusion largely on a fundamental rights interpretation of the due process clause. However, it also suggested, as an additional limitation, that the Fourteenth Amendment due process clause, to be construed consistently with Fifth Amendment due process clause, could not encompass any of the fundamental rights that were specifically enumerated in the Bill of Rights. (If the Fifth Amendment clause had been intended to encompass such rights, the majority reasoned, there would have been no need for including in the Bill of Rights both those specific guarantees and a due process clause.) This additional limitation was rejected shortly thereafter, and the broader fundamental rights interpretation, as described at pp. 5–6, was firmly established as the prevailing view. *Chicago, B. & Q. Ry. v. Chicago,* 166 U.S. 226 (1897). That interpretation continued to command majority support through the early 1960's, although several justices over the years advocated total incorporation.

The Court's application of the fundamental rights approach can be divided roughly into two periods. Prior to the early 1930's, the Supreme Court reviewed comparatively few criminal cases arising from state courts and generally ruled against Fourteenth Amendment protection of interests encompassed within the specific guarantees of the Bill of Rights. Although these decisions usually dealt with a single aspect of a general right, the opinions often seemed to characterize all aspects of the right as "not fundamental." Thus, a decision dealing with prosecutorial comment upon defendant's refusal to take the stand was commonly characterized as holding that due process did not guarantee any element of the privilege against self-incrimination. The early 1930's, however, marked a change in direction. The Supreme Court began to display increasing interest in state criminal procedure and state criminal cases soon occupied a significant portion of its docket. During this period the Supreme Court held that elements of several rights guaranteed by the first eight Amendments were also fundamental rights protected by the Fourteenth Amendment. In *Powell v. Ala.,* 287 U.S. 45 (1932), for example, the Court recognized that the indigent's right to appointed counsel, an element of the Sixth Amendment guarantee of assistance of counsel, was a fundamental right as applied to certain types of state cases. At the same time, the Court rejected claims that elements of several other guarantees were fundamental. Most of these decisions, however, were carefully limited to the particular problem before the Court. Thus, in *Palko v. Conn.,* supra, the Court held that due process did not bar a state appeal on a question of law following an acquittal, but its opinion also indicated that other forms of double jeopardy might well violate the Fourteenth Amendment.

Developments during the 1960's. The fundamental rights approach of *Palko* lost majority support during the early 1960's, although *Palko* itself was not overruled until 1970. In 1961, Mr. Justice Brennan advanced the selective incorporation interpretation, relying in part upon earlier cases that afforded fundamental substantive rights (e. g., freedom of speech) the same scope under the Fourteenth Amendment as they had under the Bill of Rights. *Cohen v. Hurley*, supra. By 1963, this position had the support of at least three justices. In addition, two Justices, Black and Douglas, while remaining supporters of total incorporation, accepted selective incorporation as a lesser evil than the fundamental rights interpretation. As a result, the post-1963 decisions consistently followed the selective incorporation standard. Because of the particular composition of the majority, opinions for the Court generally did not discuss the selective incorporation doctrine as such, but those opinions made clear that a selective incorporation standard was being applied. See, e. g., *Benton v. Md.*, 395 U.S. 784, 795 (1969). ("Once it is decided that a Bill of Rights guarantee is fundamental * * *, the same constitutional standards apply against both the State and Federal Governments.") Very frequently, the results reached in applying this standard were also supported by the remaining justices, who favored the traditional fundamental rights analysis. Indeed, at least one of the justices in this group appeared to follow the view that a Bill of Rights guarantee held to be within the Fourteenth Amendment ordinarily would take on the same dimension as applied to the federal government, and contrary rulings, like *Palko* or *Powell,* only would be justified by a special showing of the unique needs of the states in the areas involved. See *Benton v. Md.,* 395 U.S. at 808, n. 12 (collecting the opinions of Stewart, J.).

The adoption of the selective incorporation position during the early 1960's was accompanied by a movement towards a broader view of the nature of a "fundamental procedural right." Consistent with selective incorporation, the Court's assessment was directed at the significance of the right when viewed as a whole, rather than concentrating solely upon the particular aspect presented in the case at hand. In addition, the right was viewed with reference to its operation within the "common law system of [criminal procedure] * * * that has been developing * * * in this country, rather than its theoretical justification as a necessary element of a 'fair

and equitable procedure.' " *Duncan v. La.,* supra.
Finally, greater emphasis was placed upon the
very presence of a right within the Bill of Rights
as strong evidence of its fundamental nature.

Applying this approach, the Supreme Court
during the 1960's held fundamental (and therefore applicable to the states under the same
standards applied to federal government) the following Bill of Rights guarantees: the freedom
from unreasonable searches and seizures and the
right to have excluded from criminal trials any
evidence obtained in violation thereof, *Mapp v.
Ohio,* 367 U.S. 643 (1961), and *Ker v. Cal.,* 374
U.S. 23 (1963); the privilege against self-incrimination, *Malloy v. Hogan,* 378 U.S. 1 (1964); the
guarantee against double jeopardy, *Benton v. Md.,*
395 U.S. 784 (1969); the right to the assistance
of counsel, *Gideon v. Wainwright,* 372 U.S. 335
(1963); the right to a speedy trial, *Klopfer v. N.
C.,* 386 U.S. 213 (1967); the right to jury trial,
Duncan v. La., supra; the right to confront opposing witnesses, *Pointer v. Texas,* supra; the
right to compulsory process for obtaining witnesses, *Washington v. Texas,* 388 U.S. 14 (1967);
and the prohibition against cruel and unusual
punishment, *Robinson v. Cal.,* 370 U.S. 660
(1962). Moreover, in light of these rulings, two
earlier cases are now viewed as incorporating
within the Fourteenth Amendment the Sixth
Amendment rights to a public trial and to notice

of the nature and cause of the accusation. See *In re Oliver,* 333 U.S. 257 (1948) (cited in *Duncan* as incorporating the right to public trial); *Cole v. Ark.,* 333 U.S. 196 (1948). The only remaining guarantees addressed specifically to criminal procedure are the Eighth Amendment prohibition against excessive bail and the Fifth Amendment requirement of prosecution of infamous crimes by grand jury indictment. The Supreme Court has not ruled directly on the bail clause, but the court's characterization of that clause in *Schlib v. Kuebel,* 404 U.S. 357 (1971), suggests that it would be incorporated within the Fourteenth Amendment if the issue were squarely presented. Prosecution by grand jury indictment, on the other hand, was found not to be fundamental, and therefore not required of the states, in *Hurtado v. Cal.,* supra; that decision continues to be followed as valid precedent and appears unlikely to be overruled.

Future developments. Several new justices have been added to the Court since the last major selective incorporation decision of the 1960's, and it is doubtful whether a majority of the current Court would have supported selective incorporation as a matter of first impression. Nevertheless, the various decisions of the 1960's incorporating particular Bill of Rights guarantees are not likely to be overturned in the near future. The Court as a whole appears more favorably inclined toward reexamining the scope of specific guarantees than rearguing the relationship of those guarantees to the Fourteenth Amendment. The decisions treating the Sixth Amendment right to jury trial are illustrative.

In holding that the Fourteenth Amendment fully absorbed the jury trial right, the majority in *Duncan v. La.,* supra, noted the state's contention that incorporation would disrupt long established state practices by requiring adherence to past interpretations of the Sixth Amendment that were developed solely in terms of federal court practice. The majority responded that, in part, those past interpretations were "always subject to reconsideration" in light of new developments. Subsequently, in *Williams v. Fla.,* 399 U.S. 78 (1970), the Court reconsidered the scope of the Sixth Amendment, ruled that it did not require a twelve-person jury as utilized in the federal courts, and consequently upheld the state's use of a six person jury in a non-capital felony case. A similar approach was taken in *Apodaca v. Ore.,* 406 U.S. 404 (1971), although there the division over incorporationist theory did influence the result. In *Apodaca,* four justices, including three appointed after *Duncan,* found that the Sixth Amendment did not require unanimous jury verdicts and therefore a state's acceptance of 10–2 verdicts did not violate the Fourteenth Amendment. Four justices, relying in part upon past

Sixth Amendment decisions, held that unanimity was constitutionally required. Only one Justice (Powell, J.) challenged the premise that the same constitutional standards would apply to federal and state cases. He concluded that while the Sixth Amendment did require unanimity, that element of the jury trial right was not essential and therefore should not apply to the states under a traditional fundamental rights analysis of the Fourteenth Amendment.

As *Apodaca* and *Williams* suggest, through redefinition of the basic guarantee, justices opposed to selective incorporation may substantially reduce the impact of that doctrine without overruling the selective incorporation decisions of the 1960's. Moreover, redefinition does not always require alteration of the standards applied in federal courts; more restrictive standards in many areas could still be applied in federal courts pursuant to the Court's supervisory power over those courts. Cf. Fed.Crim.P. 31(a) (requiring unanimous jury verdicts). However, as Justice Powell's opinion in *Apodaca* indicates, the "reexamination route" may not always be viewed as satisfactory, and future developments might revive the incorporation issue as a major point of division among the justices.

3. EXPANSION OF INDIVIDUAL PROVISIONS

Introduction. The decisions of the past fifteen years not only made most of the Bill of Rights guarantees applicable to the states via the Fourteenth Amendment, but they also dramatically expanded the scope of those guarantees as applied to both federal and state procedure. Several constitutional guarantees were applied to new, previously uncovered areas of criminal procedure. Other guarantees were extended to apply more comprehensive and detailed restrictions in areas that had long been subject to constitutional limitations. Of course, not all of the major decisions imposed new constitutional restrictions. In a number of cases, the Court refused to impose new limitations, and, in a few instances, it overturned previously established limitations. The general trend of the decisions, however, was to further "constitutionalize" criminal procedure, and the decisions contributing to this trend may well have produced more significant new developments in criminal procedure than all of the decisions of the previous century.

The sections that follow present an overview of the current constitutional limitations imposed upon different areas of criminal procedure, with primary emphasis upon the Supreme Court decisions of the last fifteen years. The reader should

[24]

keep in mind that these sections describe only the general thrust of the current limitations and a far more complete analysis of specific rulings and the rationale advanced in both majority and dissenting opinions is needed to fully appreciate the scope of the limitations applied in a particular area.

4. POLICE INVESTIGATION

The general trend. Probably the most highly publicized group of Supreme Court decisions of the past fifteen years have been those imposing new limitations upon basic police investigatory techniques, such as interrogation, physical searches, electronic eavesdropping, eye-witness identification procedures, etc. Several of these police techniques had already been subjected to considerable constitutional regulation prior to the 1960's. In the area of searches, a series of decisions based upon the Fourth Amendment and dating back to 1914 had established an extensive body of constitutional rules regulating federal officers. The practice of police interrogation had also been examined in a significant number of cases. The decisions since 1960 revised and expanded the limitations previously imposed in both areas. In addition, those decisions imposed restraints upon practices, such as lineup identification and wiretapping, that had not previously been subject to constitutional regulation. With these new limitations added to the extensive body of prior law, the area of police investigation has become one of two phases of the criminal process (the other being the trial itself) that are most extensively regulated by constitutional limitations. The specific limitations currently imposed in this area are discussed in detail in Chapters 2–5.

The exclusionary rule. The one major development common to the imposition of constitutional limitations on all aspects of police investigatory techniques has been the so-called "exclusionary rule." This rule provides for the exclusion from a criminal prosecution of evidence obtained in violation of the Constitution. Today, the question of the constitutionality of particular police practices is ordinarily presented to the courts via a motion to exclude evidence pursuant to this rule. The exclusionary rule was not always recognized, however, as an appropriate remedy for all constitutional violations. It has traditionally been applied to violations of the Fifth Amendment privilege against self-incrimination, since that provision specifically prohibits the use of such "compelled" testimony in a criminal case. *Boyd v. U. S.,* 116 U.S. 616 (1886). The Supreme Court readily supported also the application of the exclusionary rule where unconstitutional police activities produced inherently unreliable evidence

(e. g., a confession obtained by torture). The Court had difficulty, however, with the application of the rule to exclude relevant and trustworthy evidence obtained in violation of a constitutional command that did not refer, even indirectly, to the admissibility of evidence. This problem was considered initially in ruling on the admissibility of evidence obtained in violation of the Fourth Amendment prohibition against unreasonable searches and seizures.

The Court held in *Weeks v. U. S.*, 232 U.S. 383 (1914), that any evidence obtained by federal officers in violation of the Fourth Amendment would be barred from a federal prosecution. Subsequently, in *Wolf v. Colo.*, 338 U.S. 25 (1949), the Court ruled that, although Fourteenth Amendment due process encompassed the "security of one's privacy * * * which is at the core of the Fourth Amendment," it did not require that state courts exclude all evidence obtained in violation of the Fourth (and Fourteenth) Amendment. The Court created a narrow exception to *Wolf* in *Rochin v. Cal.*, 342 U.S. 165 (1952), holding that the Fourteenth Amendment did require exclusion of evidence obtained by police activities that were so flagrantly abusive of individual privacy as "to shock * * * the conscience" of a "civilized society." *Wolf* remained the predominant ruling, however, until the early 1960's, when the Court held both that the

Fourteenth Amendment fully incorporated the Fourth Amendment guarantee and that the exclusionary rule was an essential element of that guarantee. The latter point was made in *Mapp v. Ohio,* 367 U.S. 643 (1961), which overruled *Wolf.* The *Mapp* court rejected the "factual grounds upon which *Wolf* was based"; it noted that other remedies against unreasonable searches (e. g., tort suits) had proven ineffective, the trend in the state courts was now toward adoption of the exclusionary rule (over one half of the states had adopted the rule as a matter of state law), and various inconsistencies in the prior application of the rule had been removed. The Court concluded that the exclusionary rule, by removing the incentive to disregard the Fourth Amendment, constituted "the only effectively available way * * * to compel respect for the constitutional guarantee." It discounted Justice Cardozo's argument that the rule permitted the "criminal * * * to go free because the constable had blundered," noting that "another consideration, the imperative of judicial integrity," must prevail. "Nothing," it noted, "can destroy a government more quickly than its failure to observe its own laws."

The *Mapp* rationale was subsequently extended to require exclusion of evidence obtained through other unconstitutional practices. *Wong Sun v. U. S.,* 371 U.S. 471 (1963), excluded an oral statement of a defendant made in direct response to an unconstitutional entry and arrest. Evidence obtained in violation of defendant's Sixth Amendment right to counsel was also held constitutionally inadmissible. *Massiah v. U. S.,* 377 U.S. 201 (1964) (confession) (see § 25); *U. S. v. Wade,* 388 U.S. 218 (1967) (lineup identification) (see § 29). Additionally, in *Miranda v. Ariz.,* 384 U.S. 436 (1966), the Fifth Amendment privilege against self-incrimination was applied to custodial interrogation, thereby extending the Fifth Amendment's exclusionary requirement to statements unconstitutionally obtained from such interrogation without regard to whether those statements were inherently untrustworthy (see § 26).

Although the exclusionary rule is now well established in Supreme Court precedent, its use outside the Fifth Amendment area has remained a subject of considerable controversy. That controversy has centered primarily on the comparative costs and gains resulting from the exclusion of evidence obtained through illegal searches. At least two of the current justices have indicated that they would be prepared to modify substantially or overturn *Mapp v. Ohio,* supra, if a "meaningful" legislative or regulatory alternative could be developed. See *Bivens v. Six Unknown Agents,* 403 U.S. 443 (1971) (Burger, C. J., dis.); *Coolidge v. N. H.,* 403 U.S. 510 (1971) (Blackmun, J., dis.). Cf. *Schneckloth v. Bustamonte,*

412 U.S. 218 (1973) (Powell, J., joined by Burger, C. J., and Rehnquist, J., con.).

5.   PRE–TRIAL PROCEEDINGS

Many pre-trial proceedings have far more practical significance in the criminal process than the trial itself. Viewed as a whole, however, these proceedings are subject to considerably less extensive constitutional regulation than either the trial or police investigatory stages of the criminal process. Although the Supreme Court decisions of the past several years suggest increased concern as to the operation of pre-trial proceedings generally, those decisions have varied considerably in their treatment of different pre-trial determinations. The Court has reaffirmed that constitutional limits are largely inapplicable to certain determinations, suggested the possible application of new limits to others, and actually applied significant new restrictions to still others.

Bail. The Eighth Amendment provides that "excessive bail shall not be required," but the standards for determining what constitutes "excessive bail" have not been fully developed by the Supreme Court. Indeed, only one major decision deals directly with that issue. In *Stack v. Boyle,* 342 U.S. 1 (1951), the Court stated that bail set "at a figure higher than an amount reasonably calculated" to provide assurance that the accused will be present at trial was "excessive under the Eighth Amendment." The specific ruling of the case, however, was rather narrow; the court below had violated "statutory and constitutional standards" in fixing bail of petitioners (indicted for conspiring to advocate overthrow of the government) "in a sum much higher than that usually imposed for offenses with like penalties" without any "factual showing to justify such action."

The *Stack* opinion, in noting that "traditional standards" require consideration of individual factors in setting bail, raises serious doubts as to the constitutionality of the practice, followed in many courts, of imposing a standard bail based solely on the seriousness of the crime charged. See *Ackies v. Purdy*, 322 F.Supp. 38 (S.D.Fla. 1970). *Stack's* emphasis on potential flight as the key determinant in setting bail also raises doubts as to reliance upon the accused's potential dangerousness in determining conditions of pretrial release; this issue is often hidden by the magistrate's failure to state the basis for his bail decision, but is directly presented by so-called "preventive detention" legislation. See *Blunt v. U. S.*, 322 A.2d 579 (D.C.App.1974). The discussion of bail in *Stack* also leaves open to question the imposition of bail in excess of defendant's capacity to pay. Justice Douglas has suggested, in an individual opinion, that a defendant who cannot afford to post bail must be released on his own recognizance where other relevant factors indicate that he will "comply with the conditions of his release." *Bandy v. U. S.,* 81 S.Ct. 197 (1960). So far, none of these issues have been resolved by the Court (possibly because an attack on bail does not easily reach the level of Supreme Court review before the trial is completed and the issue becomes moot).

The prosecutor's decision to prosecute. The primary constitutional restriction upon a federal prosecutor's determination to press charges is the Fifth Amendment requirement that all prosecutions for infamous crimes be commenced by grand jury indictment. Thus, a prosecutor's decision to charge a person with an infamous crime (encompassing all federal offenses carrying a term of imprisonment in excess of one year) will not be given effect unless the grand jury accepts his recommendation and itself issues the charge in the form of an indictment. A major function of the grand jury, the Court has said, is "to stand * * * between the accuser and the accused * * * to determine whether a charge is founded upon reason or was dictated by an intimidating power or by malice and personal ill will." *Wood v. Ga.,* 370 U.S. 375, 390 (1962). Whether the grand jury provides effective "screening" or acts more as a "rubber stamp of the prosecutor" is a matter of considerable dispute. The Court nevertheless has refused to review the evidence before a grand jury to ensure that it properly performed its screening function in approving an indictment. *Costello v. U. S.,* 350 U.S. 359 (1956).

The requirement of prosecution by grand jury indictment, unlike other constitutional restrictions upon prosecutorial discretion, does not apply to the states. The Supreme Court held in *Hurtado v. Cal.,* 110 U.S. 516 (1884), that state prosecution of infamous crimes on the basis of an information (a formal charge issued by the prosecutor) did not violate the Fourteenth Amendment, and *Hurtado* continues to be accepted as valid precedent. The prosecution by information in *Hurtado* did include another "screening process"—a preliminary examination, conducted by a magistrate, at which the prosecution had to justify its information by establishing probable cause to believe the defendant committed the offense charged. The Supreme Court has held, however, that the states are not under a constitutional duty to grant the defendant such an examination. *Lem Woon v. Ore.,* 229 U.S. 586 (1913). Although the Fourth Amendment requires that an arrested person be provided a prompt ex parte judicial determination as to whether probable cause exists for his continued detention, it does not mandate a substantial, adversary hearing to determine whether the prosecutor has sufficient evidence to initiate prosecution. *Gerstein v. Pugh,* p. 120).

Despite the absence of a constitutional mandate, almost all states provide for screening by preliminary examination in felony cases, and approximately one-half also require grand jury indictment. Of course, either process, once provided, must meet constitutional standards of due process and equal protection. Thus, the Court has held that the grand jury cannot be selected on a racially discriminatory basis. *Cassell v. Texas*, 339 U.S. 282 (1950). See also *Coleman v. Ala.*, (p. 342) (requiring appointed counsel at preliminary examination).

The only other major constitutional limit upon the prosecutor's discretion in deciding to prosecute lies in the application of the equal protection clause. Several opinions have indicated that the Court would recognize as a defense, at least to a non-violent, minor offense, that the prosecutor arbitrarily selected the defendant for prosecution while refusing to prosecute others who violated the statute in the same manner. See *Oyler v. Boles,* 368 U.S. 448 (1962). None of the opinions, however, involve direct holdings on that ground, and the nature of "arbitrary discrimination" has not been defined beyond reference to "discrimination based on race or religion." Also, the Court has noted that "the conscious exercise of some selectivity in enforcement is not in itself a federal constitutional violation" and the arbitrary basis for discriminatory treatment must be specifically alleged. Id.

Scope of the prosecution. In many cases, the prosecutor's discretion is not limited to the single decision whether to prosecute. Where a particular defendant has committed several separate offenses, the prosecutor may have a choice under state law as to whether to consolidate the charges in a single prosecution or to bring them separately. Similarly, where several persons are involved in an offense, the prosecutor may have a choice as to whether to prosecute them jointly or separately. Until recently, Supreme Court decisions did not impose any significant limitations upon such choices. See *Hoag v. N. J.,* 356 U.S. 464 (1958) (overruled in *Ashe v. Swenson,* infra). *Ashe v. Swenson,* 397 U.S. 436 (1970), and *Bruton v. U. S.,* 391 U.S. 123 (1968), though not imposing any direct restrictions, do establish substantial procedural burdens that may significantly influence the prosecutor's choice on joinder. Moreover, each provides a possible foundation for the future imposition of direct restrictions on joinder.

Ashe relates primarily to compulsory joinder of offenses. The Court there held that the doctrine of collateral estoppel is embodied in the Fifth Amendment's double jeopardy prohibition, and, accordingly, an acquittal based on a factual issue that is also presented as an essential element of a second charge necessarily bars trial on that charge. Thus, in *Ashe*, a defendant charged with robbing the initial victim in a single, multi-victim robbery and acquitted by the jury on the ground that he had not participated in the event could not subsequently be convicted on a charge of robbing another victim. As the Court noted, the effect of the collateral estoppel doctrine is to prevent the prosecutor from "treat[ing] the first trial as no more than a dry run for [a] second prosecution" on a related charge. With this tactic eliminated, the prosecutor may find less advantage in separate prosecutions of closely related offenses arising out of a single transaction. Moreover, the opinions in *Ashe* indicate that the Court might well impose a considerably more restrictive limitation on the use of separate charges in the future. Several Justices, writing concurring opinions, were divided over whether "the Double Jeopardy Clause requires the prosecution, except in most limited circumstances, to join at one trial all the charges against a defendant which grow out of a single criminal act, occurrence, episode or transaction." (Brennan, J., con.). The majority found no need to consider this issue, but its discussion of pre-selective-incorporation precedent clearly indicates that a prior ruling rejecting compulsory joinder, *Ciucci v. Ill.*, 356 U.S. 571 (1958), is subject to reconsideration.

Compare *P. v. White,* 212 N.W.2d 222 (Mich. 1973) with *S. v. Conrad,* 243 So.2d 174 (Fla.App. 1971).

Bruton relates to joinder of parties, but unlike *Ashe,* it tends to discourage rather than encourage joinder. Relying on the confrontation clause of the Sixth Amendment (p. 58), *Bruton* held that where the confession of one co-defendant contained references to a second co-defendant, and the confessor refused to take the stand, the second co-defendant's constitutional rights were violated even though the jury had been informed that the confession could only be used against the confessor. While *Bruton* does not bar joinder of accomplices where the prosecution intends to use a confession, it imposes as a significant price the deletion of all prejudicial references to the other accomplice, which often will substantially undercut the effectiveness of the statement against the confessor. It also suggests a potential constitutional ground for other challenges to joinder of parties. The Court has not yet determined, as a constitutional matter, the extent to which an individual defendant has a right to a severance on the ground that (1) the alleged illegal activities of the joined defendants were not sufficiently related, (2) these activities, although allegedly related, were not proven to have been related at trial, or (3) the evidence likely to be introduced against one defendant is so highly inflammatory as to prejudice the co-defendants. *Bruton* expressed considerable doubt as to the capacity of the jury to follow instructions that it disregard the references to the second defendant in the first defendant's confession. If this concern is extended to the jury's ability to keep separate other types of evidence, the Court may well recognize at least minimal constitutional restraints on joinder, particularly where the request for severance is based on the introduction of highly inflammatory evidence against a co-defendant. Cf. *Kotteakos v. U. S.*, 328 U.S. 750 (1946).

Location of the prosecution. In federal cases the prosecutor's discretion regarding the location of the prosecution is limited by Article III, § 2, which requires trial in the state where the offense "shall have been committed," and the Sixth Amendment, which guarantees an impartial jury "of the state and district wherein the crime shall have been committed." In applying these limitations, the Court has relied heavily on Congressional designation of the place or places where a particular offense "is committed," in part because this factor depends largely on the definition of the offense. Congress, in turn, has provided for quite extensive prosecutorial discretion without raising significant constitutional objections. For example, where the use of an agency of interstate commerce (e. g., a common carrier) is an element of the offense, prosecution has been authorized in any state through which the agency passed. *Armour Packing Co. v. U. S.,* 209 U.S. 56 (1908); *U. S. v. Johnson,* 323 U.S. 273 (1944).

The Supreme Court has not had occasion since the selective incorporation of the jury trial guarantee to determine whether that guarantee imposes any special limits on state choice of venue. State law ordinarily requires prosecution in the state judicial district (e. g. county) in which the offense was "committed," but constitutional difficulties may be presented by occasional state provisions permitting prosecution of particular offenses in other districts. See *P. v. Jones,* 510 P.2d 705 (Cal.1973). Moreover, although venue initially may be appropriate, the constitution may require a change in venue to avoid the consequences of prejudicial pretrial publicity (see p. 56).

Timing of the prosecution. Prosecutorial discretion relating to the timing of the prosecution is limited by the Sixth Amendment requirement that "the accused shall enjoy the right to a speedy trial." The Court has held that denial of the right automatically requires dismissal of the delayed prosecution with prejudice; the impact of the denial is too diffuse to permit trial courts to seek to tailor the remedy (e. g., by reducing defendant's sentence) to the hardship caused in the particular case. *Strunk v. U. S.,* 412 U.S. 434 (1973). Flexibility has been the governing philosophy, however, in determining whether delay

constitutes a denial of the right. Thus, the leading speedy trial decision, *Barker v. Wingo*, 407
U.S. 514 (1972), rejected what it described as
"inflexible approaches" (e. g., imposing a specific
time limitation) in favor of "a balancing test, in
which the conduct of both the prosecution and
the defendant are weighed." *Barker* listed four
factors to be considered in the particular case:
(1) length of delay; (2) the government's justification for the delay; (3) whether and how the
defendant asserted his right to a speedy trial;
and (4) prejudice caused by the delay, such as
lengthened pretrial incarceration, lengthened anx-
iety, and possible impairment of the presentation
of a defense. In balancing these factors, the
Court suggested that while a defense demand for
a speedy trial was not essential, the absence of a
demand would work strongly against the defendant who had counsel. The speedy trial right, it
noted, was unlike most other constitutional rights
in that the "deprivation of the right through delay may work to the accused's advantage."

Most of the speedy trial cases before the Court
have involved lengthy delays following defense
demands for a prompt trial, and the primary emphasis has been on evaluating the cause for the
delay. While each ruling has been tied to the
facts of the particular case, the decisions clearly
indicate that the state must offer some affirmative justification, not merely the absence of a de-

liberate attempt to pressure the defendant. Thus, *Smith v. Hooey,* 393 U.S. 374 (1969), and *Dickey v. Fla.,* 398 U.S. 30 (1970), found a constitutional violation where the state failed to make any effort to respond to the demand of a defendant, then serving a federal sentence, for a prompt trial on pending state charges. The state's failure to even request that federal officials make the defendant available could not be justified by its lack of authority to compel such cooperation. Neither could its failure be justified on the ground that the cost of transporting the prisoner would have had to be borne by the state. On the other hand, in *U. S. v. Ewell,* 383 U.S. 116 (1966), the Court rejected a speedy trial claim where the delay was attributed to the dismissal of an earlier indictment relating to the same transaction. See also *Barker v. Wingo,* supra, (upholding delay caused by a combination of the illness of the chief investigating officer and defendant's willingness to await the outcome of his accomplice's trial).

The speedy trial guarantee traditionally has protected the defendant only against undue delay between the institution of prosecution and trial. *U. S. v. Marion,* 404 U.S. 307 (1971). Yet, undue delay in the institution of charges on a fully investigated case may interfere with defendant's ability to defend himself in much the same way as the denial of a speedy trial—e. g., the delay may impair memories, cause evidence to be lost, or deprive the defendant of witnesses. In *Marion*, a divided Court recognized this potential, but refused to reach it by extending the scope of the speedy trial right. The *Marion* majority did note, however, that dismissal of charges might be required under the due process clause upon a showing of "actual prejudice resulting from pre-accusation delays."

Defendant's choice of plea. Following the filing of the information or indictment, the defendant is "arraigned"; that is, he is advised of the formal charges against him and is called upon to enter his plea—guilty, nolo contendere (where permitted), or not guilty. The Court has long recognized that the defendant's choice of plea is often the most crucial decision he makes, particularly if he enters a plea of guilty (as occurs in 70–85% of the cases reaching this stage in most jurisdictions). Accordingly, it has stressed the need for insuring that his choice represents a free and reasoned response to the charges, and several constitutional provisions have been construed to serve that end. Thus, the Sixth Amendment requirement that the defendant "be informed of the nature and cause of the accusation" has been viewed as requiring, at a minimum, that the indictment or information be sufficiently specific in describing the charges to permit the defendant to enter a reasoned plea thereto. *Russell v. U. S.,*

369 U.S. 749 (1962). Similarly, the Sixth Amendment right to the assistance of counsel, including the indigent defendant's right to the services of court-appointed counsel, has been held to require assistance in determination of plea as well as at trial (see p. 348).

The defendant's free choice of plea is also protected by the long-standing constitutional prohibition against acceptance of guilty pleas that are not "voluntary." This prohibition has been imposed pursuant to the due process clause and has been likened by the Court to the prohibition against admission of involuntary confessions. *Waley v. Johnston,* 316 U.S. 101 (1942). Application of the voluntariness standard largely rests on a "totality of circumstances" analysis similar to that employed in determining the voluntariness of confessions (see § 24), although certain factors might be given somewhat different weight as applied to guilty pleas. See, e. g., *N. C. v. Alford,* (p. 46). Since a plea reflects a waiver of various trial rights, voluntariness necessarily includes, in addition to the absence of coercion, awareness of what is being relinquished. *Brady v. U. S.,* infra.

Perhaps the most important issue relating to the application of the voluntariness standard is the appropriate treatment of pleas induced by concessions offered by the prosecution (e. g., reduction of the charge, dismissal of other charges, or a specific sentence approved by the court). A rigid definition of "voluntariness," tied strictly to the standard of confession cases, might invalidate most, if not all, pleas resulting from such "plea bargaining."   However, in *Brady v. U. S.*, 397 U. S. 742 (1970), the Supreme Court rejected that approach, at least with respect to defendants represented by counsel. Although the court was divided on the validity of the plea before it, both the majority and dissenting opinions indicated that negotiated pleas are not inherently incompatible with the voluntariness standard.

The defendant in *Brady* had entered a guilty plea under a federal kidnapping statute that provided for imposition of the death penalty only upon jury recommendation [a penalty provision held unconstitutional subsequent to defendant's plea, *U. S. v. Jackson,* 390 U.S. 55 (1968)]. Defendant argued that his plea has been "coerced" by operation of the statute since the trial court had refused to waive a jury trial and a guilty plea therefore had been his only means of avoiding a possible death penalty. The Court noted that Brady's case could not appropriately be differentiated from that of the defendant who pleads guilty in response to prosecution concessions or the defendant who pleads guilty upon counsel's advice that the trial judge is "normally more lenient with defendants who plead guilty."   The Court noted that to reject pleas produced by such

[44]

inducements would be, in large part, to "forbid guilty pleas altogether." It stressed that the granting of concessions to those pleading guilty was consistent with the administrative as well as rehabilitative goals of the criminal justice system. The state was "extend[ing] a benefit to a defendant who in turn extends a substantial benefit to the state and who demonstrates by his plea that he is ready and willing to admit his crime and to enter the correctional system in a frame of mind which affords hope for success in rehabilitation over a shorter period of time than might otherwise be necessary." The pleas could not be treated as involuntary simply because they were "motivated by the defendant's desire to accept the certainty * * * of a lesser penalty rather than * * * [a trial that might result in] conviction and a higher penalty."

While upholding negotiated pleas in general, *Brady* clearly indicated that such pleas could still be involuntary under particular circumstances. The majority opinion noted that *Brady* had been assisted by competent counsel and "had full opportunity to assess the advantages and disadvantages of a trial as compared with those attending a plea of guilty." Also, there was "no claim that the prosecutor threatened prosecution on a charge not justified by the evidence or that the trial judge threatened Brady with a harsher sentence if convicted after trial." In addition, the

Court stated that a negotiated plea could not be accepted if based on "misrepresentation (including unfulfilled or unfulfillable promises) or threats."

Post-*Brady* decisions reflect both *Brady's* basic acceptance of the negotiated plea and its warning against prosecutorial or judicial misconduct in negotiations. Thus, *N. C. v. Alford,* 400 U.S. 25 (1970), upheld a negotiated guilty plea to a lesser offense even though the plea was accompanied by defendant's protestation of his innocence. The Court noted that defendant, represented by counsel, clearly expressed his desire to plead guilty in order to avoid a potentially higher sentence, and the evidence against him, as examined by the trial judge, was substantial. In *Santobello v. N. Y.,* 404 U.S. 257 (1971), on the other hand, the Court held a negotiated plea invalid where the prosecution failed to keep its promise to make no recommendation on sentence. Although the prosecution's breach of its commitment may not have influenced the sentence imposed and the breach was the product of inadvertence rather than malice, the "interests of justice" required that the state court either permit withdrawal of the plea or grant specific enforcement of the plea agreement, as appropriate.

The voluntariness standard necessarily imposes a duty upon the trial judge to determine that the plea is made knowingly and without coercion.

The Court has emphasized that the scope of that duty, like the definition of voluntariness itself, is governed by constitutional standards. However, the leading case on this point, *Boykin v. Ala.*, 395 U.S. 238 (1969), held only that that duty was not fulfilled where, "so far as the record shows, the judge asked no questions of the [defendant] concerning his plea and [defendant] did not address the court." The trial judge must, the Court noted, employ the "utmost solicitude in canvassing the [plea] with the accused to make sure he has a full understanding of what the [plea] connotes and its consequences." Conceivably, if the trial courts fail to embrace fully this responsibility, the Supreme Court could adopt a more detailed constitutional standard specifying the type of information that must be given the defendant (e. g., elements of offense charged, potential defenses, trial rights, maximum and minimum penalties) and the type of factual inquiry that must be made before accepting a plea. Although the *Boykin* opinion provides only slight evidence of an inclination to impose such standards, the Court has prescribed specific procedural standards in analogous areas. See *Miranda v. Ariz.* (p. 213); *Von Moltke v. Gillies* (p. 357).

Pretrial preparation. The Supreme Court recognized in *Powell v. Ala.*, 287 U.S. 45 (1932), that due process requires that defendant and his counsel have an adequate opportunity to prepare for trial. As the *Powell* opinion noted: "It is vain to give the accused a day in court, with no opportunity to prepare for it, or to guarantee him counsel without giving the latter any opportunity to acquaint himself with the facts or law of the case." For many years, almost all of the decisions concerning pretrial preparation dealt, like *Powell,* with the timing of the appointment of counsel. More recent rulings, however, indicate that constitutional limitations will also play a significant role in the regulation of pretrial discovery.

The Court so far had not directly recognized a constitutional right of defendant to pretrial discovery. It has noted that, "in some circumstances, it may be a denial of due process for a defendant to be refused any [pretrial] discovery of his statements to the police." *Clewis v. Texas,* 386 U.S. 707 (1967). In the only two cases involving a state's refusal to afford such pretrial discovery, due process objections were rejected on the ground that there was "no showing of prejudice." Id. On the other hand, several decisions establishing a prosecutorial duty to disclose exculpatory evidence, while not speaking directly to pretrial discovery, do appear to provide a constitutional base for such discovery.

The prosecutor's duty to disclose was originally recognized in a series of cases holding that the prosecutor's deliberate failure to correct the perjured testimony of his own witness, which the prosecutor knew to be perjured, violated due process. *Mooney v. Holohan*, 294 U.S. 103 (1935). Later cases held that the prosecutor must reveal any known, contrary statements of his witnesses even though he may believe their current testimony to be true. *Giles v. Md.*, 386 U.S. 66 (1967). *Brady v. Md.*, 373 U.S. 83 (1963), further suggested that the duty to disclose was not limited to clarification of the testimony of prosecution witnesses. The majority noted that, at least where defense counsel requested disclosure, "the suppression by the prosecution of evidence favorable to an accused upon request violates due process where the evidence is material either to guilt or to punishment irrespective of the good or bad faith of the prosecution." Although the request for disclosure in *Brady* (of the statement of a co-defendant) initially was made prior to trial, the opinions in *Brady* and other disclosure cases are concerned primarily with disclosure at trial. Pretrial disclosure presents greater potential for attempts by defendants to manufacture evidence, bribe witnesses, or otherwise seek by improper means to negate the discovered evidence, and that factor, along with others, could lead a court to require broader disclosure at trial than at pretrial. Nevertheless, disclosure of certain types of "material" evidence "favorable to the accused" may be of little assistance unless made sufficiently before trial to permit defense counsel to seek supplementary evidence. Lower courts have suggested that, at least as to such evidence, *Brady* establishes a constitutional right to pretrial discovery. *U. S. v. Eley*, 335 F.Supp. 353 (N.D.Ga.1972).

Another major constitutional concern in the area of pretrial discovery is the validity of court rules or statutes requiring the defendant to grant discovery to the prosecution. *Williams v. Fla.*, 399 U.S. 78 (1970), upheld a limited form of prosecution pretrial discovery as imposed by a state alibi rule. A divided Court held that the Florida requirement that defendant give advance notice of an alibi defense (including the names and addresses of alibi witnesses) did not violate the privilege against self-incrimination. The majority stressed that the Florida rule only required the defendant to disclose evidence that he intended to produce subsequently at trial, and, if he changed his mind, the rule permitted the defendant to abandon the alibi defense without any harm to his case. Although the opinion was limited to alibi discovery, the majority's analysis of the self-incrimination issue arguably could be extended to uphold provisions granting the prosecution pretrial discovery of various other matters (e. g., scientific reports, expert witnesses) that defendant intends eventually to produce at trial. *Wardius v. Ore.*, 412 U.S. 470 (1973), establishes, however, that any state rule providing for prosecution discovery must be reciprocal to meet due process requirements. Thus, *Wardius* held invalid an alibi-notice provision that failed to require the prosecution to provide reciprocal disclosure of its rebuttal witness on the alibi issue. Moreover, both *Wardius* and *Williams* leave open the question of what sanctions might be applied where defendant refuses to comply with a discovery provision; it remains to be seen whether the defense could be barred from introducing evidence because it failed to provide pretrial discovery of that evidence as required under a reciprocal discovery provision.

6. THE TRIAL STAGE

Almost half of the Bill of Rights guarantees dealing with criminal procedure specifically refer to the trial stage. Moreover, several other guarantees have a less direct, but very significant impact on the trial. It is not surprising, therefore, that the trial is one of the two major stages of the criminal process most extensively regulated by constitutional limitations and that many of the major decisions of the past fifteen years relate to the trial. Those decisions generally followed a pattern of extending the scope of constitutional regulation, but they varied considerably in their treatment of different rights and different elements of the same right.

Jury trial. The scope of the jury trial right had been fairly well defined prior to 1960 by a series of cases interpreting the Sixth Amendment. Post-1960 decisions reexamined various aspects of the jury trial right with mixed results. The right was expanded in some areas, narrowed in some, and left as it was in others. The Court reaffirmed that the right to jury trial extends to all offenses that may not be characterized as "petty" (i. e., all offenses that carry a potential imprisonment in excess of six months). *Baldwin v. N. Y.,* 399 U.S. 66 (1970). It also reaffirmed that the right did not include a correlative right to insist upon a trial before a judge sitting alone; Congress could condition defendant's waiver of a jury trial upon the consent of the prosecutor. *Singer v. U. S.,* 380 U.S. 24 (1965). Primary expansion of the right occurred in a series of cases holding that a criminal contempt proceeding is a "criminal prosecution" and the contemnor therefore has a right to a jury trial if the sentence imposed exceeded six months imprisonment. *Bloom v. Ill.,* 391 U.S. 194 (1968). See also *Codispoti v. Pa.,* 418 U.S. 506 (1974) (jury trial right applicable when aggregate sentences for contemptuous acts during a single trial exceeded six months and determination of contempt was made in a single post-trial hearing). The Court narrowed the scope of the jury trial right, however, in two other cases, holding that the jury could consist of less than twelve persons, *Williams v. Fla.* (p. 22), and that a less than unanimous verdict was acceptable in state cases. *Apodaca v. Ore.* (p. 22).

Perhaps the most significant recent developments in the constitutional regulation of jury trials relate to the jury selection process. Here again, though several post-1960 decisions established substantial new constitutional limitations, others considered and rejected equally far-reaching proposed limitations. In the area of racial discrimination, for example, the Court largely adhered to previously established limitations. The prohibition against racial discrimination in jury selection was first recognized in 1880, but the problems relating to the proof of discrimination have remained a continuing source of litigation. *Turner v. Fouche,* 396 U.S. 346 (1970), reaffirmed that a prima facie case of discrimination could be established by showing that only a small percentage of Blacks had been called to jury duty despite a much larger percentage of Blacks in the community. However, both *Turner* and *Carter v. Jury Commission,* 396 U.S. 320 (1970), refused to hold invalid a statute limiting jury service to persons "esteemed in the community for their integrity, good character, and sound judgment," even though the jury commissioners clearly had used that law to discriminate against Blacks. The Court emphasized that there was "no suggestion that the law had been originally adopted or subsequently carried forward for the purpose of fostering racial discrimination," and that careful scrutiny of discrimination claims by federal courts provided an adequate safeguard against misuse of such laws.   In *Swain v. Ala.*, 380 U.S. 202 (1965), the Court also refused to hold unconstitutional the prosecutor's use of peremptory challenges to strike all prospective Black jurors in a particular case.   The majority stressed that the function of the peremptory challenge required that its use not be subject to inquiry, but did acknowledge that a constitutional violation might be established if it could be shown that the prosecutor systematically used the peremptory challenge to exclude Blacks from all juries.   The Court did break new ground in treating still another aspect of racial bias affecting the jury trial. *Ham v. S. C.*, 409 U.S. 524 (1973), held that, even though the trial judge may be granted broad discretion in conducting a voir dire examination, he could not deny a Black, bearded defendant the opportunity to have prospective jurors questioned on the subject of racial prejudice.   The trial court had not committed constitutional error in rejecting questions concerning possible juror prejudice against bearded persons, but racial bias was distinguishable because, *inter alia,* a principal purpose of the Fourteenth Amendment was to bar racial discrimination.

[54]

The more substantial recent constitutional developments in the jury selection area primarily concerned discrimination on grounds other than race. Most notably, a series of decisions, building upon *Duncan* (p. 22), firmly establish that a jury must be selected from a "representative cross-section of the community," and a defendant may challenge exclusion of a particular segment of the community though not a member of that "excluded class." *Taylor v. La.*, 419 U.S. 522 (1975). In *Taylor*, the court overturned a pre-*Duncan* ruling and upheld a male defendant's challenge to a state practice of excluding females unless they volunteered for jury service. Similarly, *Witherspoon v. Ill.*, 391 U.S. 510 (1968), held that, in a capital case, the state denied an impartial jury on the issue of sentence when it automatically excluded prospective jurors having "conscientious or religious scruples against capital punishment," without requiring any showing that the individual would invariably reject capital punishment in all cases. Though finding a denial of a representative jury, both *Taylor* and *Witherspoon* emphasized that the "fair cross-section principle must have much leeway in application." *Taylor v. La.*, supra. Thus, *Witherspoon* also held that defendant had not been denied a representative jury on the issue of guilt in the absence of showing that the excluded anti-capital punishment jurors differed from other jurors in their approach to that

issue. And in *Hamling v. U. S.*, 418 U.S. 87
(1974), the Court ruled that, even if "the young"
should be "an identifiable group entitled to a
group-based protection under * * * prior decisions," the defendant had not been denied a representative jury simply because the jury selection
list was compiled every four years and therefore
excluded young persons who had become eligible
during the interim period. The cross-section requirement, the Court noted, does not deny the
government sufficient "play in the joints of the
jury selection process" to accommodate "the practical problems of judicial administration."

Trial publicity. The post-1960 decisions also
significantly implemented defendant's right to an
impartial jury in a series of rulings dealing with
extensive media coverage of pending cases. Although the need for remedying prejudicial pretrial publicity had been noted previously, *Irvin v.
Dowd*, 366 U.S. 717 (1961), was the first Supreme Court decision actually reversing a conviction on that ground. *Irvin* relied heavily on the
voir dire examination, which revealed that several jurors who had read newspaper reports of the
crime were firmly convinced of defendant's guilt.
In *Rideau v. La.*, 373 U.S. 723 (1963), the Court
went a step beyond *Irvin* and reversed a conviction without requiring a particularized showing
of juror prejudice. The Court found that "it was

a denial of due process * * * to refuse a request for a change in venue" when the entire community has been "exposed repeatedly and in depth" to the "spectacle" of defendant confessing to the crime in a police interview broadcast on local television.

Both *Irvin* and *Rideau* stressed the facts of the particular case—the prejudicial nature of the pretrial publicity, the extent of its dissemination in the community, and, in *Irvin,* the responses of the jurors on voir dire examination. Neither case demanded that prospective jurors be totally unaware of the case or defendant's background. Thus *Murphy v. Fla.,* — U.S. — (1975), held that defendant had not been denied a fair trial although several jurors had learned from news accounts about defendant's prior crimes. The jurors' statements on voir dire examination revealed no hostility that would cause one to doubt their assurances of impartiality, the community atmosphere was not "inflammatory," and only about one fourth of the prospective jurors examined had been excused because of prior opinion as to defendant's guilt. The defendant must be given the opportunity, however, to establish that prejudicial pretrial publicity would deny him a fair trial. Thus, *Groppi v. Wis.,* 400 U.S. 505 (1971), held unconstitutional a state statute that barred a change in venue in all misdemeanor cases without regard to the impact of pretrial publicity.

Estes v. Texas, 381 U.S. 532 (1965), and *Sheppard v. Maxwell*, 384 U.S. 333 (1966), extended the *Irvin-Rideau* analysis to publicity during the trial. In *Estes*, a divided Court (5–4) held that the Fourteenth Amendment prohibited a state from televising courtroom proceedings over the objection of the defendant. Relying on *Rideau*, the majority found that the likely prejudicial impact of televising on the jury justified reversal of defendant's conviction without showing specific instances of "isolatable prejudice." Indeed, four members of the majority expressed the view that public television of a trial was inherently prejudicial, but the fifth justice limited his concurrence to "criminal trial[s] of great notoriety" such as that involved in *Estes*. In *Sheppard* a more substantial majority relied upon several factors in noting that massive, highly prejudicial publicity had contributed to a denial of due process. Those factors included the trial judge's failure to provide privacy for the jury, to insulate witnesses from newsmen, and to control various activities of newsmen that contributed substantially to the "carnival atmosphere" of the trial.

Right of confrontation. The Sixth Amendment right of the defendant "to be confronted with witnesses against him" had not received extensive interpretation prior to its incorporation within the Fourteenth Amendment in *Pointer v. Texas* (p. 20). Since *Pointer*, the Court has decided more than a dozen cases involving confrontation issues. These cases reveal both the potentially broad impact of the confrontation clause and the Court's emphasis upon a functional analysis relating each decision to its particular procedural setting.

A substantial number of confrontation cases have concerned the admissibility of hearsay. The Court has stressed that the crucial question under the confrontation clause is not compliance with common law hearsay rules, but fulfillment of the "mission of the confrontation clause to advance the accuracy of the truth determining process * * * by assuring that the trier of fact has a satisfactory basis for evaluating the truth of a prior statement." *Cal. v. Green*, 399 U.S. 149 (1970). Thus, the states have leeway to recognize new exceptions to the prohibition against hearsay evidence if those exceptions assure defendant an adequate opportunity for cross-examination. *Cal. v. Green*, supra (upholding a state rule that inconsistent prior statements of a witness now subject to cross-examination may be admitted to prove the truth of the matters asserted therein). On the other hand, well established hearsay exceptions will not be acceptable when applied so as to unnecessarily subvert the opportunity for cross-examination. For example, the Court has accepted as consistent with the confrontation clause the hearsay exception permitting admission of prior testimony of a currently unavailable witness, but has stressed that the testimony must have been obtained at a prior proceeding where counsel had "full and adequate opportunity for cross-examination." Compare *Cal. v. Green*, supra (prior preliminary hearing testimony admissible since counsel had full cross-examination rights at the preliminary hearing) with *Pointer v. Texas*, supra (preliminary hearing testimony inadmissible where defendant lacked counsel to assist in cross-examination at the hearing). The Court also has stressed that the witness must truly be unavailable for the prior testimony exception to be applied. While permanent transfer to a foreign country was sufficient to establish unavailability, *Mancusi v. Stubbs*, 408 U.S. 204 (1972), imprisonment in a federal prison was not sufficient when the state had made no effort to secure the prisoner's appearance through the cooperation of federal authorities, *Barber v. Page*, 390 U.S. 719 (1968).

Bruton v. U. S. (p. 37) and its progeny further illustrate the Court's tendency to limit its rulings to the particular procedural setting in which customary evidentiary rules are used to admit testimony not subject to full confrontation. *Bruton* involved the use in a joint trial of the confession of one co-defendant that implicated both co-defendants. A previous Supreme Court decision and various state decisions had recognized that where the confessor refused to take the stand, use of his confession against the other co-defendant would violate that co-defendant's right of confrontation. But those cases also established that the trial court properly could admit the confession against the confessor and direct the jury not to consider it against the co-defendant. *Bruton* found such jury directions inadequate to protect against the denial of confrontation; if the state desired to use the confession against the confessor, it would simply have to forsake a joint trial or delete all references to the co-defendant. Although the language of the *Bruton* opinion was quite broad, the decision was later limited to the one aspect of the admissibility of accomplices' statements presented in that case. In *Nelson v. O'Neil*, 402 U.S. 622 (1971), *Bruton* was held inapplicable where the co-defendant took the stand, but denied making the confession. The Court found that the accomplice's favorable testimony concerning the underlying facts more than offset the defendant's inability to cross-examine effectively with respect to the confession. Applying a similar functional analysis of the testimony in the particular case, the Court also refused to set aside a conviction where a third party had testified as to a spontaneous statement by defendant's accomplice that attributed liability to the defendant. *Dutton v. Evans*, 400 U.S. 74 (1970). See also *Frazier v. Cupp*, 394 U.S. 731 (1969).

The confrontation clause has also been recognized as having a significant bearing upon the proper scope of cross-examination. Here again, rulings tend to be tied to the facts of the particular case. *Smith v. Ill.*, 390 U.S. 129 (1968), found a constitutional violation when defendant was not allowed to ask the principal prosecution witness, a police informer, either his correct name or address. *Davis v. Alaska*, 415 U.S. 308 (1974), found that the trial judge committed constitutional error in denying defense the opportunity to raise a key witness' juvenile delinquent probationary status. The Court noted that the state has a legitimate interest in protecting the anonymity of juvenile offenders, but that interest could not be utilized to bar cross-examination as to a factor obviously relevant to the witness' possible improper motivation. *Chambers v. Miss.*, (discussed at p. 69) suggests further limits on restricting cross-examination, although the decision there was based upon the due process clause rather than the confrontation clause.

While the Court has held that various state interests do not justify restricting confrontation (see, e. g., *Davis* and *Bruton*, supra), *Ill. v. Allen*, 397 U.S. 337 (1970), marked an exception where a state interest did prevail. *Allen* upheld the exclusion of a disruptive defendant from the courtroom. The court acknowledged that defendant's presence was an essential element of the right to confront witnesses, but concluded that defendant could lose that right through his own behavior. When the effective operation of the courtroom was at stake, and the defendant had brought his banishment upon himself (after due warning), the right of confrontation would not be applied in such an absolute fashion as to force the trial court to resort to often less desirable remedies (e. g., binding and gagging the defendant) just to insure that the defendant be physically present at his trial.

Perhaps the most unique application of the confrontation clause has been to the out-of-court presentation of information to the jury. Arguably such presentations easily could be invalidated upon due process grounds analogous to those cited in the prejudicial pretrial publicity cases (p. 56). However, if the source supplying the out-of-court information is treated as a witness, the confrontation clause provides another ground for objection. That approach was taken in *Parker v. Gladden*, 385 U.S. 363 (1966), where a bailiff casually commented to the jury, "oh that wicked fellow, he is guilty" and, "if there is anything wrong [in rendering a guilty verdict] * * * the Supreme Court will fix it." The Court concluded that defendant had been denied the right of confrontation since the bailiff had become, in effect, a secret witness. Compare *Turner v. La.*, 379 U.S. 466 (1965), where the Court relied solely on the impartial jury rationale in reversing a conviction when two deputy sheriffs, who were key prosecution witnesses, were placed in charge of the jury and fraternized with them throughout the trial.

Right to compulsory process. The Court has decided only one major case relying directly upon the defendant's Sixth Amendment right to "have compulsory process for obtaining witnesses in his favor." *Washington v. Texas*, 388 U.S. 14 (1967), held that the defendant's right to compulsory process was violated by a state statute prohibiting one co-participant in an alleged offense from testifying on behalf of the other participant (although allowing him to testify against the other participant). The statute presented in *Washington* was most unique, but a recent due process decision, *Chambers v. Miss.* (discussed at p. 69) may lead to future compulsory process rulings having a far more significant impact upon trial practice.

Self-incrimination. The Fifth Amendment privilege against self-incrimination permits the defendant to refuse to take the stand at trial. Post-1960 decisions emphasize that that right cannot be undermined by placing improper burdens upon its exercise. Most significantly, *Griffin v. Cal.*, 380 U.S. 609 (1965), rejected well accepted practice in several states when it held that the privilege barred any potentially adverse comment by court or prosecutor on the defendant's failure to take the stand. *Brooks v. Tenn.*, 406 U.S. 605 (1972), held that a state could not force a defendant to make his choice as to whether to take the stand before he had heard the testimony of defense witnesses. While the state has a legitimate interest in ensuring that a defendant not color his testimony to conform to the prior testimony of defense witnesses, "pressuring the defendant to take the stand, by foreclosing [his] later testimony [if he refuses to testify as the first witness on his own behalf], is not a constitutionally permissible means of insuring his honesty."

Double jeopardy. The Fifth Amendment also provides that no person shall be "twice put in jeopardy" for the "same offense." Post-1960 decisions dealing with double jeopardy largely have involved the application of previously developed standards. The Court has adhered to the position that jeopardy attaches when the jury is sworn, but the attachment of jeopardy does not necessarily prohibit a subsequent retrial for the same offense. If the trial is terminated before verdict (i. e., a "mistrial" is declared), a retrial is permitted if the mistrial was justified by "manifest necessity." The Court has been sharply divided, however, in the evaluation of particular factors that might contribute to a finding of manifest necessity, and recent decisions largely have been limited to the facts of the individual case.   Compare *Downum v. U. S.*, 372 U.S. 734 (1963); *U. S. v. Jorn*, 400 U.S. 470 (1971); *Ill. v. Sommerville*, 410 U.S. 458 (1973).   Where the jury reaches a guilty verdict, the double jeopardy prohibition also may not bar a retrial. If the defendant appeals and gains reversal of his conviction, a new trial is permitted. *Green v. U. S.*, 355 U.S. 184 (1957), held, however, that where the jury initially convicted only on a lesser included charge, this amounted to an acquittal on the higher charge, and a new trial following reversal of the conviction must be limited to the lower charge.   In *N. C. v. Pearce* (discussed at p. 75), the Court rejected an extension of *Green* that would have restricted the trial court's authority on a retrial to imposing a sentence no more harsh than that imposed for the initial, reversed conviction.

Recent decisions also have further explored the double jeopardy limitations upon the state's authority to provide for prosecution appeals following the attachment of jeopardy. Those decisions clearly establish that double jeopardy prohibits a government appeal from a verdict of acquittal, even where the appeal is based on an alleged error at trial. On the other hand, the Court has held that double jeopardy does not prohibit a prosecution appeal where sustaining the prosecution's claim would not require a new trial (e. g., where the jury originally found guilt and the trial judge then set aside that verdict, reversal of the trial judge's ruling would simply require reinstituting the jury verdict, and therefore the trial judge's ruling can be appealed). See *U. S. v. Wilson*, 420 U.S. —— (1975); *U. S. v. Jenkins*, 420 U.S. —— (1975).

With respect to one aspect to the double jeopardy clause—determining what constitutes the "same offense"—the Court has clearly moved away from prior precedent towards an expansion of the jeopardy prohibition. *Ashe v. Swenson* (discussed at p. 35) added a collateral estoppel element that extends the jeopardy prohibition beyond a technical view of the same offense limitation. *Waller v. Fla.*, 397 U.S. 387 (1970), found that state and local prosecutions based on the same basic acts did constitute prosecutions for the "same offense"; accordingly an initial conviction under a local ordinance bars a subsequent prosecution under state law. While *Waller* distinguished prior rulings permitting successive state and federal prosecutions for the same acts [e. g., *Bartkus v. Ill.*, 359 U.S. 121 (1959)], the continuing validity of those rulings remains questionable. Concurring opinions in *Ashe*, as noted at p. 36, also left open the possibility of further expansion of the same offense concept.

Due process. The Supreme Court has long relied upon the due process clause in imposing constitutional standards upon various aspects of the criminal process that do not appear to fall readily within the reach of the more specific Bill of Rights guarantees.   Several of the post-1960 rulings relating to the trial stage continued this approach.   In a few instances, these rulings simply recognized as constitutionally based principles that had been universally accepted as a matter of state law.   Thus, *In re Winship*, 397 U.S. 358 (1970), held that the due process clause requires as a standard of proof that guilt be established beyond a reasonable doubt.   Similarly, *Drope v. Mo.*, 420 U.S. 162 (1975), held that due process prohibits trial of a defendant "whose mental condition is such that he lacks the capacity to understand the nature and the object of the proceedings against him."   Other cases noted that an improper charge to the jury or an improper summation by the prosecutor could render a trial "so fundamentally unfair" as to "rise to the level of a constitutional error."   *Donnelly v. DeChristoforo*, 416 U. S. 637 (1974); *Cool v. U. S.*, 409 U.S. 100 (1972). The impropriety, however, must be sufficiently grave as to "infect the entire trial" with unfairness. *Cupp v. Naughten*, 414 U.S. 141 (1973).

In other areas, the Court extended the application of principles of fairness recognized in previous due process rulings.   Thus, as previously noted (pp. 48–49), it expanded the duty of the prosecutor to disclose at trial potentially exculpatory material, although considerable disagreement remained as to the precise scope of that duty. See *Brady v. Md.* (p. 49); *Giles v. Md.* (p. 49); *Moore v. Ill.*, 408 U.S. 786 (1972). The Court also extended earlier rulings holding that, just as the Sixth Amendment requires an impartial jury, due process requires an "impartial" judge when the case is tried to a judge rather than a jury. Thus, a judge was held to be barred from sitting on cases in which he had a special institutional, but no personal financial, interest in the imposition of fines. See *Ward v. Village of Monroeville*, 409 U.S. 57 (1972) (mayor could not sit as judge in traffic cases where he had executive responsibility for finances of the village substantially supported by court fines). Similarly, where a contempt charge was based upon defendant's highly personal attack against the trial judge, that judge was held constitutionally precluded from presiding over the non-summary contempt proceedings even though he had not become "personally embroiled" in the controversy. *Mayberry v. Pa.*, 400 U.S. 455 (1971). The guiding standard in this area, the Court emphasized, must look to the "likelihood or appearance of bias," rather than "proof of actual bias." *Taylor v. Hayes*, 418 U.S. 488 (1974).

Finally, *Chambers v. Miss.*, 410 U.S. 284 (1973), although resting on due process grounds, may presage further extension of two Sixth

Amendment rights. Defendant Chambers was sharply restricted by the trial court in his attempts to bring before the jury evidence relating to a confession of one McDonald admitting to the commission of the homicide for which Chambers was charged. The trial court refused on hearsay grounds to allow the testimony of third persons who had heard McDonald confess, and, when defendant called McDonald as his own witness, the trial court refused to permit cross-examination of McDonald as an adverse witness. The Supreme Court noted that the first ruling interfered with defendant's right to compulsory process under the Sixth Amendment and the second ruling restricted his right of confrontation protected by the same Amendment. It found no need, however, to determine whether either ruling itself violated a Sixth Amendment guarantee because the combined impact of the two rulings resulted in a denial of due process. It remains to be seen whether *Chambers* will be treated in the future as an isolated due process ruling, limited by its special facts, or as the foundation for the development of new Sixth Amendment standards relating both to confrontation and to the presentation of defense witnesses.

7. POST–TRIAL PROCEDURES

Sentencing. Prior to the 1960's, only a few major constitutional decisions had dealt directly with sentencing procedure. These cases held that sentencing, though not "immune" from the restrictions of due process, nevertheless was not subject to the same constitutional limitations as the trial process. That conclusion was based, in part, on the historical separation of the trial and sentencing stages. It was also justified on the ground that fulfillment of the basic objectives of sentencing, particularly the emphasis on relating punishment to the individual as well as the crime, would often require more flexible procedural standards than those applied to the determination of guilt. Thus, in *Williams v. Okla.*, 358 U.S. 576 (1959), the Court held that a sentencing judge could "consider responsible unsworn or 'out-of-court' information relative to the circumstances of the crime and to the convicted person's life and characteristics." And, in *Williams v. N. Y.*, 337 U.S. 241 (1949), it held that the defendant had no constitutional right to an adversary sentencing proceeding in which he could cross-examine persons who had supplied such information to the court.

Cases decided in recent years have continued to recognize the special functions of sentencing proceedings, but they also reflect an unwillingness to assume automatically that the application of basic procedural rights would significantly disrupt these functions. *Mempha v. Rhay* (p. 348) established that the indigent defendant's Sixth

Amendment right to appointed counsel applies to the initial imposition of sentence even where sentencing has been deferred to a subsequent probation revocation proceeding. *Gagnon v. Scarpelli* (p. 349) further held that, although a probation revocation following the imposition of sentence is not part of the "criminal prosecution" governed by the Sixth Amendment, due process requires the appointment of counsel when the issues presented indicate that counsel's assistance will be necessary for a fair hearing. *Morrissey v. Brewer*, 408 U.S. 471 (1972), similarly held that, while a parole revocation proceeding "is not part of a criminal prosecution and thus the full panoply of rights due a defendant * * * does not apply," due process still requires hearings at "two important stages in the typical process of parole revocations"—a preliminary hearing at the place of the arrest and a revocation hearing at the correctional institution to which the parolee is returned. Moreover, due process requires that such hearings be conducted by independent officers (though not necessarily judicial officers), that the parolee be given ample notice, that he be allowed to present evidence on his own behalf, and that he be allowed cross-examination of adverse witnesses (unless an exception is justified by "good cause").

The Court has also examined in recent years the special problems presented by allocation of sentencing responsibility to juries (a practice followed in approximately a dozen states for noncapital crimes and in many others for capital offenses). While expressing concern, it has been reluctant to restrict jury sentencing on procedural grounds alone. In *Spencer v. Texas*, 385 U.S. 554 (1967), a divided Court held that defendant was not denied a fair trial when the jury determining guilt was fully informed in the same proceeding of defendant's past record so as to be able to apply a habitual offender sentencing provision. Similarly, in *Crampton v. Ohio*, 402 U.S. 183 (1973), the Court rejected petitioner's contention that allowing the jury to determine guilt and impose the death penalty in a single proceeding created an "intolerable tension" between defendant's right to refuse to take the stand and his right to be heard on the issue of punishment. A companion case, *McGautha v. Cal.*, 402 U.S. 183 (1971), also rejected a claim that permitting a jury to impose the death penalty without any prescribed standards violated due process. Subsequently, however, a divided (5–4) Court held that "the imposition and carrying out" of the death penalty under typical state statutes "constituted cruel and unusual punishment in violation of the Eighth and Fourteenth Amendments." *Furman v. Ga.*, 408 U.S. 238 (1972). At least three members of the majority based their separate opinions on the consequences of the statutory grants of discretion to the jury or judge in determining when the death penalty should be imposed. Two of these Justices emphasized the "infrequent imposition of the death penalty" without any "meaningful basis for distinguishing cases in which it is imposed from the many cases in which it is not" (White, J.), and the third found that "these discretionary statutes" were, as applied, "pregnant with discrimination" based upon race, wealth, and social position (Douglas J.). Consider also *Giacco v. Pa.*, 382 U.S. 399 (1966) (holding unconstitutional as unduly vague a state statute permitting the jury, at its discretion, to tax costs against an exonerated defendant).

Appeals. The Supreme Court held in *McKane v. Durston*, 153 U.S. 684 (1894), that a state was not constitutionally required to provide appellate review of criminal convictions. See also *Ross v. Moffit* (p. 328). All states now provide for appellate review, however, and the Supreme Court has held that, once established, appellate review cannot be restricted or burdened on arbitrary grounds. Thus, *Griffin v. Ill.* (p. 326)held that the availability of review cannot be conditioned on the convicted defendant's financial status; where a state requires a trial transcript for review, it must provide that transcript for the indigent. Indeed, *Douglas v. Cal.* (p. 326) held that the state must also provide the indigent with appointed counsel on his first appeal as a matter of right. Compare *Ross v. Moffit* (p. 328) (appointed counsel not necessary on discretionary appeal).

N. C. v. Pearce, 395 U.S. 711 (1969), granted further protection to the appellate process in barring potential vindictiveness against those who use the process. *Pearce* involved defendants who had appealed their initial convictions, obtained reversals, were retried on the same charges, convicted again, and then sentenced to more severe sentences than on the first conviction. *Pearce* initially rejected the contention that the double jeopardy clause applied to the first sentence and therefore absolutely barred a more severe second sentence. Due process, however, did prohibit the imposition of a more severe sentence for the purpose of discouraging defendants from exercising their statutory right to appeal. To facilitate attack on such improper motivation, the majority held that, "whenever a judge imposes a more severe sentence upon a defendant after a new trial, the reasons for his doing so must affirmatively appear." Moreover, "those reasons must be based upon objective information concerning identifiable conduct on the part of the defendant occurring after the time of the original sentencing proceeding." These "prophylactic requirements" constitute a dramatic departure from traditional sentencing practice which does not require any statement justifying the sentence or restrict consideration to defendant's behavior during a specific period.   In *Chaffin v. Stynchcombe,* 412 U.S. 17 (1973), the *Pearce* requirements were held inapplicable to jury sentencing since the jury "is unlikely to be sensitive to the institutional interests that might occasion higher sentences by a judge desirous of discouraging what he regards as meritless appeals."   The *Pearce* analogy was held applicable, however, to bar the prosecutor's initiation of a felony charge after defendant sought a trial de novo on appeal from a misdemeanor conviction based on the same activities.   *Blackledge v. Perry,* 417 U.S. 21 (1974).

8.   RETROACTIVITY

It should be emphasized that not all of the newly imposed constitutional restrictions discussed in the previous sections have been given full retroactive effect (i. e., applied on appeal and in habeas corpus proceedings to all prior convictions).   The rulings in *Mapp* (p. 28), *Griffin* (p. 326), *Coleman* (p. 342), *Miranda* (p. 29), *Gilbert* (p. 246), *Wade* (p. 246), *Katz* (p. 171), and *Duncan* (p. 22), were limited largely to prospective application.   See *Desist v. U. S.,* 394 U.S. 244 (1969); *Mich. v. Payne,* 412 U.S. 47 (1973) (collecting cases).   In determining whether a new ruling should be given retroactive effect, the Court has relied primarily upon three considerations: "(a) the purpose to be served by the new standards, (b) the extent of the reliance by law enforcement authorities on the old standards, and (c) the effect on the administration of justice of a retroactive application of the new standards." *Stovall v. Denno*, 388 U.S. 293 (1967). The Court has noted, however, that the "foremost" factor is the first. Decisions have sought to distinguish between new rulings that are designed to "avoid unfairness at the trial by enhancing the reliability of the fact-finding process" and those designed to serve other, independent interests, such as individual privacy. Rulings in the latter category have been held not to require retroactive application. Thus, the Court ruled that *Mapp* could be limited to prospective application because, inter alia, the deterrent functions of the exclusionary rule would not be enhanced by retroactive application. "[T]he misconduct of the police prior to *Mapp* had already occurred and [would] not be corrected by releasing the prisoners involved." *Linkletter v. Walker*, 381 U.S. 618 (1965).

Where the new ruling clearly is designed to enhance the reliability of the guilt determination process, it generally has been given retroactive effect. There have been a few instances, however, in which rulings at least partially serving that function, e. g., *Wade* and *Gilbert*, (providing counsel at lineups), have been applied only prospectively. Emphasis here has been on the second and third considerations noted above—reliance of law enforcement officials on prior standards and the administrative burden of retroactive application. In examining the reliance factor, the Court has looked particularly to the clarity of prior law—i. e., whether, under prior precedent, the state's practice was clearly constitutional or subject to significant doubt. In examining the administrative burden, the Court has sought to evaluate the procedural difficulties presented in applying the particular ruling to cases decided long before that ruling. *Desist v. U. S.*, supra. It has also given considerable weight to the application in such cases of prior rulings that served to ensure the reliability of the fact-finding process (although not so effectively as the new rulings). *Stovall v. Denno*, supra.

While the various decisions noted above have been denied general retroactive application, they have not all been limited in application to prosecutions brought after the date of the decision (as was the case with *Miranda* and *Escobedo*). The *Mapp* and *Griffin* rulings were also applied to all cases pending on direct review on the dates of the respective rulings. The *Katz* and *Wade* decisions, on the other hand, were applied only to future prosecutions in which the proscribed official conduct had occurred after the date of the respective decisions. This variation in treatment of "non-retroactive" rulings has been justified, in part, on the particular function of the individual ruling and the scope of the reliance upon past decisions. See *Desist v. U. S.*, supra.

9. BASIC THEMES

The Supreme Court has decided over 300 cases involving questions of constitutional-criminal procedure during the past fifteen years, and each decision was undoubtedly governed to a considerable extent by the particular issue before court. Nevertheless, viewed as a whole, the decisions do reflect certain basic policy positions, which contributed in a general fashion to individual rulings. Although several such policy positions may be suggested by the Court's opinions, four in particular stand out.

First, the opinions have consistently emphasized that criminal procedure involves important aspects of individual liberty and should be of primary concern to society and the Court itself. As Chief Justice Warren put it, "No general respect for, nor adherence to, the law as a whole can well be expected without judicial recognition of the paramount need for prompt, eminently fair and sober criminal law procedures. The methods we employ in the enforcement of our criminal law have aptly been called the measures by which the quality of our civilization may be judged." *Coppedge v. U. S.*, 369 U.S. 438 (1962).

Closely related to this theme has been the emphasis on achieving equality in the administration of the criminal law. The Court has recognized the unequal impact of criminal procedure on the poor and racial minorities and has sought to eliminate at least the official aspects of such inequality. Although only a few decisions have been based squarely on the equal protection clause, others, like *Gideon* (p. 20) and *Miranda* (p. 29) had strong equal protection overtones.

A third theme relates to the appropriate function of federal-state relations in framing constitutional limitations upon criminal procedure. Prior to the 1960's, the Court had frequently noted that "the very essence of our federalism [requires] that the states should have the widest latitude in the administration of their own system of criminal justice." *Hoag v. N. J.*, 356 U.S. 464 (1958). It was suggested that disparity in the types of crimes investigated, the nature of the communities immediately concerned, and the organization of law enforcement agencies required that more flexible constitutional standards be applied to the state than the federal government. Since the early 1960's, a majority of the Court has consistently rejected this position. The majority has emphasized that, while states may properly serve as laboratories to try novel social and economic systems, they should not be allowed the same discretion "when fundamental rights" are involved. Moreover, several justices have maintained that a uniform constitutional standard, though more restrictive, actually improves federal-state relations by (1) encouraging cooperation between federal and state police agencies through elimination of suspicion that their working arrangements "were designed to take advantage of the more flexible standards applicable to state prosecutions," and (2) eliminating the friction between state and federal courts that flows from the application of flexible constitutional standards that emphasize the totality of the circumstances and therefore are largely unpredictable in application and tend to personalize any reversals of state proceedings. See *Pointer v. Texas* (p. 5) (Goldberg, J., con.); *Mapp v. Ohio* (p. 28).

Elimination of the more flexible constitutional standards previously applied to the states has naturally tended to broaden the scope of constitutional rulings. But even aside from this tendency, the opinions of the last fifteen years often have reflected an independent movement toward more broadly stated rulings. Decisions like *Miranda* (p. 29), *Mapp* p. 28), and *Morrissey* (p. 72) reflect an inclination toward more generalized constitutional standards that extend substantially beyond the facts of the particular case. Indeed, in several cases, the Court went beyond the

proscription of particular unconstitutional practices to prescribe "prophylactic procedures" that
it viewed as needed to safeguard against such unconstitutional practices. *Miranda* held that, to
avoid the potential violation of defendant's privilege against self-incrimination during custodial
interrogation, the defendant must be warned of
his rights, and given the right to consult with
counsel (either his own or appointed counsel if he
is indigent) before and during any interrogation.
Similarly, *Pearce* (p. 75) sought to prevent vin-
dictive sentencing against defendants who exercise their right to appeal by limiting more severe
sentences after a retrial to situations in which
the judge can justify the added severity by reference to defendant's subsequent conduct.

The Court's inclination toward more general
rulings has been a subject of sharp debate within
the Court and often has not commanded the support of a majority of the justices. The Court has
on various occasions rejected the adoption of prophylactic procedures in favor of a particularized
evaluation of prosecution or police conduct in the
individual case. See, e. g., *Barker v. Wingo* (p.
40); *Schneckloth v. Bustamonte* (p. 145). Consider also the division among the majority in
Estes v. Texas (p. 58).

Moreover, where the Court has adopted broad
rulings, the policy justifications for such rulings
often seem to have varied considerably among

the justices. Some justices apparently believed that more generalized rulings were necessary to ensure the effective day-by-day implementation of constitutional rights. Their comments, often in concurring opinions, suggested that limited rulings based upon a series of variable factors were too easily evaded and therefore largely ineffective in discouraging improper practices. Compare, e. g., the several opinions in *Miranda* and *Pearce*. There is some indication, however, that, at least in certain areas, the establishment of broad rules to ensure day-by-day implementation of constitutional rights may have been viewed by the majority as largely a legislative task, but one which the Court had to take upon itself in the absence of appropriate legislation. Thus, the *Miranda* and *Wade* (p. 246) opinions both noted that the affirmative safeguards required there were not absolute constitutional necessities, and both expressly invited legislative formulation of alternative schemes that would provide equally adequate safeguards. On the other hand, it is also noteworthy that both decisions dealt with police investigatory practices. Some justices have indicated that they will be less reluctant to impose expanded restraints on the trial process, where the issues presented are raised in a relatively uniform and familiar context and fall within the traditional expertise of the courts. *In re Gault*, 387 U.S. 1, 70 (1967) (Harlan, J., con.).

The future implementation of the basic themes outlined above will depend in large measure on the particular composition of the Court, but the very presence of the decisions of the past fifteen years probably ensures that the policy issues presented in those cases will continue to occupy much of the Court's efforts over the next several years.

CHAPTER 2

ARREST, SEARCH AND SEIZURE

10. INTRODUCTION

The Fourth Amendment. The Fourth Amendment to the U. S. Constitution reads: "The right of the people to be secure in their persons, houses, papers, and effects, against unreasonable searches and seizures, shall not be violated, and no Warrants shall issue, but upon probable cause, supported by Oath or affirmation, and particularly describing the place to be searched, and the persons or things to be seized." The Amendment is applicable to the states through the due process clause of the Fourteenth Amendment (see § 2), and thus evidence obtained in violation of the Amendment is subject to exclusion in the state courts, *Mapp v. Ohio*, 367 U.S. 643 (1961), as well as the federal courts, *Weeks v. U. S.*, 232 U.S. 383 (1914). The same standards of reasonableness and probable cause govern both federal and state activities. *Ker v. Cal.*, 374 U.S. 23 (1963); *Aguilar v. Texas*, 378 U.S. 108 (1964).

Seizure of the person. Because of the exclusionary sanction, the Fourth Amendment is more

[85]

commonly thought of as a limitation on the power of police to search for and seize evidence, instrumentalities, and fruits of crime. However, an illegal arrest or other unreasonable seizure of the person is itself a violation of the Fourth and Fourteenth Amendments, *Terry v. Ohio*, 392 U.S. 1 (1968); *Henry v. U. S.*, 361 U.S. 98 (1959), although it is no defense to a state or federal criminal prosecution that the defendant was illegally arrested or forcibly brought within the jurisdiction of the court, *Frisbie v. Collins*, 342 U.S. 519 (1952), except perhaps when the circumstances are particularly shocking. *U. S. v. Toscanino*, 500 F.2d 267 (2d Cir. 1974).

Whether an arrest or other seizure of the person conforms to the requirements of the Constitution is nonetheless frequently a matter of practical importance. The police are authorized to conduct a limited search without warrant incident to a lawful arrest (see § 14B), and thus the admissibility of physical evidence acquired in this way depends upon the validity of the arrest. The same is true of certain other evidentiary "fruits" obtained subsequent to and as a consequence of the arrest (see § 32).

The major issues. Several Fourth Amendment issues of current significance are surveyed in this Chapter. Consideration is first given to the areas and interests protected by the Amendment (see § 11), for they determine what constitutes a "search" and thus what activities are subject to the requirements of the Amendment. The most pervasive requirement of the Amendment is that of "probable cause," needed for lawful arrests and searches both with and without warrant, and special attention is therefore given to the meaning and significance of this quantum-of-evidence standard (see § 12). Other constitutional requirements for obtaining physical evidence by search warrant (see § 13), without a warrant (see § 14), and with consent (see § 15) are separately considered. Finally, to illustrate the flexibility of the Fourth Amendment limitations, this Chapter covers some unique practices for which separate rules have been developed because of the limited intrusion or special need attending their use: inspections and regulatory searches (see § 16); and brief detentions for purposes of investigation (see § 17).

11. PROTECTED AREAS AND INTERESTS

Property interests vs. privacy interests. What is a search under the Fourth Amendment? The traditional approach has been to speak of intrusion into certain "constitutionally protected areas," in that the Fourth Amendment protects the "right of the people to be secure in their persons, houses, papers, and effects, against unreasonable searches and seizures." The word "houses" has not been interpreted literally, and thus the protection has been extended to such places as a store, business office, hotel room, automobile, and occupied taxicab, but not to a jail, where "official surveillance has traditionally been the order of the day." *Lanza v. N. Y.*, 370 U.S. 139 (1962).

This property approach was rejected in *Katz v. U. S.*, 389 U.S. 347 (1967), in favor of a privacy approach. In concluding that a nontrespassory eavesdropping into a public telephone booth constituted a search, the Court declined to characterize the booth as a "constitutionally protected area": "For the Fourth Amendment protects people, not places. What a person knowingly exposes to the public, even in his own home or office, is not a subject of Fourth Amendment protection * * *. But what he seeks to preserve as private, even in an area accessible to the public, may be constitutionally protected."

In light of the difficulties which have grown out of the use of property concepts (particularly the "trespass" doctrine) in resolving Fourth Amendment issues, this shift to a privacy approach is an appealing one, although it will undoubtedly require clarification in future cases. The majority opinion in *Katz* does not elaborate

[*88*]

upon the privacy approach, except for the helpful observation that defendant's activities were protected because the government intrusion "violated the privacy upon which he justifiably relied." Justice Harlan, concurring, suggests a "two-fold requirement: first, that a person have exhibited an actual (subjective) expectation of privacy; and, second, that the expectation be one that society is prepared to recognize as 'reasonable.' " [But later, dissenting in *U. S. v. White*, 401 U.S. 745 (1971), he cautioned against undue emphasis upon actual expectations, which "are in large part reflections" of what the law permits.] He also notes, quite correctly, that in asking what protection the Fourth Amendment affords people (i. e., where an expectation of privacy is reasonable), it is generally necessary to answer with reference to a place, and thus it would seem that most of the earlier property-based decisions discussed below are not disturbed by *Katz*.

The "curtilage" concept. Traditionally, the Fourth Amendment extends only to such area surrounding a dwelling as comes within the common law concept of the curtilage, which includes "all buildings in close proximity to a dwelling, which are continually used for carrying on domestic employment, or such place as is necessary and convenient to a dwelling, and is habitually used for family purposes." *U. S. v. Potts*, 297 F. 2d 68 (6th Cir. 1961). Thus, an open field some

distance from a household is not so protected.
Hester v. U. S., 265 U.S. 57 (1924).

Courts have experienced considerable difficulty
in employing the curtilage test to determine the
status of such structures as garages, barns, and
other outbuildings, although it has not infre-
quently been held that such buildings are not protected if they are detached from the residence.
Carney v. U. S., 163 F.2d 784 (9th Cir. 1947).
Other courts have severely criticized the curtilage
concept; it has been argued that a garage should
be entitled to Fourth Amendment protection
without regard to whether it is within the curtilage, *U. S. v. Hayden*, 140 F.Supp. 429 (D.Md.
1956), and that a farmer's barn is no less deserv-
ing of such protection than an urban dweller's
place of business, *Walker v. U. S.*, 225 F.2d 447
(5th Cir. 1955) (dissent). *Katz* lends considerable support to these latter views, and will undoubtedly result in protection of buildings outside
the curtilage in which there is a justified expectation of privacy. *Katz* is also somewhat inconsistent with the "open fields" doctrine of *Hester*, and
thus it would no longer seem correct to apply
Hester, as in *McDowell v. U. S.*, 383 F.2d 599
(8th Cir. 1967), to instances in which the police
enter fields in which the defendant has manifested an expectation of privacy by posting "no hunt-
ing" and "no trespassing" signs.

But the most significant impact of *Katz* is likely to be that whether the police have conducted a search within the meaning of the Fourth Amendment is not to be determined solely by whether they crossed the invisible line into the defendant's curtilage. For one thing, some police entries within the curtilage may properly be viewed as not intruding upon any reasonable privacy expectation. For example, in *P. v. Bradley*, 460 P.2d 129 (Cal.1969), where police discovered and seized marijuana growing in a planter in defendant's fenced back yard, it was held that he had no reasonable expectation of privacy with respect to the planter because it could be readily observed by delivery men and others who would come to the back door. And in *Wattenburg v. U. S.*, 388 F.2d 853 (9th Cir. 1968), the court ruled inadmissible evidence obtained from the search of a stockpile of trees located on the grounds of defendant's motel, but indicated that this was not merely because the trees were located within the curtilage, but rather because the meticulous inspection of the trees for over six hours intruded upon defendant's privacy. On the other hand, there will be cases in which the police have intruded upon the defendant's justified expectation of privacy even though they did not trespass upon property exclusively possessed by the defendant. For example, under a trespass approach it might be concluded that police observations into a fourth floor apart-

ment from a fire escape do not constitute a
search, but under the *Katz* approach it would be
necessary to inquire whether the fire escape was
used for other than emergencies and whether one
going down the fire escape in an emergency
would have a view into the apartment. *Cohen v.
Superior Court*, 85 Cal.Rptr. 354 (App.1970).

The "plain view" doctrine. Contrary to an
earlier position, courts generally recognize that
mere observation without physical entry onto
protected premises may amount to a search, *U. S.
v. Gonzales*, 388 F.2d 145 (5th Cir. 1968), a conclusion supported by the *Katz* decision. Yet, "it
has long been settled that objects falling in the
plain view of an officer who has a right to be in
the position to have that view are subject to seizure and may be introduced in evidence." *Harris
v. U. S.*, 390 U.S. 234 (1968). The plain view
doctrine has been applied in cases in which officers standing upon public property looked into
car windows, *Nunez v. U. S.*, 370 F.2d 538 (5th
Cir. 1967), or the windows of dwellings, *P. v.
Wright*, 242 N.E.2d 180 (Ill.1968), and also when
the observations were by officers while on defendant's property in the pursuit of legitimate
business, *Ellison v. U. S.*, 206 F.2d 476 (D.C.Cir.
1953). These decisions are not inconsistent with
Katz, for it may be said that the defendant
should have reasonably anticipated that such ob-

servations could be made by others in the normal pursuit of their daily activities.

The same may not be true if the police, though not on defendant's property, employ artificial means in making the observations. The notion that such observations are permissible even if by "the use of bifocals, field glasses or the telescope to magnify" it is possible to focus "upon what one supposes to be private indiscretions," *On Lee v. U. S.*, 343 U.S. 747 (1952), appears to conflict with the *Katz* rationale, and now a closer examination of the circumstances will be required to determine the reasonableness of the defendant's privacy expectation. Most subject to question are earlier cases permitting nontrespassory use of highly sophisticated and unusual devices, such as a "scintillator" (an instrument sensitive to radiation), as in *Corngold v. U. S.*, 367 F.2d 1 (9th Cir. 1966). As for the traditional view that observations by flashlight or other artificial light do not constitute a search, *U. S. v. Lee*, 274 U.S. 559 (1927), it may need to be reassessed, although these devices are so commonly employed that their nighttime use to see what would be in plain view in the daytime cannot be said to be reasonably unanticipated. *Marshall v. U. S.*, 422 F.2d 185 (5th Cir. 1970).

Abandoned property. Another longstanding doctrine is that it is permissible for the police to search for and seize property which has been abandoned, provided that the abandonment was not prompted by prior illegal police conduct. *P. v. Roebuck*, 183 N.E.2d 166 (Ill.1962). On this basis, warrantless searches of garbage cans have been upheld. *U. S. v. Minker*, 312 F.2d 632 (3d Cir. 1963). Since *Katz*, however, it is important to inquire into the nature of the abandonment in order to determine whether the defendant still had a justified expectation of privacy with respect to the abandoned property. Taking this approach, it has correctly been held that examination of the contents of a garbage can is a search, for the expectation is that the garbage will be hauled away and then lose "its identity and meaning by becoming part of a larger conglomeration of trash elsewhere." *P. v. Edwards*, 458 P. 2d 713 (Cal.1969).

What may be seized? In *Gouled v. U. S.*, 255 U.S. 298 (1921), where federal agents investigating use of the mails to defraud obtained a search warrant on probable cause for seizure of an executed contract, an unexecuted contract, and some bills for legal services, it was held that these objects were of evidential value only and that therefore their seizure violated the Fourth Amendment and their use in evidence violated the Fifth Amendment. This so-called "mere evidence" rule was later applied to the seizure of items found in a search incident to arrest. *U. S. v. Lefkowitz*, 285 U.S. 452 (1932). The rule was severely criticized and often rejected by state courts, e. g., *P. v. Thayer*, 408 P.2d 108 (Cal.1965), and was frequently circumvented in the federal courts by extreme characterizations of evidence as the instrumentalities of crime, *U. S. v. Guido*, 251 F.2d 1 (7th Cir. 1958).

The "mere evidence" rule was discarded in *Warden v. Hayden,* 387 U.S. 294 (1967), where the Court held admissible items of clothing found in a "hot pursuit" search for a robber. This rejection of the distinction between "mere evidence" and instrumentalities, fruits of crime, and contraband was based upon the conclusions that (1) nothing in the language of the Fourth Amendment supports the distinction; (2) privacy is disturbed no more by a search for evidentiary material than other property; (3) the Fourth Amendment protects privacy rather than property, so that the defendant's or the government's property interest in the items seized is not relevant; and (4) the distinction had spawned numerous exceptions and great confusion.

The Court was careful to emphasize in *Hayden* that "the items of clothing involved in this case are not 'testimonial' or 'communicative' in nature, and their introduction therefore did not compel respondent to become a witness against himself in violation of the Fifth Amendment." This suggests that there may remain some items which are not subject to seizure, such as a diary in which its author has recited his criminal conduct. One possibility is that such items are protected by the Fifth Amendment, as held *re* a doctor's records in *Hill v. Philpott*, 445 F.2d 144 (7th Cir. 1971), although it has been argued that Fifth Amendment considerations should not be controlling here in that even in the days of the "mere evidence" rule it was permissible to search for and seize items which, under the Fifth Amendment, the defendant could not be required to produce in response to a subpoena. *U. S. v. Bennett*, 409 F.2d 888 (2d Cir. 1969). Another possibility is that such items are protected by the First Amendment (compare the developments as to search for obscene literature, discussed at p. 113). As for the Fourth Amendment, the argument is that it may sometimes be unreasonable to permit search for and seizure of certain items, e. g., a diary, in that even if they are specifically described the result will be a rummaging through and official scrutiny of private writing unconnected with crime. *U. S. v. Bennett*, supra.

Notwithstanding *Hayden,* a search warrant should not ordinarily be utilized to obtain evidence from a nonsuspect; he is entitled to greater Fourth Amendment protection, given the usual lack of need to acquire the evidence by surprise, and thus should be afforded the less intrusive alternative of responding to a subpoena duces tecum. *Stanford Daily v. Zurcher*, 353 F.Supp. 124

(N.D.Cal.1972). Even if this evidence in possession of others is owned by the suspect, his Fourth and Fifth Amendment rights are not violated by the subpoena, except perhaps where his "relinquishment of possession is so temporary and insignificant as to leave the personal compulsions upon the accused substantially intact." *Couch v. U. S.*, 409 U.S. 322 (1973).

12. "PROBABLE CAUSE" AND RELATED PROBLEMS

When and why "probable cause" in issue. The Fourth Amendment provides that "no Warrants shall issue, but upon probable cause," and thus it is apparent that a valid arrest warrant or search warrant may only be issued upon an affidavit or complaint which sets forth facts establishing probable cause. Those arrests and searches which may be made without a warrant must not be "unreasonable" under the Fourth Amendment, and because the requirements in such cases "surely cannot be less stringent" than when a warrant is obtained, *Wong Sun v. U. S.*, 371 U.S. 471 (1963), probable cause is also required in such circumstances. *Draper v. U. S.*, 358 U.S. 307 (1959).

When the police act without a warrant, they initially make the probable cause decision themselves, although it will be subject to after-the-fact review by a judicial officer upon a motion to suppress evidence found because of the arrest or search. When the police act with a warrant, the probable cause decision is made by a magistrate in the first instance, but his decision may likewise be challenged in an adversary setting upon a motion to suppress.

Although there are many circumstances in which arrests and searches may be made without a warrant (see § 14), the Supreme Court has expressed a strong preference for arrest warrants, *Beck v. Ohio*, 379 U.S. 89 (1964), and search warrants, *U. S. v. Ventresca*, 380 U.S. 102 (1965), on the ground that interposing an orderly procedure whereby a neutral and detached magistrate makes the decision is better than allowing those engaged in the competitive enterprise of ferreting out crime to make hurried decisions which would be reviewable by a magistrate only after the fact and by hindsight judgment. This preference has even resulted in a subtle difference between the probable cause required when there is no warrant and that required when there is; "in a doubtful or marginal case a search under a warrant may be sustainable where without one it would fall." *U. S. v. Ventresca*, supra.

Although there is reason to question whether before-the-fact review when warrants are sought is ordinarily as cautious as presumed by the Supreme Court, the warrant process at least has the advantage of providing a before-the-fact record of the facts upon which probable cause is based. If the police have acted without a warrant, the probable cause determination must be made primarily upon the basis of the officer's testimony on the motion to suppress, and thus there is some risk that the facts brought out at that time may not be limited to those upon which the officer acted. But when the police have acted with a warrant, the factual justification is under the prevailing practice set out in a complaint or affidavit, and at the motion to suppress hearing the issue is whether those pre-recorded facts show probable cause. That is, the question is whether the magistrate acted properly, not whether the police officer did. *Jones v. U. S.*, 362 U.S. 257 (1960). Thus, a defective complaint or affidavit may not be saved by police testimony that they actually had additional facts, *Whiteley v. Warden*, 401 U.S. 560 (1971), although where not barred by statute it is possible to receive testimony that additional facts were orally presented to the magistrate at the time of the warrant application. *Frazier v. Roberts*, 441 F.2d 1224 (8th Cir. 1971). There is a split of authority on the question whether an affidavit or complaint sufficient on its face may be attacked on a motion to suppress. Some courts, stressing that the issue is whether the magistrate acted properly, confine the inquiry to whether the alleged facts, if true, would show probable cause and whether the magistrate had reason to believe the complainant or affiant, *Scarborough v. S.*, 238 A.2d 297 (Md.App.1968); others have concluded that a defendant should be permitted to show that the warrant was obtained on the basis of perjured testimony by the affiant, *P. v. Alfinito*, 211 N.E.2d 644 (N.Y.1965).

Probable cause for arrest does not necessarily constitute probable cause for a search warrant, nor does probable cause for a search warrant necessarily provide grounds for arrest; each requires the same quantum of evidence, but as to somewhat different facts and circumstances. For a search warrant, two conclusions must be supported by substantial evidence: (1) that the items sought are connected with criminal activity; and (2) that the items will be found in the place to be searched. By comparison, for arrest there must be probable cause (1) that an offense has been committed; and (2) that the person to be arrested committed it. Thus, a showing of the probable guilt of the person whose premises are to be searched is no substitute for a showing that items connected with the crime are likely to be found there, and an affidavit for a search warrant need not identify any particular person as the offender, *P. v. Meaderds*, 171 N.E.2d 638 (Ill.1961).

Information which may be considered. Probative evidence may be considered in determining whether there is probable cause, without regard to whether such evidence would be admissible at trial. Thus, it is proper to consider hearsay, *Draper v. U. S.*, supra, and a prior police record, *Brinegar v. U. S.*, 338 U.S. 160 (1949). As the Court explained in *Brinegar*, those rules of evidence at trial which exclude probative evidence because of "possible misunderstanding or misuse by the jury" have no place at the probable cause determination: "In dealing with probable cause * * *, as the very name implies, we deal with probabilities. These are not technical; they are the factual and practical considerations of everyday life on which reasonable and prudent men, not legal technicians, act. The standard of proof is accordingly correlative to what must be proved."

Information from informants. Those probable cause cases which have reached the Supreme Court have dealt almost exclusively with the troublesome question of when probable cause may be established solely upon the basis of information from an informant or upon such information plus some corroborating facts. If probable cause is to be based solely upon the informant's information, then the warrant application, or the testimony at the suppression hearing if there was no warrant, *Beck v. Ohio*, supra, must reveal (1) underlying circumstances showing reason to believe that the informant is a credible person, and (2) underlying circumstances showing the basis of the conclusions reached by the informant. *Aguilar v. Texas*, 378 U.S. 108 (1964). Thus, for example, a search warrant affidavit which merely states that a credible informant reported that narcotics are concealed in certain premises (as in *Aguilar*) is defective in two respects. First, there should have been a disclosure of why the informant is believed to be a credible person, such as that he provided information on past occasions which investigation proved to be correct, *McCray v. Ill.*, 386 U.S. 300 (1967), or that his statement constituted an admission against his own penal interest, *U. S. v. Harris*, 403 U.S. 573 (1971). But, this alone is not enough, for even a credible person may reach unjustified conclusions on the basis of circumstantial evidence or information from unreliable sources. That is, even if it were established that the informant was a credible person, it would still be unclear whether he asserted that there were narcotics in the house because (a) he saw them there, (b) he assumed they were there because of defendant's suspicious conduct, or (c) he was told by someone that they were there. Probable cause cannot be determined without deciding which is the case, for while an informant's direct observation of criminal conduct would suffice, *McCray v. Ill.*, supra, it cannot be decided whether the suspicious conduct is adequate unless the precise nature of that conduct is revealed to the judge, *U. S. v. Ventresca, supra,* while hearsay-upon-hearsay can hardly be adequate unless it is determined that the ultimate source of the information was also credible and in a position to know of what he speaks.

If the underlying circumstances concerning the informant's credibility, the source of his information, or even both are not disclosed, the informant's tip may nonetheless be considered in determining whether there is probable cause, although the tip clearly needs "some further support." The question then is whether the tip, when partially corroborated, is "as reliable as one which passes *Aguilar*'s requirements when standing alone." *Spinelli v. U. S.,* 393 U.S. 410 (1969). Thus, when an informant who had given reliable information in the past indicated that one Draper was peddling narcotics and that he would return from Chicago by train on one of two days with narcotics, and also described Draper and his clothing and said he would be carrying a tan zipper bag and that he habitually walked fast, agents possessing this information had probable cause to arrest the described person carrying such a bag and walking fast when he alighted from a train from Chicago on one of these days. *Draper v. U. S.,* supra. The officers knew from their past experience that the informant was credible, but they did not know whether he had a basis for believing that Draper would be in possession of narcotics, and this is what required corroboration. As the Court later explained in *Spinelli*, because the agents corroborated all of the many details stated by the informant except that Draper actually possessed narcotics, they could "reasonably infer that the informant had gained his information in a reliable way."

The difficulty in determining just how much corroborating information is sufficient is illustrated by *Spinelli*. A search warrant for gambling paraphernalia was obtained on an affidavit which indicated that: (1) defendant had been observed on several occasions going to a certain apartment; (2) a check with the telephone company disclosed that there were two telephones in this apartment listed in the name of another person; (3) defendant was "known to this affiant and to federal law enforcement agents and local law enforcement agents as a bookmaker"; and (4) affiant had been "informed by a confidential reliable informant that [the defendant] is operating a handbook and accepting wagers and disseminating wagering by means of the telephones" located in the apartment. The Court first noted that the last allegation was insufficient by itself, in that no underlying circumstances about either the informant's credibility or his source of information were revealed, and thus inquired whether the corroborating evidence was adequate. Disregarding the third item because it was only "a bald and unilluminating assertion of suspicion that is entitled to no weight," the Court concluded that the FBI had only established that the informant was correct in placing defendant and two telephones at the apartment, which did not warrant the inference that the informant had come by his information in a reliable way instead of "from an offhand remark heard at a neighborhood bar." Although *Draper* and *Spinelli* are not easily reconciled, it is at least clear that when the source of the informant's information is not directly disclosed, the informant must have given enough details to justify the conclusion, when they are corroborated, that his source was reliable—either direct observation, admissions by the defendant, fair conclusions drawn from circumstantial evidence, or information given by another who was reliable and in a position to know.

When probable cause is based in whole or in part upon information from an informant, his identity need not always be disclosed at the motion to suppress hearing. Disclosure is not required when the officer has testified in full and has been cross-examined as to what the informant told him and as to why the information was believed trustworthy. *McCray v. Ill.*, supra. Compare *P. v. Verrechio*, 245 N.E.2d 222 (N.Y. 1969), requiring disclosure in the "rare" case in which the information was vague and defense counsel questioned the existence and reliability of the informer.

Information from other sources. The reliability of informants used to uncover narcotics and gambling offenses has been a matter of special concern because they are often engaged in criminal conduct themselves. Thus, when the facts are provided by a police officer, *U. S. v. Ventresca,* supra, a crime victim, *Brown v. U. S.,* 365 F.2d 976 (D.C.Cir. 1966), a cooperative citizen, *Jaben v. U. S.,* 381 U.S. 214 (1965), or an informant not from the criminal milieu, *In re Boykin,* 237 N.E. 2d 460 (Ill.1968), there is no need for establishing credibility. It is still necessary to show why the person giving the information has a basis for his knowledge, although the number of details which need be disclosed varies depending upon the circumstances. See *Jaben v. U. S.,* supra, pointing out that tax evasion is not a crime which one might directly observe and that therefore there need not be disclosure of the details of the investigation into defendant's income. A warrantless arrest based upon the conclusory statements or directive of another policeman (i. e., that a certain person should be arrested) is not per se illegal, but will be upheld only upon a subsequent showing that the instigating official possessed facts constituting probable cause. *Whiteley v. Warden,* 401 U.S. 560 (1971).

When information is provided by sources other than informers, it usually goes to past, completed crimes rather than to future or continuing criminal conduct, and any doubts which exist are not likely to be based upon whether the source is reliable or knows what he claims to know, but rather upon whether the information is complete enough to justify the conclusion that certain evidence is to be found in a certain place or that a certain individual is the offender. It is these cases which most directly raise the issue of what probabilities are required to establish probable cause. Although there may be exceptions (e. g., the classic case in which a murdered man is found in a locked room with two other persons, each of whom accuses the other), it may generally be said that there must exist a more than 50% probability of the ultimate facts needed to justify arrest or search. For example, if police at the scene of a recent crime obtain only a general description of the offender, whether there is probable cause to arrest a person fitting this description and found in the general area shortly thereafter depends upon the likelihood that the description would fit only one person in that area. *P. v. Gibson*, 33 Cal.Rptr. 775 (App.1963). Some courts, however, view probable cause as a variable concept (as suggested by Justice Jackson in *Brinegar v. U. S.*, supra), and thus require a less than 50% probability when the need for action is greater, as when the crime in question is murder. *P. v. Schader*, 401 P.2d 665 (Cal.1965).

Even with this qualification, it must be conceded that the more-than-50%-probability test has not been followed in all arrest cases.   This is most likely attributable to the fact that an arrest serves several different functions, for the particular function being served appears to have entered into the consideration of whether the arrest was lawful.   For example, the Supreme Court has been more demanding when the arrest was viewed as apprehension of a person to be charged, *Mallory v. U. S.*, 354 U.S. 449 (1957), or as a basis for nocturnal entry of private premises, *Wong Sun v. U. S.*, supra, than when (as in *Draper v. U. S.*, supra) the arrest merely justified an on-the-street search which could be expected immediately to prove or disprove the suspicion.   The underlying notion that the amount of evidence required to satisfy the probable cause test varies depending upon the contemplated degree of intrusion, has been explicitly recognized in other contexts (see §§ 16, 17).

13.   SEARCH WARRANTS

A.   ISSUANCE

Who may issue.   Where a state attorney general, as authorized by state law, issued a search warrant in the context of an investigation of which he had taken personal charge, this procedure violated the Fourth Amendment, as he "was not the neutral and detached magistrate required by the Constitution." *Coolidge v. N. H.*, 403 U.S. 443 (1971). But it is not necessary "that all warrant authority must reside exclusively in a lawyer or judge"; an issuing magistrate need only be "neutral and detached" and "capable of determining whether probable cause exists," and thus a clerk of court could be authorized to issue arrest warrants for municipal ordinance violations. *Shadwick v. City of Tampa*, 407 U.S. 345 (1972). It does not necessarily follow that a clerk could be permitted to issue search warrants, as to which the probable cause issues are often much more complex.

Passage of time since facts gathered. If information showing probable cause that a crime was committed is gathered, and assuming no other evidence to the contrary is later uncovered, this probable cause will still be present weeks, months, or years later. The same is not true, however, as to information showing probable cause to believe that certain items are to be found at a particular place. As time passes, the chances increase that the goods have since been removed from that location. For this reason, an affidavit in support of a search warrant must contain a statement as to the time when the facts relied upon occurred. *Chin Kay v. U. S.*, 311 F. 2d 317 (9th Cir. 1962). This statement of time must be reasonably definite, but declarations that the observations were made "recently" or "within" or "during" a named period have been approved. *Rugendorf v. U. S.*, 376 U.S. 528 (1964); *Waggener v. McCanless*, 191 S.W.2d 551 (Tenn. 1946).

Just how long a time period may elapse without probable cause vanishing depends in large measure upon the extent of the criminal scheme involved. If it is an extensive operation which by its nature could be expected to continue for a substantial period of time at the same location, then probable cause may still be present after the passage of several weeks. Thus, the passage of 49 days between the purchase of cigarettes with forged tax stamps and the obtaining of a warrant to search for forged stamps at the place of business of the wholesaler who distributed those cigarettes was held not excessive, as the evidence of repeated sales and deliveries of such cigarettes over an extensive territory justified the belief that the criminal operation was a continuing one. *P. v. Dolgin*, 114 N.E.2d 389 (Ill.1953). By contrast, a passage of only six days between the observation of gambling and the unlicensed sale of liquor at defendant's club and the obtaining of a search warrant for liquor and gambling paraphernalia was held excessive, as there was no evidence that the conduct was continuing. *P. v. Wright*, 116 N.W.2d 786 (Mich.1962).

Particular description of place or person to be searched. The Fourth Amendment provides that no warrants shall issue except those "particularly describing the place to be searched." This means the description must be such that the executing officer will not be left with any doubt or discretion as to where to search. *McCormick v. S.*, 331 S.W.2d 307 (Tex.Crim.1960).

In describing premises to be searched, more care is generally required in urban areas than in rural areas. Farm property, for example, might merely be described in a general way and identified by section, township and range number. *P. v. Lavendowski*, 160 N.E. 582 (Ill.1928). In a city, however, a building must be identified by street and number or by an equally specific description. *Steele v. U. S.*, 267 U.S. 498 (1925). Minor errors in description, such as an incorrect street number, will not invalidate a warrant if it is still apparent what building or what part of a building is to be searched. *S. v. Daniels*, 217 A. 2d 610 (N.J.1966). In multiple-occupancy structures, the particular unit to be searched must be identified by occupant, room number, or apartment number, *U. S. v. Brown*, 151 F.Supp. 441 (E.D.Va.1957), unless the multi-unit character of the property was not known to the officers applying for or executing the warrant and was not externally apparent. *U. S. v. Santore*, 290 F.2d 51 (2d Cir. 1959).

Similarly, if a search warrant is obtained for search of an automobile, the description must direct the executing officer to one specific vehicle, either by license number, *Hines v. S.*, 275 P.2d 355 (Okla.Crim.1954), or by the make of the car and the name of the operator, *Carnaggio v. S.*, 109 So. 732 (Miss.1926). As to misdescription, the question again is whether the officer could select the proper vehicle, and thus a license number is sufficient notwithstanding a mistake as to the color and model year of the car. *Bowling v. S.*, 408 S.W.2d 660 (Tenn.1966).

A valid warrant for the search of a certain person must indicate the person's name, if known, *Garrett v. S.*, 270 P.2d 1101 (Okla.Crim.1954). If his name is not known, an otherwise complete description, listing such facts as the individual's aliases, approximate age, height and weight, race, and clothing, is adequate. *Dow v. S.*, 113 A.2d 423 (Md.1955).

Particular description of things to be seized. The Fourth Amendment also provides that no search warrants shall issue except those "particularly describing the * * * things to be seized." "The requirement that warrants shall particularly describe the things to be seized

makes general searches under them impossible
* * *. As to what is to be taken, nothing is
left to the discretion of the officer executing the
warrant." *Marron v. U. S.*, 275 U.S. 192 (1927).

The degree of particularity required varies
somewhat depending upon the nature of the materials to be seized. Greater leeway is permitted
in describing contraband (property the possession
of which is a crime), and thus during Prohibition
a description merely of "cases of whiskey" would
suffice. *Steele v. U. S.*, supra. By comparison,
innocuous property must be described more specifically so that executing officers will not be confused between the items sought and other property of a similar nature which might well be found
on the premises. *U. S. v. Quantity of Extract,
Bottles, Etc.*, 54 F.2d 643 (S.D.Fla.1931). Because of First Amendment considerations, this
constitutional requirement "is to be accorded the
most scrupulous exactitude when the 'things' are
books, and the basis for their seizure is the ideas
they contain." *Stanford v. Texas*, 379 U.S. 476
(1965). Also, in obscenity cases a search warrant may not authorize the seizure of great quantities of the same publication before the owner
has had an opportunity to litigate the question of
obscenity, for this would be an unconstitutional
prior restraint. *A Quantity of Copies of Books v.
Kansas*, 378 U.S. 205 (1964).

B.   EXECUTION

Time of execution.   Even where statutes or court rules purport to authorize execution within a fixed period of time, e. g., 10 days, the better view is that execution even within that time is permissible only if "the probable cause recited in the affidavit continues until the time of execution, giving consideration to the intervening knowledge of the officers and the passage of time," *U. S. v. Nepstead*, 424 F.2d 259 (9th Cir. 1970).   Three members of the Court have suggested that a search warrant may be executed at night only upon a special showing of a need to do so, as provided by law in several jurisdictions, because of the "Fourth Amendment doctrine that increasingly severe standards of probable cause are necessary to justify increasingly intrusive searches."   *Gooding v. U. S.*, 416 U.S. 430 (1974). A search warrant may be executed in the absence of the occupant, *U. S. v. Gervato*, 474 F.2d 110 (3d Cir. 1973).

Entry without notice.   18 U.S.C. § 3109 provides that an officer may break into premises to execute a search warrant only "if, after notice of his authority and purpose, he is refused admittance," and many states have comparable statutes.   The breaking referred to in such statutes includes any unannounced intrusion, even by opening a closed but unlocked door, *Sabbath v. U. S.*, 391 U.S. 585 (1968), but apparently not entry by subterfuge, *S. v. Valentine*, 504 P.2d 84 (Ore. 1973). By analogy to the cases dealing with entry for purposes of arrest (see pp. 129–130), it may be concluded that these statutes state the requirements of the Fourth Amendment, subject to exceptions when exigent circumstances are present. *Ker v. Cal.*, 374 U.S. 23 (1963); *Sabbath v. U. S.*, supra.

The exigent circumstances most likely to be present when a search warrant is to be executed is the risk that notice would result in destruction of the evidence sought. However, entry without notice cannot be so justified merely by the type of crime or evidence involved, but instead requires a specific showing of facts and circumstances involved in that particular case indicating there was a risk that the evidence would be destroyed. *P. v. Gastelo*, 432 P.2d 706 (Cal.1967). "Just as the police must have sufficient particular reason to enter at all, so must they have some particular reason to enter in the manner chosen."

Detention and search of persons on the premises to be searched. In *U. S. v. DiRe*, 332 U.S. 581 (1948), in holding that a passenger in an automobile could not be searched incident to the right to search the vehicle upon probable cause, the Court noted that while "an occupant of a house could be

[*115*]

used to conceal this contraband on his person quite as readily as can an occupant of a car," the government conceded that, armed with a search warrant for a residence only, it could not search all persons found in that residence. On this basis, some courts have held that a warrant for search of premises provides no basis for search of a person who merely happens to be present on the premises and who is not connected in any other way with the premises being searched. *S. v. Bradbury*, 243 A.2d 302 (N.H.1968).

Of course, in serving the search warrant a person might be discovered within as to whom there are grounds for arrest, in which case a search of the person could be undertaken incident to arrest and without reliance upon the search warrant. *Marron v. U. S.*, 275 U.S. 192 (1927). Or, if there are not grounds to arrest but yet probable cause that the person has in his possession the items named in the search warrant, this would appear to be an additional basis for the search, for there would not be time to seek an additional warrant. *S. v. Ryan*, 1 P.2d 893 (Wash.1931). In other circumstances, it might be proper to detain briefly for investigation a person who attempts to leave during execution of a warrant naming items which could easily be removed from the premises, *U. S. v. Festa*, 192 F.Supp. 160 (D.Mass.1960), cf. *Terry v. Ohio*, 392 U.S. 1 (1968), and perhaps to look into packages or containers carried by that person, *Clay v. U. S.*, 246 F.2d 298 (5th Cir. 1957).

A second justification given for search of persons on the premises where a search warrant is being executed is self-protection of the officer. *P. v. Pugh*, 217 N.E.2d 557 (Ill.App.1966). If there is some basis for thinking that the person may be armed, and if only a frisk is undertaken, this would seem proper. Cf. *Terry v. Ohio*, supra (discussed in § 17).

Seizure of items not named in the warrant. Even if, as required, the police look within the described place only where the described items might be located, *U. S. v. White*, 122 F.Supp. 664 (D.D.C.1954), and terminate the search once those items are discovered, *U. S. v. Highfill*, 334 F.Supp. 700 (E.D.Ark.1971), they may discover supposed incriminating evidence other than that named in the warrant. As to this situation, the Court stated in *Marron v. U. S.*, supra: "The requirement that warrants shall particularly describe the things to be seized * * * prevents the seizure of one thing under a warrant describing another. As to what is to be taken, nothing is left to the discretion of the officer executing the warrant." The *Marron* rule, frequently criticized and often disregarded, was abandoned in *Coolidge v. N. H.*, 403 U.S. 443 (1971): "Where, once an otherwise lawful search is in progress, the police inadvertently come upon a piece of evidence [in plain view], it would often be a needless inconvenience, and sometimes dangerous—to the evidence or to the police themselves—to require them to ignore it until they have obtained a warrant particularly describing it."

The requirement of inadvertent discovery, which may not actually have been accepted by a majority of the Court, see *North v. Superior Court*, 502 P.2d 1305 (Cal.1972), was explained on the ground that if the warrant fails to mention a particular object but "the police know its location and intend to seize it," then there is a violation of the Fourth Amendment requirement that warrants particularly describe the things to be seized. It would seem that discovery is anticipated only where there was "pre-existing knowledge of the identity and location of an item sufficiently in advance of the seizure to permit the warrant to be applied for and issued." *U. S. v. Welsch*, 446 F.2d 220 (10th Cir. 1971). Even if the discovery was inadvertent, the item may be seized only if there is probable cause it constitutes the fruits, instrumentalities or evidence of crime, *C. v. Wojcik*, 266 N.E.2d 645 (Mass.1971).

14. WARRANTLESS SEARCHES AND SEIZURES

A. PERSONS

Arrest. The prevailing view, as a matter of state law, is that an arrest warrant is not required in serious cases notwithstanding the practicability of obtaining one before arrest. Arrest without warrant was lawful at common law when the officer had "reasonable grounds to believe" that a felony had been committed and that the person to be arrested had committed it, and this is the prevailing rule today either as a matter of statute or court decision. This "reasonable grounds" test and the "probable cause" requirement of the Fourth Amendment "are substantial equivalents." *Draper v. U. S.*, 358 U.S. 307 (1959). On the other hand, warrants are sometimes required for minor offenses notwithstanding the need for immediate action. The prevailing law is that an officer may arrest without warrant for all misdemeanors committed in his presence, but that he must obtain a warrant even when he has overwhelming evidence of a misdemeanor which occurred out of his presence. This requirement, even when interpreted to mean that the officer must only have reasonable grounds to believe that a misdemeanor occurred in his presence, *Bursack v. Davis*, 225 N.W. 738 (Wis.1929), is sometimes too restrictive, in that there may be a need for immediate arrest even though the officer did not witness the misdemeanor. Some jurisdictions have thus provided by statute for arrest without warrant on "reasonable grounds" for all offenses.

With the possible exception of the case in which private premises must be entered to make the arrest (see pp. 128–129), there is presently no constitutional requirement that an arrest warrant be obtained when it is practicable to do so. As noted in *Gerstein v. Pugh*, 320 U.S. 103 (1975), "while the Court has expressed a preference for the use of arrest warants when feasible, * * * it has never invalidated an arrest supported by probable cause solely because the officers failed to secure a warrant." *Gerstein* held, however, that though "a policeman's on-the-scene assessment of probable cause provides legal justification for arresting a person suspected of crime, and for a brief period of detention to take the administrative steps incident to arrest," the Fourth Amendment "requires a [prompt] judicial determination of probable cause as a prerequisite to extended restraint on liberty following [the warrantless] arrest." That determination, upon a standard which "is the same as that for arrest," may be made without an adversary hearing or participation by defense counsel.

Search incident to arrest. "When an arrest is made, it is reasonable for the arresting officer to search the person arrested in order to remove any weapons that the latter might seek to use in order to resist arrest or effect his escape [and to] seize any evidence on the arrestee's person in order to prevent its concealment or destruction." *Chimel v. Cal.*, 395 U.S. 752 (1969). Given this justification, doubt existed for some time as to whether a search could be undertaken incident to an arrest for a lesser offense, such as a minor traffic violation, where there would be no evidence to search for and a relatively lesser risk that the arrestee would be armed. But in *U. S. v. Robinson*, 414 U.S. 218 (1973), the Court held that a full search of the person incident to a "full custody arrest" (i. e., one made for the purpose of taking the person to the station) may be undertaken without regard to "what a court may later decide was the probability in a particular arrest situation that weapons or evidence would in fact be found upon the person of the suspect," apparently on the ground that it would be unwise to have courts second-guessing such a "quick *ad hoc* judgment" by arresting officers. The limited frisk alternative of *Terry* (see § 17) was deemed insufficient in the case of arrest, as "the danger to an officer is far greater in the case of the extended exposure which follows the taking of a suspect into custody and transporting him to the police station."

Robinson makes more significant the long-standing issue of what items are subject to seizure once discovered. Clearly seizure is not limited to the items sought; "when an article subject to lawful seizure properly comes into an officer's possession in the course of a lawful search it would be entirely without reason to say that he must return it because it was not one of the things it was his business to look for." *Abel v. U. S.*, 362 U.S. 217 (1960). But in *Abel* there was probable cause to seize the item in question, and on this ground *Abel* was distinguished in *S. v. Elkins*, 422 P.2d 250 (Or.1966), where the officer seized an unlabeled bottle of pills from the pocket of a defendant arrested for public intoxication. The court, noting the absence of cases in point, concluded that the seizure was improper because the officer acted only upon suspicion that the pills might be narcotics and not upon "reasonable grounds to believe that the article he has discovered is contraband." Compare the situation as to seizure of items not named in a search warrant, § 13B, which likewise raises the question of how much discretion should be left to the searching officer; and consider *Warden v. Hayden*, 387 U.S. 294 (1967), where the court, in rejecting the contention that abolition of the "mere evidence" rule would result in indiscriminate seizures, empha-

sized that there "must, of course, be a nexus
* * * between the item to be seized and criminal behavior," and that "probable cause must be
examined in terms of cause to believe that the evidence sought will aid in a particular apprehension or conviction."

Time of search; inventory. It is clear that a
search cannot be justified as being "incident" to
arrest if the search is conducted without arrest
and at a time when a lawful arrest could not be
made because sufficient grounds are lacking, *P. v.
Edge*, 94 N.E.2d 359 (Ill.1950), or because of
physical inability to make an arrest at that time,
Mosco v. U. S., 301 F.2d 180 (9th Cir. 1962).
Some courts have asserted a broader rule: if the
search comes before the arrest, then for that reason alone the search is invalid. *U. S. v. Waller*,
108 F.Supp. 450 (N.D.Ill.1952). The better view
is to the contrary, as a search before arrest when
there are grounds to arrest involves no greater
invasion of the person's security and privacy, and
has the advantage that if the search is not productive the individual may not be arrested at all.
P. v. Simon, 290 P.2d 531 (Cal.1955). If there
was no present intent to arrest and arrest does
not promptly follow the search, then the search is
not properly characterized as "incident" to arrest,
but it is still lawful if made upon probable cause
and limited to the extent "necessary to preserve

highly evanescent evidence [e. g., fingernail scrapings]." *Cupp v. Murphy*, 412 U.S. 291 (1973).

Courts have generally upheld delayed searches of the person arrested (such as those made on the way to or at the station), either on the theory that police control of the person by arrest is so substantial that it of necessity carries with it a continuing right of search, or on the ground that the police are entitled to inventory the property found on a person before placing him in a cell. *Westover v. U. S.*, 394 F.2d 164 (9th Cir. 1968); *C. v. Querubin*, 236 A.2d 538 (Pa.1967). A contrary result has sometimes been reached because of a prior failure of the police to permit the defendant to exercise his right of stationhouse release. *P. v. Overlee*, 483 P.2d 222 (Colo.1971). In *U. S. v. Edwards*, 415 U.S. 800 (1974), the Court held that "once the defendant is lawfully arrested and is in custody, the effects in his possession at the place of detention that were subject to search at the time and place of his arrest may lawfully be searched and seized without a warrant even though a substantial period of time has elapsed between the arrest and subsequent administrative processing on the one hand and the taking of the property for use as evidence on the other," at least where such searches are not unreasonable "either because of their number or their manner of perpetration." This qualification suggests that neither *Robinson* nor *Edwards* disturb the holding in *Schmerber v. Cal.*, 384 U.S. 757 (1966), that, except where delay would threaten loss of the evidence, a search warrant is required to intrude into an arrestee's body.

"Subterfuge" arrests. *Robinson* has been criticized on the ground that it opens the door to "subterfuge" arrests for minor offenses made to support searches of persons for evidence of more serious offenses as to which probable cause is lacking, particularly in light of the fact that *Robinson* was applied in the companion case of *Gustafson v. Fla.*, 414 U.S. 260 (1973), to a situation in which the officer had complete discretion as to whether to arrest or give a citation and whether to search if an arrest was made. Evidence has been suppressed upon a showing that the desire to seek such evidence was the motivation behind arrest for such minor crimes as vagrancy, *Green v. U. S.*, 386 F.2d 953 (10th Cir.1967), or a traffic violation, *Amador-Gonzales v. U. S.*, 391 F.2d 308 (5th Cir. 1968). But some courts have overlooked strong evidence of such a "subterfuge." See *P. v. Watkins*, 166 N.E.2d 433 (Ill.1960) (officers assigned to gambling squad who suspected defendant possessed gambling paraphernalia arrested him for parking too close to a crosswalk, searched his person and found policy slips); *Anderson v. S.*, 444 P.2d 239 (Okla.Crim.1968) (officer who arrested defendant for making improper right turn and then found marijuana in search was accompanied by federal narcotics agent).

The significance of booking. "Booking" is an administrative step taken after the arrested person is brought to the police station, which involves entry of the person's name, the crime for which the arrest was made, and other relevant facts on the police "blotter," and which may also include photographing, fingerprinting, and the like. Because booking results in a record of some of the circumstances of arrest, the question has arisen whether the entries made are relevant in determining the lawfulness of the arrest. A few courts have taken the position that an entry that the defendant was arrested "on suspicion of" or "for investigation of" a certain offense shows that the arrest was without probable cause, *Staples v. U. S.*, 320 F.2d 817 (5th Cir. 1963), but in practice such entries are often made solely for the purpose of identifying those cases being referred to the detective division. It has been held that if a person was booked for one offense, his arrest may thereafter be upheld on the ground that the police had sufficient evidence of a quite different offense, *U. S. v. Traceski*, 271 F.Supp. 883 (D.Conn.1967). A contrary conclusion, it is argued, would prevent arrest "on a trumped-up charge," *Wainwright v. New Orleans*, 392 U.S. 598 (1968) (dissent of Chief Justice to dismissal of writ of certiorari), and on this basis some courts have declined to inquire into the existence of probable cause for an offense unrelated to that for which the defendant was booked. *U. S. v. Atkinson*, 450 F.2d 835 (5th Cir.1971).

B. PREMISES

Entry to arrest. Police may enter premises without a warrant when they are in hot pursuit of an offender. This was the holding *Warden v. Hayden*, 387 U.S. 294 (1967), where the police were informed that an armed robbery had taken place and that the suspect had entered a certain house five minutes before they reached it. Because delay under these circumstances would endanger the lives of the police and others, the "exigent circumstances" justified entry without notice. Once inside, the Court concluded, the police were justified in looking everywhere in the house where the suspect might be hiding and also (before his capture) where weapons might be hidden.

In contrast to *Hayden*, many cases have involved warrantless police entry solely on the basis that it was the home of a person they had grounds to arrest. It is often assumed that there must be a reasonable belief the suspect is home, *U. S. v. Shye*, 492 F.2d 886 (6th Cir. 1974), although it has also been asserted that "rudimentary police procedure dictates that a suspect's residence be eliminated as a possible hiding place before a search is conducted elsewhere." *P. v. Sprovieri*, 238 N.E.2d 115 (Ill.App.1968), aff'd, 252 N.E.2d 531 (Ill.1969).

In *Coolidge v. N. H.*, 403 U.S. 443 (1971), the Court, though finding it unnecessary to decide the question in that case, noted "that the notion that the warrantless entry of a man's house in order to arrest him on probable cause is *per se* legitimate is in fundamental conflict with the basic principle of Fourth Amendment law that searches and seizures inside a man's house without warrant are *per se* unreasonable in the absence of some one of a number of well defined 'exigent circumstancees.'" The Court cited *Dorman v. U. S.*, 435 F.2d 385 (D.C.Cir. 1970), where the court, en banc, adopted the "basic principle," subject to exceptions, that a warrant must be obtained before entry of premises "not only in case of entry to search for property, but also in case of entry to arrest a suspect." (An exception was found to exist in *Dorman*, based upon these factors: (1) a crime of violence was involved; (2) the suspect was reasonably believed to be armed; (3) there was a very clear showing of probable cause; (4) there was strong reason to believe the suspect was within the premises; (5) there was a likelihood the suspect would escape if not swiftly apprehended; and (6) the entry was made peaceably.) *Dorman* rests upon the notion that essentially the same limitations should govern the grave step of entering private premises whether the objective is to search for a person or an object.

In both *Coolidge* and *Dorman*, the reference is to an arrest warrant rather than a search warrant. This is significant, for (unlike a search warrant) an arrest warrant does not identify any particular premises nor require a prior judicial determination that what is sought is within those premises (see p. 100). The assumption may be that an arrest warrant should suffice where entry of the defendant's own premises are involved, in that the police should be left with some discretion in deciding whether he might be found there. But if a wanted person is to be sought in the homes of third parties, it is then consistent with *Coolidge* and *Dorman* to suggest that a search warrant is required. The cases are not in agreement on this issue; compare *U. S. v. Brown*, 467 F.2d 419 (D.C.Cir. 1972), with *England v. S.*, 488 P.2d 1347 (Okla.Crim.1971).

Entry without notice. Many jurisdictions have statutes which expressly provide that an officer may not break into private premises for purposes of arrest unless he has been denied admittance after giving "notice of his office and purpose." However, these statutes have generally been interpreted as codifying the common law rule with its exceptions for "exigent circumstances." These laws apply to actual breaking of doors and windows as well as merely opening an unlocked door, but not to entry by subterfuge. *Leahy v. U. S.*, 272 F.2d 487 (9th Cir. 1960). Courts have excused notice and demand when it reasonably appeared that: (1) the occupants were already aware of the presence of the police and their objective, *U. S. v. Frierson*, 299 F.2d 763 (7th Cir. 1962); (2) prompt action was required for the protection of a person within, *P. v. Woodward*, 190 N.W. 721 (Mich.1922); (3) unannounced entry was required for protection of the officer, *P. v. Hammond*, 357 P.2d 289 (Cal.1960); (4) unannounced entry was required to prevent the destruction of evidence, *P. v. Maddox*, 294 P. 2d 6 (Cal.1956); (5) by unannounced entry actual commission of the offense could be observed, *P. v. Ramsey*, 320 P.2d 592 (Cal.App.1958); or (6) by unannounced entry escape of the person to be arrested could be prevented, *P v. Maddox,* supra. Such belief must be based upon the facts of the particular case, and cannot be justified by a general assumption that certain classes of persons are more likely than others to resist arrest, attempt escape, or destroy evidence. *Meyer v. U. S.*, 386 F.2d 715 (9th Cir. 1967).

The Supreme Court has yet to speak clearly to the issue. In *Ker v. Cal.*, 374 U.S. 23 (1963), four members of the Court concluded that entry without notice and demand was proper because the evidence (narcotics) could easily be disposed of and it appeared from the defendant's earlier furtive conduct that he was expecting the police. Another justice concurred on the ground that state searches and seizures should be judged by "concepts of fundamental fairness," while the remaining members of the Court argued that under the Fourth Amendment the only exceptions to the demand-notice requirements were "(1) where the persons within already know of the officers' authority and purpose or (2) where the officers are justified in the belief that persons within are in imminent peril of bodily harm, or (3) where those within, made aware of the presence of someone outside (because, for example, there has been a knock at the door) are then engaged in activity which justifies the officers in the belief that an escape or the destruction of evidence is being attempted."

Search incident to and after arrest. For many years, it could be said that the right to make a warrantless search incident to arrest was one exception which came close to swallowing up the search warrant requirement. Per *Harris v. U. S.*, 331 U.S. 145 (1947), and *U. S. v. Rabinowitz*, 339 U.S. 56 (1950), such searches were permitted of the premises where the arrest occurred, without regard to the practicality of obtaining a search warrant. Under the *Harris-Rabinowitz* rule, the scope of the search was not limited to places the

arrestee might reach to obtain a weapon or destroy evidence, but extended to the entire premises in which the defendant had a possessory interest. *Smith v. U. S.*, 254 F.2d 751 (D.C.Cir.
1958). It was sometimes said that "the right to
search and the validity of the seizure are not de-
pendent on the right to arrest, but on the reasonable cause the arresting officer has to believe
that articles subject to seizure are concealed at
the place of arrest," *U. S. v. Antonelli Fireworks
Co.*, 53 F.Supp. 870 (W.D.N.Y.1943), but most
cases failed to consider the issue. "The same meticulous investigation which would be appropriate
in a search for two small cancelled checks could
not be considered reasonable where agents are
seeking a stolen automobile or illegal still." *Harris v. U. S.*, supra. But this limit on the intensity
of the search was of minor significance, given the
general lack of concern over requiring grounds to
look for particular objects. In *Chimel v. Cal.*,
395 U.S. 752 (1969), the Court, noting that in
more recent decisions such searches had been justified solely upon the need to prevent the arrested
person from obtaining a weapon or destroying evidence, overruled *Harris* and *Rabinowitz* and limited the scope of warrantless searches incident to
arrest consistent with that purpose:

"When an arrest is made, it is reasonable for
the arresting officer to search the person arrested
in order to remove any weapons that the latter

might seek to use in order to resist arrest or effect his escape. * * * In addition, it is entirely reasonable for the arresting officer to search for and seize any evidence on the arrestee's person in order to prevent its concealment or destruction. And the area into which an arrestee might reach in order to grab a weapon or evidentiary items must, of course, be governed by a like rule. A gun on a table or in a drawer in front of one who is arrested can be as dangerous to the arresting officer as one concealed in the clothing of the person arrested. There is ample justification, therefore, for a search of the arrestee's person and the area 'within his immediate control'—construing that phrase to mean the area from within which he might gain possession of a weapon or destructible evidence." A broader search of the place of arrest "may be made only under the authority of a search warrant."

Chimel involved a search of an entire house, but the Court made it clear that the new rule would also bar more limited searches, such as the one-room search in *Rabinowitz* and the four-room search in *Harris*. However, many lower courts have applied the *Chimel* "immediate control" test broadly by assuming that defendants maintain control over a considerable area even after they have been arrested. For example, in *U. S. v. Wysocki*, 457 F.2d 1155 (5th Cir. 1972), a search into a box inside a closet was upheld although the arrestee was seated in a chair with one of the two officers immediately behind him.

Chimel is not inconsistent with the notion that if it is necessary for the arrestee to put on clothing or do other things before he is taken to the station, then the police may examine closets and other places to which the arrestee is permitted to move. *Giacalone v. Lucas*, 445 F.2d 1238 (6th Cir. 1971). Similarly, if a "potential accomplice" is also present, he may be frisked for weapons, *P. v. Roach*, 93 Cal.Rptr. 354 (App.1971), and the area within his immediate control may also be searched for weapons and evidence, *U. S. v. Manarite*, 448 F.2d 583 (2d Cir. 1971). Other cases have recognized that subsequent to the arrest the police may sometimes be justified in walking through other parts of the premises, either because other offenders are reasonably believed to be present, *P. v. Block*, 491 P.2d 9 (Cal.1971), or to see if there are others present who might constitute a security risk, *U. S. v. Biddle*, 436 F.2d 4 (8th Cir. 1970).

Plain view. As noted in *Coolidge v. N. H.*, supra, "an object which comes into view during a search incident to arrest that is appropriately limited in scope under existing law may be seized without a warrant." Thus, if an object is discovered by the officer from a place where he is lawfully present, that discovery is not illegal, and this is so even if an arrest has been made but the

[*134*]

object itself is not within the control of the arrestee under *Chimel*. *P. v. Block*, supra. But in
Coolidge it was indicated, though perhaps not by
a majority of the Court, see *North v. Superior
Court*, 502 P.2d 1305 (Cal.1972), that the item
may be seized only if its discovery was "inadvertent," for if the police knew of the identity and location of the object in advance they should have
obtained a search warrant for it. This suggests
that discovery is anticipated only where there
was "pre-existing knowledge of the identity and
location of an item sufficiently in advance of the
seizure to permit the warrant to be applied for and
issued." *U. S. v. Welsch*, 446 F.2d 220 (10th Cir.
1971). Even so limited, the feasibility of the inadvertent discovery test has been questioned by some
commentators on the ground that it creates an
anomolous situation in which the police will have
to show the absence of probable cause. Another
devise which has been utilized to prevent abuse of
the power to enter to arrest is the "timed" arrest
doctrine of *McKnight v. U. S.*, 183 F.2d 977 (D.
C.Cir. 1950), holding that when the police pass up
a convenient opportunity to arrest on the street
and "time" the arrest to occur when the defendant is within premises in order to find evidence
therein, the evidence found in the premises must
be suppressed.

Assuming no problems in the manner in which
the plain view is acquired, it does not necessarily

follow that the observed object may be seized. As stated in *Coolidge*, it must be "an incriminating object," which would appear to mean that there must be probable cause that the object is the fruits, instrumentality, or evidence of crime. And that determination must be made by the police without exceeding their authority. See, e. g., *Eiseman v. Superior Court*, 98 Cal.Rptr. 342 (App.1971), holding illegal the seizure of vials observed on a dresser at the time of arrest, as the incriminating nature of their contents was discovered only after the police picked them up and examined them.

Search to prevent loss of evidence. In *Agnello v. U. S.*, 269 U.S. 20 (1925), the Court held that "belief, however well founded, that an article sought is concealed in a dwelling house furnishes no justification for a search of that place without a warrant." But in *Johnson v. U. S.*, 333 U.S. 10 (1948), and *Chapman v. U. S.*, 365 U.S. 610 (1961), reference was made to the possibility of a warrantless dwelling search being upheld upon a showing of a need for immediate action. This issue also took on increased importance because of the *Chimel* decision, and was not directly confronted in *Chimel* because no emergency was present there; the police had sufficient opportunity to obtain a search warrant before they tipped their hand by making an arrest.

But in *Vale v. La.*, 399 U.S. 30 (1970), the circumstances were different; the police had come to arrest the defendant on another matter, observed what reasonably appeared to be a sale of narcotics by the defendant to a person who drove up to his house, arrested the defendant in front of his house, made a cursory inspection of the house to determine if any one else was there, and then (after the defendant's mother and brother entered the house during the inspection) made a warrantless search of the house for the additional narcotics they believed were hidden there. Yet the Court concluded that the state had not met its burden "to show the existence of such an exceptional situation" as to justify a warrantless search, as the goods seized were not actually in the process of destruction or removal from the jurisdiction. The Court also asserted that because the officers had arrest warrants for Vale, "there is thus no reason * * * to suppose that it was impracticable for them to obtain a search warrant as well," but this is a questionable conclusion in view of the fact that here (unlike *Chimel*) the probable cause for search did not exist until the officers on the scene observed the illegal transaction. *Vale*, therefore, cannot easily be squared with the search-of-vehicles cases (see § 14C), but does show that the Court is much more protective of dwellings then vehicles. Also underlying *Vale* may be the notion expressed in

Davis v. U. S., 423 F.2d 974 (5th Cir. 1970), that recognition of a general exception to the warrant requirement on the basis of a risk of destruction of evidence by a third party "would result in the evaporation of an arrestee's Fourth Amendment rights" in that "there is almost always a partisan who might destroy or conceal evidence."

Nonetheless, some lower courts have upheld entry and search of premises on probable cause but without a search warrant on the ground that the risk of loss of evidence was sufficient to justify such immediate action. *U .S. v. Doyle*, 456 F.2d 1246 (5th Cir. 1972) (warrantless search of garage for stolen drugs where reason to believe suspects would leave city before search warrant could be obtained); *U. S. v. Rubin*, 474 F.2d 262 (3d Cir. 1973) (warrantless search of house after one defendant, upon arrest nearby, shouted to friends to call home about the arrest). And in *P. v. Sirhan*, 497 P.2d 1121 (Cal.1972), a warrantless search of defendant's home even without probable cause that evidence would be found was upheld on the ground that prompt action was necessary to discovery whether there was a conspiracy to assassinate several political leaders.

C. AUTOMOBILES

Search incident to arrest. Although *Chimel* involved search of premises, the more limited rule of that case is equally applicable to a search of an automobile incident to arrest. *Thompson v. S.*, 488 P.2d 944 (Okla.Crim.1971). Here as well, however, some courts have taken a broad view of what is within the defendant's "immediate control." In *Application of Kiser*, 419 F.2d 1134 (8th Cir. 1969), the court upheld a search under a blanket on the back seat of the car because the arrestee, in the custody of several officers, was "within leaping range."

Search to prevent loss of evidence. In *Carroll v. U. S.*, 267 U.S. 132 (1925), the Court upheld a warrantless search of a vehicle being operated on the highway upon probable cause that it contained contraband, because it could be quickly moved out of the locality. The *Carroll* rule has seldom been utilized, for most vehicle searches have been justified as incident to the arrest of the driver, and thus it was not until the *Chimel* decision that the precise reach of the *Carroll* rule became a matter of importance. The basic question was whether *Carroll* could be relied upon to justify a warrantless search of the car after arrest of the driver. One court answered in the negative on the ground that "exigencies do not exist when the vehicle and the suspect are both in police custody," *Ramon v. Cupp*, 423 F.2d 248 (9th Cir. 1970), but in *Chambers v. Maroney*, 399 U.S. 42 (1970), the Supreme Court reached a contrary conclusion. In response to the contention that *Carroll* was not applicable on these facts because the car in which the defendant was arrested could simply be held until a search warrant was obtained, the Court in *Chambers* responded: "For constitutional purposes, we see no difference between on the one hand seizing and holding a car before presenting the probable cause issue to a magistrate and on the other hand carrying out an immediate search without a warrant." This would seem somewhat inconsistent with the rationale of *U. S. v. VanLeeuwen*, 397 U.S. 249 (1970), permitting the lesser intrusion of delaying a mailed package for a day until a search warrant could be obtained.

But *Chambers* does not mean that vehicles are always subject to search without a search warrant. In *Coolidge v. N. H.*, supra, concerning the warrantless seizure and subsequent search of defendant's car following his arrest in his nearby home, the culmination of several weeks of investigation into a murder, the plurality opinion noted that the instant case was distinguishable from *Chambers* in that there the car was discovered being operated shortly after the crime, so that there was no prior opportunity to obtain a search warrant, while in the instant case the police had the grounds for a warrant well in advance and knew where the vehicle might be found. Other bases of distinction mentioned by the *Coolidge* plurality, such as that there the objects being sought "were neither stolen nor contraband nor dangerous" and that neither Coolidge (who was under arrest) nor his wife (who was accompanied by police to another town) could gain access to the car, are less than convincing.

Precisely what constitutes an emergency justifying a warrantless search of a vehicle is a matter which continues to divide the Court, as illustrated by *Cardwell v. Lewis*, 417 U.S. 583 (1974), where, after defendant's arrest at the police station, his car was seized from a nearby parking lot and later subjected to an examination of its exterior. Four members of the Court concluded that there was a need for immediate action because the defendant might otherwise have given the car keys to his wife, and that it made no difference that the police had grounds to obtain a search warrant in advance of the arrest; four others concluded there was no emergency because the police had the car keys in their custody and because, as in *Coolidge*, there was ample opportunity to obtain a warrant before the arrest. (Powell, J., did not reach this issue in his concurring opinion.)

Inventory. When there is not probable cause to search the vehicle, so that *Chambers* cannot be invoked in support of an at-the-station search, the question is whether the vehicle may be inventoried after its seizure at the time of the arrest of the operator. In *Cooper v. Cal.*, 386 U.S. 58 (1967), where the car was seized at the time of arrest and kept in police custody pending forfeiture proceedings, the Court concluded it "would be unreasonable to hold that the police, having to retain the car in their garage for such a length of time, had no right, even for their own protection, to search it." And in *Harris v. U. S.*, 390 U.S. 234 (1968), seizure of evidence found in plain view while securing a vehicle seized earlier incident to arrest was upheld, but in *Dyke v. Taylor Impl. Mfg. Co.*, 391 U.S. 216 (1968), a search of a vehicle after arrest was held unlawful where the car had not been impounded and the defendant was taken immediately to court to make bail.

This leaves the case in which the car is not being held for forfeiture proceedings but has been impounded because the arrestee is in jail and the evidence is not found in plain view but is discovered in the course of a regular inventory procedure. Most lower courts have held evidence found under these circumstances admissible, absent a showing that the inventory was a subterfuge to conduct an exploratory search. *U. S. v. Pennington*, 441 F.2d 249 (5th Cir. 1971). But in *Mozzetti v. Superior Court*, 484 P.2d 84 (Cal. 1971), the court found the argument that inven-

tory is for the benefit of the arrestee "unpersua-
sive" given the general practice not to ask him
whether he desires an inventory, and the argument
that it protects the police from tort claims "even
less convincing" because the duty of slight care
owed by the police could be met by merely locking
up the car. The issue was not resolved in *Cady v.
Dombrowski*, 413 U.S. 1074 (1973), because of
the unusual facts there present; rural police had
to leave defendant's car unguarded where it was
towed after an accident, and thus it was held that
they were justified in making a warrantless
search of the car in an attempt to prevent a gun
they reasonably believed was inside from falling
into the hands of vandals.

15. "WAIVER" OR "CONSENT"
vs. PEACEFUL SUBMISSION

A. THE NATURE OF CONSENT

Background.   Where effective consent is given,
a search may be conducted without a warrant and
without probable cause. At one time, the consent
doctrine was assumed to be grounded on the concept of waiver, *Stoner v. Cal.*, 376 U.S. 483 (1964).
But in *Schneckloth v. Bustamonte*, infra, the Court
concluded that "a [traditional] 'waiver' approach
to consent searches would be thoroughly inconsistent with our decisions," and thus held that the

issue is whether the person's consent was "voluntary." Although this voluntariness test would appear to focus primarily upon the state of mind of the person allegedly consenting, the Court in *Schneckloth* did not have occasion to consider the notion that because it is the Fourth Amendment prohibition against unreasonable searches which is at issue, the question is whether "the officers, as reasonable men, could conclude that defendant's consent was given." *P. v. Henderson,* 210 N. E.2d 483 (Ill.1965).

Most federal courts have said that consent to search "is not lightly to be inferred," *Rosenthall v. Henderson,* 389 F.2d 514 (6th Cir. 1968), and thus have viewed consent given by a defendant in custody as almost per se invalid, *Judd v. U. S.,* 190 F.2d 649 (D.C.Cir. 1951), and have often expressed the view that, except where the suspect has confessed or not denied his guilt, it is incredulous to say that he actually consented to search of a place where he knew the incriminating evidence to be. *Higgins v. U. S.,* 209 F.2d 819 (D. C.Cir. 1954). By contrast, the typical state decision recognizes no presumption of lack of waiver from custody or the fact that incriminating articles were easily located in the place searched, and often the search is upheld by merely concluding that the trial judge's finding of consent was not "clearly unreasonable." *P. v. Peterson,* 162 N.E. 2d 380 (Ill.1959).

Warning of rights. *Schneckloth v. Bustamonte*, 412 U.S. 218 (1973), holds that, while a person's knowledge of his right to refuse is a factor to be taken into account in determining (based on the totality of the circumstances) whether his consent was voluntary, the prosecution is not required to prove that he was so warned or otherwise had such knowledge where the consent was obtained while the person was not in custody. The *Johnson v. Zerbst* (p. ——) test of waiver, "an intentional relinquishment or abandonment of a known right or privilege," was distinguished as applicable only to those constitutional rights which, unlike the Fourth Amendment, are intended to protect a fair trial and the reliability of the truth-determining process; the *Miranda* requirement of Fifth Amendment warnings (see § 26) was distinguished because it only governs interrogation of those in custody. While this latter distinction suggests that the *Miranda* analogy might be persuasive as to a consent to search given by one in custody, most courts view the *Schneckloth* totality of circumstances test as equally applicable in that situation. *U. S. v. Garcia*, 496 F.2d 670 (5th Cir. 1974).

If some warning is required in a custody situation, is it sufficient that the defendant was warned of his *Miranda* rights, submitted to orderly interrogation and subsequently consented to a search? In *Gorman v. U. S.*, 380 F.2d 158 (1st

Cir. 1967), the court answered in the affirmative on the ground that a warning that "things which might be found in a search could be used against an accused seems implicit in the warning of the right to remain silent." The contrary view was taken in *U. S. v. Moderacki*, 280 F.Supp. 633 (D. Del.1968), because a frightened or confused suspect, most in need of protection, might not understand the *Miranda* warnings to be applicable to a search.

Consent subsequent to a claim of authority. A search may not be justified on the basis of consent when that "consent" was given only after the official conducting the search asserted that he possessed a search warrant, but in fact there was no warrant or an invalid warrant. Such a claim of authority is, in effect, an announcement that the occupant has no right to resist the search, and thus acquiescence under these circumstances cannot be construed as consent. *Bumper v. N. C.*, 391 U.S. 543 (1968). The courts are not in agreement as to whether the same result is required when the officer only threatens to obtain a search warrant. Compare *Hamilton v. N. C.*, 260 F.Supp. 632 (E.D.N.C. 1966), with *U. S. v. Boukater*, 409 F.2d 537 (5th Cir. 1969). In such a case it may be relevant whether the officer could in fact obtain a warrant. Even when there is no assertion of a warrant or threat to obtain one, submission to such declarations as "I am here to search your house" or "I have come to search your house" are almost certain to be viewed as coercive. *Amos v. U. S.*, 255 U.S. 313 (1921).

Other relevant factors. The voluntariness of a consent to search is "to be determined from the totality of all the circumstances," *Schneckloth v. Bustamonte*, supra. Among the other factors to be considered in determining the effectiveness of an alleged consent to search are whether (1) the defendant was under arrest at the time it was given, *P. v. Kaigler*, 118 N.W.2d 406 (Mich.1962); (2) he was overpowered by arresting officers, handcuffed, or similarly subject to physical restrictions, *P. v. Zazzetta*, 189 N.E.2d 260 (Ill. 1963); (3) the keys to the premises searched had already been seized by the police from the defendant, *P. v. Porter*, 236 N.Y.S.2d 162 (Sup.Ct. 1962); (4) the defendant employed evasive conduct or attempted to mislead the police, *Castaneda v. Sup. Ct.*, 380 P.2d 641 (Cal.1963); (5) he denied guilt or the presence of any incriminatory objects in his premises, *U. S. v. Kidd*, 153 F.Supp. 605 (W.D.La.1957); (6) the defendant initiated the search, or at least the investigation leading to the search, *S. v. Kotka*, 152 N.W.2d 445 (Minn. 1967); or (7) he was hesitant in agreeing to the search, *S. v. Leavitt*, 237 A.2d 309 (R.I.1968). The presence of some of these factors is not controlling, however, as each case "must stand or fall on its own special facts." *U. S. v. Dornblut*, 261 F.2d 949 (2d Cir. 1959).

Scope of consent. Assuming a valid consent, the police may not exceed the physical bounds of the area as to which consent was granted, such as by looking through private papers after a consent to allow search for narcotics. *U. S. v. Dichiarinte*, 445 F.2d 126 (7th Cir. 1971). There is disagreement as to whether a voluntary consent may be used to justify a second search of the same place after a fruitless first search; compare *P. v. Nawrocki*, 148 N.W.2d 211 (Mich.App.1967), with *S. v. Brochu*, 237 A.2d 418 (Me.1967). At least where, as in *Brochu*, there has been a significant passage of time, the second search involves re-entry of defendant's home, and defendant's status has changed from suspect to accused, the second search cannot be justified on the assumption that defendant's consent is continuing.

Consent by deception. A somewhat related problem concerning the scope of the consent arises when the consent was obtained by deception, as where the suspect gives the policeman a gun on the representation that the officer will aid him in selling it, but the officer then has a ballistics test run on the weapon, as in *C. v. Brown*, 261 A.2d 879 (Pa.1970), or where the suspect gives a blood sample to the police on the representation that it will be tested for alcohol content but it is in fact matched with blood found at the scene of a rape, as in *Graves v. Beto*, 424 F.2d 524 (5th Cir. 1970). The "misplaced trust" cases, upholding the admissibility of voluntary disclosures of criminal conduct to an undercover officer or police agent, *Lewis v. U. S.*, 385 U.S. 206 (1966), *Hoffa v. U. S.*, 385 U.S. 293 (1966), are probably distinguishable. Situations such as *Brown* and *Graves* are more like *Gouled v. U. S.*, 255 U.S. 298 (1921) (where an old acquaintance acting for the police obtained defendant's consent to enter his office, but then conducted an extensive search when defendant left the room), in that the officer exceeded the reasonably anticipated scope of the consensual intrusion. That is, in *Lewis* and *Hoffa* the defendant voluntarily revealed his criminal activity to another, but this was not so in *Gouled, Brown,* or *Graves*. See *C. v. Brown,* supra (dissent).

B.   THIRD PARTY CONSENT

Background. In the area of consent searches, courts have long recognized that certain third parties may give consent which will permit use of the seized evidence against the defendant. Various theories have been utilized to explain this result. An agency theory was relied upon in *Stoner v. Cal.*, 376 U.S. 483 (1964), where the Court held that Fourth Amendment rights can only be waived by the defendant "either directly or through an agent." But in *Bumper v. N. C.*, supra, the Court seemed to rely upon a property theory in intimating that the grandmother's consent to search of her house for a rifle, had it been voluntary, would have been effective against the grandson who lived there because she "owned both the house and the rifle." And in *Frazier v. Cupp*, 394 U.S. 731 (1969), consent by defendant's cousin Rawls to search of a duffel bag jointly used by them was held to be effective against the defendant because he "must be taken to have assumed the risk that Rawls would allow someone else to look inside." Similarly, in *U. S. v. Matlock*, 415 U.S. 164 (1974), the Court indicated that where two or more persons have joint access to or control of premises "it is reasonable to recognize that any of the co-inhabitants has the right to permit the inspection in his own right and that the others have assumed the risk that one of their number might permit the common area to be searched." The assumption-of-risk theory is consistent with the new justified-expectation-of-privacy approach to the Fourth Amendment in *Katz v. U. S.*, 389 U.S. 347 (1967) (see § 11).

The choice of theory may affect the result. For example, the holding that the wife's consent would not be effective against her husband when she called the police because she was angry at him, *Kelley v. S.*, 197 S.W.2d 545 (Tenn.1946), or the holding that one co-tenant could not given consent effective against the other co-tenant who was present and objected to the search, *Dorsey v. S.,* 232 A.2d 900 (Md.App.1967), are more readily understandable under the agency theory.   However, such rulings have sometimes been explained on the ground that "a joint occupant's right of privacy in his home is not completely at the mercy of another with whom he shares legal possession." *Tompkins v. Superior Ct.,* 378 P.2d 113 (Cal.1963).

Relationship of third party to defendant and place searched. Most of the third party consent cases have involved the husband-wife relationship, and the prevailing view is that when a husband and wife jointly own or occupy the premises in question, either may consent to a search of those premises for items which may incriminate the other.   *Coolidge v. N. H.,* 403 U.S. 443 (1971).   Recent decisions have also upheld consents given by paramours who actually shared the premises on a continuing basis.   *U. S. v. Matlock,* supra.   But in these and other cases based upon joint occupation of the premises, one occupant may not consent to search of areas kept private by the other occupant.   For example, in *S. v. Evans,* 372 P.2d 365 (Hawaii 1962), it was held that a wife in joint occupancy of a home could not authorize a search of her husband's personal effects in a bedroom bureau drawer.

If a child is living at the home of his parents, the head of the household may consent to a search of the child's living quarters. *Maxwell v. Stephens*, 229 F.Supp. 205 (E.D.Ark.1964). On the other hand, a child may not give effective consent to a full search of the parents' home, *P. v. Jennings*, 298 P.2d 56 (Cal.App.1956), although where it is not unusual or unauthorized for the child to admit visitors into the home, the mere entry of police on the premises with the consent of the child is not improper. *Davis v. U. S.*, 327 F.2d 301 (9th Cir. 1964).

A landlord may not consent to the search of rented premises occupied by a tenant, and this is so even though the landlord may have some limited right of entry for purposes of inspecting or cleaning the premises. *Chapman v. U. S.*, 365 U. S. 610 (1961). A person who rents a hotel room is treated as any other tenant, *Stoner v. Cal.*, supra, although once the time of occupancy has expired and the guest has checked out, a hotel representative may then consent to a search for anything the guest has left behind. *P. v. Van Eyk*, 364 P.2d 326 (Cal.1961). However, the landlord or his agents (such as a building custodian or superintendent) may consent to a search of hallways, basements, and other area to which all tenants have common access. *Gillars v. U. S.*, 182 F.2d 962 (D.C.Cir. 1950). A tenant may not consent to search of the part of the premises retained by the landlord, *Weeks v. U. S.*, 232 U.S. 383 (1914), but may consent to search of the premises rented to him for items the landlord may have hidden there. *Vejih v. S.*, 200 N.W. 659 (Wis.1924). A person sharing a house or apartment with another may consent to a search of rooms of common usage, *P. v. Palmer*, 187 N. E.2d 236 (Ill.1962), and a person in lawful possession of premises may give consent to search of the premises which will be effective against a nonpaying guest, *Crosland v. S.*, 203 A.2d 876 (Md.App.1964), or a casual visitor, *P. v. Kortwright*, 236 N.Y.S.2d 385 (Sup.Ct.1962).

Although there is authority to the effect that an employer may consent to a search of an employee's work and storage areas on the employer's premises, *S. v. Zuehlke*, 300 N.W. 746 (Wis. 1941), the better view is that the employer may not consent to a search of areas in which the employee is permitted to keep personal items not connected with the employment. *U. S. v. Blok*, 188 F.2d 1019 (D.C.Cir. 1951). Whether an employee can give a valid consent to a search of his employer's premises depends upon the scope of his authority. Generally, the courts have been of the view that the average employee, such as a clerk, janitor, driver, or other person temporarily in charge, may not give consent. *U. S. v. Lagow*, 66 F.Supp. 738 (S.D.N.Y.1946). However, if the employee is a manager or other person of considerable authority who is left in complete charge for a substantial period of time, then the prevailing view is that such a person can waive his employer's rights. *U. S. v. Antonelli Fireworks Co.,* 155 F.2d 631 (2d Cir. 1946).

Whether a bailee, who does not own the property but has lawful possession of it, can consent to a police search of the property which will be effective against the bailor depends upon the nature of the bailment. The extent to which the bailor has surrendered control and the length of the bailment are most important. Thus, a brief bailment of papers by the defendant to his sister for the limited purpose of her doing some clerical work on them would not support her surrender of the papers to the police, *Pielow v. U. S.,* 8 F.2d 492 (9th Cir. 1925), in contrast to a case in which boxes were stored in the bailee's garage for an indefinite period of time and the bailee had the only key. *Von Eichelberger v. U. S.,* 252 F.2d 184 (9th Cir. 1958). Often, the nature of the bailment must be considered against the extent of the search; perhaps an attendant in a public garage may consent to the opening of the car door to see items on the floor of the car, *Casey v. U. S.,* 191 F.2d 1 (9th Cir. 1951), but for the bailee to consent to search of the trunk it must appear that the bailee was authorized to open the trunk. *Potman v. S.,* 47 N.W.2d 884 (Wis.1951).

Apparent authority. In *Stoner v. Cal.*, supra, in response to the state's contention that a police search of defendant's hotel room was proper because they reasonably believed that the clerk had authority to consent, the Court emphasized "that the rights protected by the Fourth Amendment are not to be eroded by strained applications of the law of agency or by unrealistic doctrines of 'apparent authority.'" As a consequence, it is unclear what remains of the apparent authority rule, which rests upon the notion that police have not conducted an unreasonable search if they acted upon the consent of a person who reasonably appeared to be in a position to give consent. *P. v. Gorg*, 291 P.2d 469 (Cal.1955). It may only be that reasonable mistakes of law (e. g., whether a hotel clerk can consent to search of a hotel room), as opposed to reasonable mistakes of fact (e. g., whether the person giving consent actually has the property interest in the premises searched which he claims or otherwise appears to have), are not sufficient.

16. INSPECTIONS; REGULATORY SEARCHES

Border searches. Dictum in *Carroll v. U. S.*, 267 U.S. 132 (1925), quoted with approval in *Almeida-Sanchez v. U. S.*, 413 U.S. 266 (1973), states: "Travellers may be stopped in crossing an international boundary because of national self protection reasonably requiring one entering the country to identify himself as entitled to come in, and his belongings as effects which may be lawfully brought in." Border searches are considered unique, and a person crossing the border may be required to submit to a search of his person, baggage, and vehicle without the slightest suspicion. *Henderson v. U. S.*, 390 F.2d 805 (9th Cir. 1967). However, some evidence short of probable cause must exist to justify more intrusive and embarrassing searches; "a real suspicion" is said to be required for a strip search, and a "clear indication" for examination of body cavities. *Henderson v. U. S.*, supra. The special rules on border searches also apply to persons who have already travelled some distance into the country, if the circumstances indicate that any contraband which might be found was in the place searched at the time of entry. *Alexander v. U. S.*, 362 F. 2d 379 (9th Cir. 1966). But, a border search must occur at the border or "its functional equivalent," and thus a car found near the border but not known to have crossed the border may not be subjected to a warrantless search for illegal aliens, either by a roving patrol or at a fixed checkpoint, in the absence of consent or probable cause. *Almeida-Sanchez v. U. S.*, supra; *U. S. v. Ortiz*, —— U.S. —— (1975). Such a vehicle may be stopped briefly to enable questioning of the occupants about their citizenship and immigration status if the officer is aware of specific articulable facts which, together with rational inferences from those facts, reasonably warrant suspicion that the car contains aliens who may be illegally in the country. *U. S. v. Brignoni-Ponce,* —— U.S. —— (1975).

Supervision of probationers and parolees. Probation and parole officers may subject probationers and parolees to searches without arrest or a search warrant and upon evidence which falls short of the usual probable cause requirement. *P. v. Hernandez,* 40 Cal.Rptr. 100 (App.1964); *P. v. Chinnici,* 273 N.Y.S.2d 538 (Nassau Co.Ct. 1966). Although this has sometimes been explained on the ground that probation and parole are acts of grace which are bestowed in exchange for the curtailment of constitutional rights, this is inconsistent with the principle that a state may not attach unconstitutional conditions to the grant of state privileges. Somewhat more convincing is the argument that without such close supervision there would be reluctance to grant parole and probation to those who are reasonable risks for such conditional release. If this is so, it would seem that the fruits of such close scrutiny should not be admissible in new criminal prosecutions, but only in revocation proceedings, particularly when there is some evidence that the probation or parole agent acted on behalf of the police. *P. v. Coffman*, 82 Cal.Rptr. 782 (App.1969).

Inspection of premises. Administrative inspections of residential and commercial premises for fire, health and safety violations may not be undertaken without a search warrant unless the occupant consents to the inspection or the inspection is made in an emergency. The occupant is thus usually free to challenge the inspector's decision to search without the risk of suffering criminal penalties for his refusal. However, a search warrant for such an inspection does not require a showing of probable cause that a particular dwelling contains violations of the code being enforced, but only that reasonable legislative or administrative standards for conducting an area inspection are satisfied with respect to a particular building. This special probable cause test was arrived at "by balancing the need to search against the invasion which the search entails," considering (1) the long history of acceptance of such inspection programs; (2) the public interest in abating all dangerous conditions, even those which are not observable from outside the building; and (3) the fact that the inspections are neither personal in nature nor aimed at discovery of evidence of crime, and thus involve a relatively limited invasion of privacy. *Camara v. Mun. Ct.*, 387 U.S. 523 (1967); *See v. City of Seattle*, 387 U.S. 541

(1967). The *Camara-See* warrant requirement is inapplicable to inspection of licensed premises, at least where the business is such that effective regulation requires frequent unannounced inspections. *U. S. v. Biswell*, 406 U.S. 311 (1972) (weapons dealer).

17. STOP–AND–FRISK AND OTHER BRIEF DETENTION

Background. Police have long followed the practice of stopping suspicious persons on the street or other public places for purposes of questioning them or conducting some other form of investigation, and, incident to many stoppings, of searching the person for dangerous weapons. Because this investigative technique, commonly referred to as stop-and-frisk, is ordinarily employed when there are not grounds to arrest the suspect and to search him incident to arrest, it was often questioned whether the practice could be squared with the Fourth Amendment. The Supreme Court provided some answers in *Terry v. Ohio*, 392 U.S. 1 (1968), and the companion cases of *Sibron v. N. Y.* and *Peters v. N. Y.*, 392 U.S. 40 (1968).

In *Terry*, where an officer observed three men who appeared to be "casing" a store for a robbery and then approached them for questioning and frisked them, finding weapons on two of them, the Court held "that where a police officer observes unusual conduct which leads him reasonably to conclude in light of his experience that criminal activity may be afoot and that the persons with whom he is dealing may be armed and presently dangerous; where in the course of investigating this behavior he identifies himself as a policeman and makes reasonable inquiries; and where nothing in the initial stages of the encounter serves to dispel his reasonable fear for his own or others' safety, he is entitled for the protection of himself and others in the area to conduct a carefully limited search of the outer clothing of such persons in an attempt to discover weapons which might be used to assault him." *Sibron* involved the search of a man observed consorting with narcotic addicts, and there the Court found the officer did not have a reasonable fear for his own safety or that of others; *Peters* was disposed of on the ground that the officer had made a lawful arrest prior to the search which uncovered burglary tools.

The result in *Terry* rests upon three fundamental conclusions the Court reached concerning Fourth Amendment theory. First of all, the Court concluded that restraining a person on the street is a "seizure" and that exploring the outer surfaces of his clothing is a "search," and thus rejected "the notions that the Fourth Amendment does not come into play at all as a limitation upon police conduct if the officers stop short of something called a 'technical arrest' or a 'full-blown search.'" Secondly, after noting that the police conduct here was without a warrant and thus subject to the reasonableness rather than the probable cause part of the Fourth Amendment, the Court utilized the balancing test of the *Camara* case to conclude that a frisk could be undertaken upon facts which would not support an arrest and full search. (Justice Douglas objected in dissent that the Court had in effect said that the police have more power without a warrant than with a warrant, which could have been answered—but was not—by observing that the balancing test applies in determining both the reasonableness of warrantless searches and seizures and, as in *Camara*, the probable cause for those with warrant.) Finally, in response to the defendant's observation that some stops and frisks are employed for harassment and other improper purposes, the Court noted that the exclusionary rule is ineffective when the police have no interest in prosecution and that consequently a flat prohibition of all stops and frisks would not deter those undertaken for improper objectives.

Temporary seizure for investigation. In *Terry*, the Court declined to rule upon "the constitutional propriety of an investigative 'seizure' upon less than probable cause." Yet, it seems that the

Court approved such seizures by implication, for (as Justice Harlan observed in his concurring opinion) the conclusion that an officer was entitled to frisk for his own protection must rest upon the assumption that the officer was justified in creating the danger in the first instance by stopping the suspect for investigation. *Terry* was later relied upon in upholding "the officer's forcible stop" in *Adams v. Williams*, 407 U.S. 143 (1972).

It remains unclear what Fourth Amendment evidentiary test is to be applied to temporary seizures, although a clue may be provided by the Court's emphasis in *Terry* upon the situation "where a police officer observes unusual conduct which leads him reasonably to conclude in light of his experience that criminal activity may be afoot." If this language is compared with that usually employed to describe the evidentiary test for arrest, it appears that some difference exists in the degree of probability required. As to the probability required for arrest, it may generally be stated that it must be more probable than not that the person has committed an offense; that is there must be a more than 50% probability that a crime has been committed, *P. v. Ingle*, 348 P.2d 577 (Cal.1960), and a more than 50% probability that the person arrested committed it, *Wong Sun v. U. S.*, 371 U.S. 471 (1963) (see pp. 107–108). The language in *Terry* suggests that a substantial possibility that a crime has been or is about to be committed and that the suspect is the person who committed or is planning the offense would suffice for a temporary seizure for investigation. See, e. g., *P. v. Mickelson*, 380 P.2d 658 (Cal.1963), holding that a stopping of a suspect near the scene of a recent robbery because he fitted the general description given by the victim was proper, though arrest would not have been proper because the description might have also fit others in the area.

In *Adams v. Williams,* supra, the Court, 6–3, upheld a stop based upon information the suspect possessed a gun and narcotics, given by a known informant who had provided information in the past. Because the informer could have been prosecuted for making a false complaint if his tip proved false, the tip (though insufficient for arrest) was deemed to have sufficient "indicia of reliability" to justify a stop. The dissenters objected to extending *Terry* so as to permit a stop where the information did not amount to probable cause because of its possible unreliability rather than its incompleteness, and one dissenter added that the power to stop would be subject to abuse if permitted for "mere possessory offenses."

A detention for investigation of a somewhat different kind was involved in *U. S. v. Van-Leeuwen*, 397 U.S. 249 (1970), where the Court, citing *Terry*, upheld the holding of mailed packages for approximately one day while the police promptly investigated the suspicious circumstances of the mailing and obtained a search warrant for the packages.

Protective search. *Terry* makes it clear that whether it is proper to make a protective search incident to a stopping for investigation is a question separate from the issue of whether it is permissible to stop the suspect. For a protective search, it must reasonably appear that the suspect "may be armed and presently dangerous," which would again appear to require only a substantial possibility, rather than the more than 50% probability which would justify an arrest and full search for carrying a concealed weapon. Although *Terry* also emphasizes that the officer frisked only after he had made some initial inquiries and the responses did not "dispel his reasonable fear," the frisk upheld in *Adams* was not preceded by inquiries.

Terry indicates that a two-step process must ordinarily be followed: the officer must pat down first and then intrude beneath the surface of the suspect's clothing only if he comes upon something which feels like a weapon. In *Adams*, the Court approved the officer's conduct in reaching directly into the suspect's pocket, apparently because the informant had indicated the precise location of the weapon. But in any event, the search is limited by its recognized purpose, that is, "to an intrusion reasonably designed to discover guns, knives, clubs, or other hidden instruments for the assault of the police officer." This means that the search must be limited to those places to which the suspect has immediate access.

Brief detention at the station. It remains unclear whether the *Terry* balancing test may be utilized to support a brief detention for investigation at the station on grounds slightly short of that required for arrest. In *Davis v. Miss.*, 394 U.S. 721 (1969), holding fingerprints inadmissible because obtained after an illegal arrest, the Court noted it was arguable "that because of the unique nature of the fingerprinting process, such detention might, under narrowly defined circumstances, be found to comply with the Fourth Amendment even though there is no probable cause in the traditional sense," in that it "may constitute a much less serious intrusion upon personal security than other types of police searches and detentions." The Court added that a warrant would be required for such a detention, a matter which concurring Justice Harlan preferred to leave open.

Davis suggests that the intended investigative technique is a relevant consideration; the Court emphasized that detention for fingerprinting "involves none of the probing into an individual's private life and thoughts which marks an interrogation or search," cannot "be employed repeatedly to harass any individual," and "is an inherently more reliable and effective crime-solving tool than eyewitness identifications or confessions and is not subject to such abuses as the improper line-up and the 'third degree.'" But in *Wise v. Murphy*, 275 A.2d 205 (D.C.App.1971), the court stated that a properly conducted lineup would be reliable and that therefore detention to facilitate it would be permissible on less than the grounds needed for arrest. And in the pre-*Davis* case of *P. v. Morales*, 238 N.E.2d 307 (N.Y.1968), brief stationhouse detention for questioning on less than probable cause was approved; the Supreme Court remanded for an evidentiary hearing on other issues, preferring "not to grapple with the question of the legality of custodial questioning on less than probable cause for a full-fledged arrest," *Morales v. N. Y.*, 396 U.S. 102 (1969). Other courts have declined to approve detention at the station on less than grounds for arrest even where more reliable investigative methods were used. *U. S. v. Jennings*, 368 F.2d 111 (9th Cir. 1972) (fingerprinting); *U. S. v. Bailey*, 327 F.Supp. 802 (N.D.Ill.1971) (handwriting exemplars); *U. S. v. Askins*, 351 F.Supp. 408 (D.Md. 1972) (voice exemplars).

These decisions must be distinguished from *U. S. v. Dionisio*, 410 U.S. 1 (1973), and *U. S. v. Mara*, 410 U.S. 19 (1973), upholding the subpoenaing of witnesses to appear before a grand jury to give voice and handwriting exemplars without a prior showing of probable cause. The Court there emphasized that "a subpoena to appear before a grand jury is not a 'seizure' in the Fourth Amendment sense" and the obtaining of exemplars is not a search because "no person can have a reasonable expectation that others will not know" the characteristics of his voice or handwriting.

CHAPTER 3

WIRETAPPING, ELECTRONIC EAVESDROPPING, AND THE USE OF SECRET AGENTS

18. HISTORICAL BACKGROUND; APPLICATION OF FOURTH AMENDMENT

The Olmstead case. In *Olmstead v. U. S.*, 277 U.S. 438 (1928), the first wiretap case to reach the Supreme Court, the police intercepted communications by placing a tap on defendant's telephone line. In a 5–4 decision, the majority read the Fourth Amendment literally in concluding that the police conduct did not constitute a search and seizure. Two reasons were given: (1) at no time did the police trespass upon defendant's premises, so that no "place" was searched; and (2) only conversations were obtained, so that no "things" were seized.

As indicated herein, both of these grounds have since been rejected, and thus it is not surprising that in recent years the forceful dissents in *Olmstead* have more often been quoted. Justice Brandeis argued that the Amendment did cover wiretapping, and also that the government, as "the omnipresent teacher," should not be upheld in its admitted violation of a state wiretapping law.   Justice Holmes, dissenting on the latter ground only, characterized wiretapping in violation of state law as "dirty business" and contended that "it is a less evil that some criminals should escape than that the government should play an ignoble part."

Section 605.   Congress later enacted the Federal Communications Act of 1934, which provided in § 605: "[N]o person not being authorized by the sender shall intercept any communication and divulge or publish the existence, contents, substance, purport, effect, or meaning of such intercepted communication to any person."   On the basis of this language, it was held that a person with standing, i. e., a party to the conversation, *Goldstein v. U. S.*, 316 U.S. 114 (1942), could suppress in a federal prosecution evidence obtained by state or federal officers, *Nardone v. U. S.*, 302 U.S. 379 (1937); *Benanti v. U. S.*, 355 U.S. 96 (1957), by wiretapping interstate or intrastate communications, *Weiss v. U. S.*, 308 U.S. 321 (1939), unless done with the consent of one of the parties to the conversation.   *Rathbun v. U. S.*, 355 U.S. 107 (1957).   The ruling that wiretap evidence gathered by state officials was admissible in state prosecutions, *Schwartz v. Texas*, 344 U.S. 199 (1952), was finally overruled in *Lee v. Fla.*, 392 U.S. 378 (1968), where the Court em-

phasized the constitutional extension of the exclusionary rule in *Mapp v. Ohio* (p. 28), and the
lack of other effective sanctions for violation of §
605. *Lee* was decided just two days before the
Crime Control Act (see § 19) superceded the
wiretapping prohibition of § 605.

Non-telephonic electronic eavesdropping. *Goldman v. U. S.*, 316 U.S. 129 (1942), was the "bugging" counterpart of *Olmstead*: because federal
officers had merely placed a detectaphone against
the outer wall of a private office, the Court held
there had been no trespass and thus no Fourth
Amendment violation. Similarly, in *On Lee v. U.
S.* (p. 183), where incriminating statements were
picked up via a "wired for sound" acquaintance
of defendant, a 5–4 majority rejected the contention that a trespass by fraud had occurred and
thus found no constitutional violation.

That the Constitution does furnish some protection against the electronic seizure of conversations was made plain by *Silverman v. U. S.*, 365
U.S. 505 (1961). There, a unanimous Court held
that listening to incriminating conversations
within a house by inserting a "spike mike" into a
party wall and making contact with a heating
duct serving the house occupied by defendants,
amounted to an illegal search and seizure. Although the Court asserted it was irrelevant
"whether or not there was a technical trespass

under the local property law relating to party walls," the opinion did not clearly indicate whether the "intrusion" by the spike into defendants' premises was a critical fact.

Any remaining doubts were dispelled by *Katz v. U. S.*, 389 U.S. 347 (1967). The issue in *Katz* was whether recordings of defendant's end of telephone conversations, obtained by attaching an electronic listening and recording device to the outside of a public telephone booth, had been obtained in violation of the Fourth Amendment. In a 7–1 decision, the Court expressly rejected the "trespass" doctrine of *Olmstead* and *Goldman*, and held that the government action constituted a search and seizure within the meaning of the Fourth Amendment because it "violated the privacy upon which [the defendant] justifiably relied while using the telephone booth." *Katz* thus made it clear that, with the possible exception of the case in which a conversation is overheard or recorded with the consent of a party to the conversation (see § 20), wiretapping and electronic eavesdropping are subject to the limitations of the Fourth Amendment.

19. CONSTITUTIONALITY OF TITLE III OF THE CRIME CONTROL ACT

Under what circumstances, then, may wiretapping and electronic eavesdropping without the prior consent of a party to the conversations be conducted consistent with the Fourth Amendment? Because such surveillance is authorized in limited circumstances by Title III of the Omnibus Crime Control and Safe Streets Act of 1968, 18 U.S.C. §§ 2510–2520, the appropriate inquiry is into the constitutionality of that legislation. The Supreme Court has not yet passed upon the Act, but some guidance on the issues involved may be found in recent decisions of the Court: *Osborn v. U. S.*, 385 U.S. 323 (1966), upholding a judicially authorized use of an undercover agent with a concealed tape recorder; *Berger v. N. Y.*, 388 U.S. 41 (1967), holding the New York eavesdropping law unconstitutional; and *Katz v. U. S.*, 389 U.S. 347 (1967), indicating that the limited eavesdropping undertaken there would have been constitutional if a warrant had first been obtained.

Summary of Title III. Under the Act, the Attorney General or a specially designated Assistant Attorney General may authorize application to a federal judge for an order permitting interception of wire or oral communications (i. e., wiretapping or electronic eavesdropping) by a federal agency having responsibility for investigation of the offense as to which application is made, when such interception may provide evidence of certain enumerated federal crimes. A comparable provision permits, when authorized by state law, application by a state or county prosecutor to a state judge when the interception may provide evidence of "murder, kidnapping, gambling, robbery, bribery, extortion, or dealing in narcotic drugs, marijuana or other dangerous drugs, or other crime dangerous to life, limb, or property, and punishable by imprisonment for more than one year." The judge may only grant an interception order as provided in § 2518 of the Act, and evidence obtained in the lawful execution of such order is admissible in court. Other willful interception or disclosure of any wire or oral communication without the prior consent of a party thereto is made criminal, and evidence so obtained is inadmissible in any state or federal proceedings.

The Act expressly provides that it does not limit the constitutional power of the President to take such measures as he deems necessary "to protect the Nation against actual or potential attack or other hostile acts of a foreign power, to obtain foreign intelligence information deemed essential to the security of the United States, * * * to protect national security information against foreign intelligence activities, [or] to protect the United States against the overthrow of the Government by force or other unlawful means, or against any other clear and present danger to the structure or existence of the Government," and communications intercepted by authority of the President in the exercise of those powers may be received in evidence "where such interception was reasonable." Those powers do not extend to warrantless tapping in *domestic* security cases, as Fourth Amendment protections are "the more necessary" for "those suspected of unorthodoxy in their political beliefs." *U. S. v. U. S. District Court*, 407 U.S. 297 (1972).

Under § 2518, an interception order may be issued only if the judge determines on the basis of facts submitted that there is probable cause for belief that an individual is committing, has committed, or is about to commit one of the enumerated offenses; probable cause for belief that particular communications concerning that offense will be obtained through such interception; that normal investigative procedures have been tried and have failed or reasonably appear to be unlikely to succeed if tried or to be too dangerous; and probable cause for belief that the facilities from which, or the place where, the communications are to be intercepted are being used, or are about to be used, in connection with the commission of such offense, or are leased to, listed in the name of, or commonly used by such person. Each interception order must specify the identity of the person, if known, whose communications are to be intercepted; the nature and location of the communications facilities as to which, or the place where, authority to intercept is granted; a particular description of the type of communication sought to be intercepted, and a statement of the particular offense to which it relates; the identity of the agency authorized to intercept the communications and of the person authorizing the application; and the period of time during which such interception is authorized, including a statement as to whether or not the interception shall automatically terminate when the described communication has been first obtained. No order may permit interception "for any period longer than is necessary to achieve the objective of the authorization, nor in any event longer than thirty days." Extensions of an order may be granted for like periods, but only by resort to the procedures required in obtaining the initial order.

Interception without prior judicial authorization is permitted whenever a specifically designated enforcement officer reasonably determines that "(a) an emergency situation exists with respect to conspiratorial activities characteristic of organized crime that requires a wire or oral communication to be intercepted before an order authorizing such interception can with due diligence be obtained, and (b) there are grounds upon which an order could be entered." In such a case, application for an order must be made within 48 hours after the interception commences, and, in the absence of an order, the interception must terminate when the communication sought is obtained or when the application for the order is denied, whichever is earlier.

Within a reasonable time but not later than 90 days after the filing of an application which is denied or the termination of an authorized period of interception, the judge must cause to be served on the persons named in the order or application and other parties to the intercepted communications, an inventory which shall include notice of (1) the fact of the entry of the order or application; (2) the date of the entry and the period of authorized interception, or the denial of the application; and (3) the fact that during the period communications were or were not intercepted. A similar inventory is required as to interceptions terminated without an order having been issued.

Continued surveillance. The most obvious difference between a search for tangible items and the search for wire or oral communications allowed under Title III is the time dimension of the latter kind of search. A search warrant for some physical object permits a single entry and prompt search of the described premises, while Title III permits continuing surveillance up to 30 days, with extensions possible. During the authorized time, all conversations over the tapped line or within the bugged room may be overheard and recorded without regard to their relevance.

As reflected in *Berger*, this striking difference accounts for the major constitutional obstacle to legalized electronic surveillance. In holding a New York law unconstitutional, the Court emphasized that it (1) permitted installation and operation of surveillance equipment for 60 days, "the equivalent of a series of intrusions, searches, and seizures pursuant to a single showing of probable cause"; (2) permitted renewal of the order "without a showing of present probable cause for the continuance of the eavesdrop"; and (3) placed "no termination date on the eavesdrop once the conversation sought is seized." While Title III permits extensions only upon a new showing of probable cause and requires that interception cease once "the objective of the authorization" is achieved, it does permit continued surveillance for up to 30 days upon a single showing of probable cause, and thus goes well beyond the kind of with-warrant electronic surveillance the Supreme Court has approved or indicated would be permitted.

As emphasized in *Berger*, the bugging of a secret agent upheld in *Osborn* was pursuant to an order which "authorized one limited intrusion rather than a series or a continuous surveillance.

And, we note that a new order was issued when the officer sought to resume the search and probable cause was shown for the succeeding one. Moreover, the order was executed by the officer with dispatch, not over a prolonged and extended period." And in *Katz* the Court noted that the "surveillance was so narrowly circumscribed that a duly authorized magistrate * * * clearly apprised of the precise intrusion * * * could constitutionally have authorized * * * the very limited search and seizure that the Government asserts in fact took place." The surveillance was limited in that the agents had probable cause to believe defendant was using certain public telephones for gambling purposes about the same time almost every day and thus activated the surveillance equipment attached to the outside of the phone booth only when defendant entered the booth.

Decisions holding that continued surveillance may also be squared with the Fourth Amendment, e. g., *U. S. v. Cafero*, 473 F.2d 489 (3d Cir. 1973), rely upon the analysis of Justices Harlan and White, dissenting in *Berger*. First, they contend that an electronic surveillance which is continued over a span of time is no more a general search than the typical execution of a search warrant over a described area. As Justice White argued: "Petitioner suggests that the search is inherently overbroad because the eavesdropper

[178]

will overhear conversations which do not relate to criminal activity. But the same is true of almost all searches of private property which the Fourth Amendment permits. In searching for seizable matters, the police must necessarily see or hear, and comprehend, items which do not relate to the purpose of the search. That this occurs, however, does not render the search invalid, so long as it is authorized by a suitable search warrant and so long as the police, in executing that warrant, limit themselves to searching for items which may constitutionally be seized."

This analogy holds only if it may be concluded that the overhearing or recording of a series of conversations is merely a search, from which certain particularly described conversations will thereafter be seized, as Justice Harlan contended: "Just as some exercise of dominion, beyond mere perception, is necessary for the seizure of tangibles, so some use of the conversation beyond the initial listening process is required for the seizures of the spoken word." A majority of the Court has yet to speak clearly on this point, although in *Katz* there is language characterizing the "electronically listening to and recording" of defendant's words as a "search and seizure."

Lack of notice. The Court in *Berger* also found the New York law "offensive" because it "has no requirement for notice, as do conventional warrants, nor does it overcome this defect by requiring some showing of special facts. On the contrary, it permits uncontested entry without any showing of exigent circumstances. Such a showing of exigency, in order to avoid notice would appear more important in eavesdropping, with its inherent dangers, than that required when conventional procedures of search and seizure are utilized." This criticism goes to the heart of all eavesdropping practices, as the Court noted, in that success depends upon secrecy.

The *Berger* Court did not explore this matter in greater detail, and thus it is not entirely clear whether Title III might be challenged on this basis. In decisions upholding the statute, e. g., *U. S. v. Cafero*, supra, the following arguments have been made: (1) One reason for advance notice, as emphasized by four members of the Court in *Ker v. Cal.*, 374 U.S. 23 (1963), is to guard the entering officer from attack on the mistaken belief he is making a criminal entry, and this danger is not present in most eavesdropping cases— including all which do not require a trespass. (2) Another reason for notice is so that the individual will be aware that a search was conducted, but in the more typical search case this notice may come only after the event by discovery of the warrant and a receipt at the place searched, which is comparable to the Title III requirement of service of an inventory within 90 days. (3)

Prior notice is not required when there is reason to believe it would result in destruction of the evidence sought (see p. 114), and while the Court in *Berger* may have been unwilling to uphold all eavesdropping without notice on this ground, this "exigency" is sufficiently established upon a showing that "normal investigative procedures have been tried and have failed or reasonably appear to be unlikely to succeed if tried or to be too dangerous," as required by Title III. An extensive footnote (n. 16) on the subject in *Katz* suggests that the Court finds these arguments compelling.

Other considerations. An exhaustive analysis of Title III would reveal a number of other problems, primarily going to how the Act must be construed in light of the Fourth Amendment. Three of these problems deserve brief mention here. First of all, what meaning is to be given to the "probable cause" requirement in this context? If, as discussed earlier, the Fourth Amendment has some flexibility, so that somewhat less evidence is needed to justify such lesser intrusions as a building inspection, stop-and-frisk, or brief seizure for fingerprinting (see §§ 16, 17), then it may be equally true that more evidence than usual will be required to establish probable cause for the unusual degree of intrusion which results from electronic surveillance. Justice Stewart, concurring in *Berger*, took this approach and thus found the affidavits in that case adequate for a "conventional search or arrest" but insufficient for a 60-day eavesdrop.

Title III requires a particular description of the "type of communication sought to be intercepted, and a statement of the particular offense to which it relates," but it is unclear how this language is to be interpreted. The statute in *Berger* merely required the naming of "the person or persons whose communications * * * are to be overheard or recorded"; the Court held this did not meet the Fourth Amendment requirement that the things to be seized be particularly described and declared that the "need for particularity * * * is especially great in the case of eavesdropping [because it] involves an intrusion on privacy that is broad in scope." Yet, as Justice Harlan noted in dissent, the cases on search for tangible items make it clear that the particularity requirement of the Amendment is a flexible one, depending upon the nature of the described things and whether the description readily permits identification by the executing officer (see p. 112). From this it might be argued that specification of conversations as relating to a certain kind of criminal activity should suffice.

Finally, there is the provision in Title III which permits interception without prior judicial approval when there are grounds for an interception order but an emergency exists with respect to conspiratorial activities threatening national security or characteristic of organized crime that require interception before an order could with due diligence be obtained. If strictly construed to ensure that warrantless interceptions are not being upheld after the fact on the basis of what was discovered, this provision is consistent with Fourth Amendment decisions on search for physical evidence without warrant to prevent loss of the evidence (see § 13C). *Katz* condemned the warrantless eavesdropping challenged in that case, but the facts make it clear that there was ample time to secure a warrant.

20. THE USE OF SECRET AGENTS TO OBTAIN INCRIMINATING STATEMENTS

"Wired" agents: On Lee and Lopez. In *On Lee v. U. S.*, 343 U.S. 747 (1952), a wired-for-sound informant entered the laundry of the defendant, an old acquaintance, and engaged him in conversation, resulting in defendant's incriminating statements being transmitted to a narcotics agent outside. At trial, the agent testified as to these statements, but the informer was not called as a witness. A 5–4 majority rejected the claim that the informant committed a trespass by fraud, dismissed as "verging on the frivolous" the contention that the narcotics agent was trespassing by use of the transmitter and receiver, and concluded that in the absence of a trespass there was no Fourth Amendment violation.

Lopez v. U. S., 373 U.S. 427 (1963), concerned an internal revenue agent who, after receiving a bribe offer from the defendant, engaged defendant in subsequent incriminating conversations in the agent's office while equipped with a pocket recorder. The recordings were admitted at trial in support of the agent's testimony. In a 6–3 decision, the Court held no eavesdropping had occurred, in that there had been no invasion of the defendant's premises and the recording revealed only what the defendant willingly disclosed to the agent and what the agent in turn was entitled to disclose to others. The Chief Justice, concurring specially, asserted that *On Lee* was "wrongly decided" and was distinguishable from *Lopez* because in *On Lee* the eavesdropping deprived the defendant of an opportunity to cross-examine the informer. The three dissenters saw no difference between the two cases, and asserted that the Fourth Amendment should protect a person against the risk that third parties may give independent evidence of conversations engaged in with another.

Without "bugging": Lewis and Hoffa. In *Lewis v. U. S.*, 385 U.S. 206 (1966), a federal narcotics agent misrepresented his identity and expressed a willingness to purchase narcotics, which resulted in his being invited into defendant's home, where an unlawful narcotics sale occurred. Because the agent did not "see, hear, or take anything that was not contemplated and in fact intended by petitioner as a necessary part of his illegal business," but merely entered a home "converted into a commercial center to which outsiders are invited for purposes of transacting unlawful business," the Court found no Fourth Amendment violation. *Gouled v. U. S.*, 255 U.S. 298 (1921), was distinguished in that there a business acquaintance, acting on police order, gained entry to defendant's office as a social visitor and then searched for and seized papers in the defendant's absence.

In *Hoffa v. U. S.*, 385 U.S. 293 (1966), the defendant unsuccessfully challenged on Fourth, Fifth, and Sixth Amendment grounds the admission of evidence obtained by a Teamsters official who at government instigation visited Hoffa during the latter's earlier trial and overheard conversations between Hoffa and his associates concerning an attempt to bribe jurors. As to the contention that the failure of the informer to disclose his role vitiated the consent to his entry of a constitutionally protected area, Hoffa's hotel suite, the Court noted that Hoffa "was not relying on the security of the hotel room [but rather] upon his misplaced confidence that [the informer] would not reveal his wrongdoing," which is not protected by the Fourth Amendment. The Fifth

Amendment claim was summarily dismissed with the observation that "a necessary element of compulsory self-incrimination is some kind of compulsion," absent here because Hoffa's conversations with and in the presence of the informer were "wholly voluntary." As to the Sixth Amendment claim that the informer had intruded upon the confidential attorney-client relationship, the Court concluded that, at least on these facts, such a violation of Sixth Amendment rights in one trial does not render evidence obtained thereby inadmissible in a different trial on other charges. Another Sixth Amendment argument, that from the time when there was evidence for arrest Hoffa was entitled to the same protection afforded an arrested person under *Massiah* and *Escobedo* (see §§ 25, 26), was quickly disposed of on the ground that "there is no constitutional right to be arrested," for otherwise the police would be in the perilous position of having to guess at the precise moment they had probable cause.

The impact of Katz. The thrust of these four cases is that such uses of secret agents, with or without listening or recording devices, are not covered by the Fourth Amendment. It is apparently on this basis that the electronic eavesdropping provisions of Title III expressly exclude from the warrant requirement the interception of communications with the consent of a party to the conversation. However, doubts about the continued vitality of *On Lee, Lopez, Lewis*, and *Hoffa* emerged when the Court in *Katz v. U. S.* (p. 88), rejected the old trespass-into-constitutionally-protected-areas analysis in favor of an expectation-of-privacy approach to Fourth Amendment issues.

The question reached the Court in *United States v. White*, 401 U.S. 745 (1971), where an informer, carrying a concealed transmitter, engaged the defendant in conversations in a restaurant, defendant's home and the informer's car. The informer did not testify at the trial, but the narcotics agents who electronically overheard the conversations did, resulting in defendant's conviction. In a 4-man plurality opinion by White, J., it was concluded (1) that one may not have a "justifiable" expectation that his trusted associates neither are nor will become police agents, and (2) that a different result is not called for when the agent has recorded or transmitted the conversations: "Given the possibility or probability that one of his colleagues is cooperating with the police, it is only speculation to assert that the defendant's utterances would be substantially different or his sense of security any less if he also thought it possible that the suspected colleague is wired for sound." Black, J., concurred on the basis of his *Katz* dissent, which contended the Fourth Amendment did not apply to intangibles.

Brennan, J., concurred in the result in *White* on the ground that *Katz* should not be applied retroactively, but contended that *On Lee* and *Lopez* both should be viewed as overruled by *Katz*, the position apparently taken in each of the three dissenting opinions. None of the dissenters specifically questioned the status of *Lewis* and *Hoffa*, and Harlan, J., in particular, emphasized the difference between the practices involved in those cases and the instant case: "The interest *On Lee* fails to protect is the expectation of the ordinary citizen, who has never engaged in illegal conduct in his life, that he may carry on his private discourse freely, openly, and spontaneously without measuring his every word against the connotations it might carry when instantaneously heard by others unknown to him and unfamiliar with his situation or analyzed in a cold, formal record played days, months, or years after the conversation."

21. DISCLOSURE OF ELECTRONIC SURVEILLANCE RECORDS

If conversations have been overheard or recorded by electronic surveillance in violation of the Fourth Amendment, testimony concerning or recordings of these conversations may be suppressed by a defendant with standing. Under the "fruit of the poisonous tree" doctrine (see § 32), other evidence which was the product of illegal surveillance is also subject to suppression. This has given rise to the issue of what procedures are required to facilitate a determination whether other evidence is in fact the fruit of such a surveillance.

This issue was decided in *Alderman v. U. S., Ivanov v. U. S.,* and *Butenko v. U. S.,* 394 U.S. 165 (1969); *Alderman* involved convictions for conspiring to transmit murderous threats in interstate commerce, while the other cases concerned convictions for transmitting national defense information to the Soviet Union. The defendants sought disclosure of all surveillance records so that they might show that some of the evidence admitted against them grew out of illegally overheard conversations. The government urged that in order to protect innocent third parties participating or referred to in irrelevant conversations overheard by the government, surveillance records should first be subjected to in camera inspection by the trial judge. He would then turn over to defendants and their counsel only those materials "arguably relevant" to defendants' convictions, in the sense that the overheard conversations arguably underlay some item of evidence offered at trial.

The Court, in a 5–3 decision, held that a defendant should receive all surveillance records as to which he has standing (see p. 300). The government's proposal was rejected on the ground that the trial judge often would not be in a position to determine what conversations were relevant: "An apparently innocent phrase, a chance remark, a reference to what appears to be a neutral person or event, the identity of a caller or the individual on the other end of a telephone, or even the manner of speaking or using words may have special significance to one who knows the more intimate facts of an accused's life. And yet that information may be wholly colorless and devoid of meaning to one less well acquainted with all relevant circumstances. Unavoidably, this is a matter of judgment, but in our view the task is too complex, and the margin for error too great, to rely wholly on the in camera judgment of the trial court to identify those records which might have contributed to the Government's case." To protect innocent third parties, the Court added, the trial court could place defendants and counsel under enforceable orders against unwarranted disclosure of the materials they would be entitled to inspect.

Justice Fortas, dissenting in part, argued that the in camera screening procedure should be followed when the trial judge makes written and sealed findings "that disclosure would substantially injure security interests." Justice Harlan, dissenting in part, subscribed to a narrower view that such screening would be appropriate whenever the defendant is charged with spying for a foreign power, in which case protective orders would not deter disclosure to others and the location of listening devices crucial to espionage work would otherwise be needlessly disclosed. In an unsuccessful petition for rehearing, the Attorney General argued against disclosure of records of surveillance activities to gather "foreign intelligence information" on the ground that such activity was practiced by all nations and thus not unreasonable.

In *Giordano v. U. S.*, 394 U.S. 310 (1969), the Court emphasized that the disclosure required in *Alderman* was expressly limited to situations where the surveillance had been determined to be in violation of the Fourth Amendment. Justice Stewart, concurring, suggested that this preliminary determination might sometimes be made in ex parte, in camera proceedings. And in *Taglianetti v. U. S.*, 394 U.S. 316 (1969), the Court rejected defendant's contention that he was entitled to examine additional surveillance records to establish that he might be a party to some other conversations. Distinguishing *Alderman*, the Court concluded that the trial judge could be expected to identify defendant's voice without the defendant's assistance.

By Title VII of the Organized Crime Control Act of 1970, 18 U.S.C. § 3504, Congress has attempted to limit the impact of *Alderman* in the federal courts. For one thing, records of an unlawful surveillance which occurred prior to June 19, 1968, (the date that the Omnibus Crime Control and Safe Streets Act of 1968 became law) need not be disclosed "unless such information may be relevant to a pending claim of * * * inadmissibility," which presumably is to be determined by the judge in camera. For another, on the legislative finding that "there is virtually no likelihood" that evidence offered to prove an event would have been obtained by exploitation of an unlawful surveillance occurring more than five years prior to that event, no such claim is to be considered. The constitutionality of these provisions is open to some doubt, considering the fact that the *Alderman* decision was cast in terms of "the scrutiny which the Fourth Amendment exclusionary rule demands."

22. THE USE OF SECRET AGENTS TO "ENCOURAGE" CRIMINAL CONDUCT

Entrapment. Secret agents—sometimes undercover police officers but very often private citizens acting as informants—are frequently utilized to "encourage" others to engage in criminal conduct. Such tactics are for the most part confined to the crimes of prostitution, homosexuality, liquor and narcotic sales, and gambling; normal detection methods are virtually impossible as to these offenses, as they are committed privately with a willing victim who will not complain. The encouragement very frequently involves little more than a feigned offer by the agent to purchase criminal services from the suspect, but on occasion the agent may use considerably more pressure to gain the suspect's agreement to commit an offense.

The Supreme Court has held that techniques of encouragement may not reach the point where they constitute "entrapment"; if they do, the presence of entrapment constitutes a defense to the defendant's otherwise criminal act. The exact definition of entrapment is a matter of dispute, but it clearly includes the situation in which "the criminal design originates with the [police agents] and they implant in the mind of an innocent person the disposition to commit the offense and induce its commission in order that they may prosecute." *Sorrells v. U. S.*, 287 U.S. 435 (1932). So far, the Court has based the defense upon other than constitutional grounds; some of the Justices have relied upon general principles of substantive criminal law and others upon the supervisory power of the Court over the administration of justice in federal courts. *U. S. v. Russell*, 411 U.S. 423 (1973); *Sherman v. U. S.*, 356 U.S. 369 (1958).

Possible constitutional bases. While the entrapment defense is also recognized in the state courts, which for the most part purport to use the *Sorrells-Sherman* test, state convictions are sometimes affirmed notwithstanding evidence of what would constitute entrapment under those decisions, e. g., *P. v. Toler*, 185 N.E.2d 874 (Ill. 1962). This has given rise to the question of whether freedom from entrapment is a federal constitutional right for which relief may be granted upon federal habeas corpus, to which the courts have so far responded in the negative. *U. S. ex rel. Toler v. Pate*, 332 F.2d 425 (7th Cir. 1964).

In support of the contention that freedom from entrapment is a right protected under the due process clause, commentators have suggested that: (1) by analogy to the Fourth Amendment protection against unreasonable searches or by application of the penumbral "right of privacy," *Griswold v. Conn.*, 381 U.S. 479 (1965), secret agents may encourage only those individuals as to whom there exists "probable cause" (under the balancing approach, see §§ 16, 17, a lesser quantum of evidence than would be required for arrest) ; (2) by analogy to the constitutional prohibition on illegally obtained confessions, under which ruses and appeals to sympathy are relevant considerations, *Spano v. N. Y.*, 360 U.S. 315 (1959), secret agents may not overbear a person's will to get him to perpetrate a crime; (3) by analogy to the doctrine that it is cruel and unusual punishment to convict for mere status and without the proof of any act, *Robinson v. Cal.*, 370 U.S. 660 (1962), the acts which serve as the basis for conviction must be attributable to the defendant rather than to the police or their agents; (4) by analogy to the constitutional limitation on abolition of *mens rea*, *Lambert v. Cal.*, 355 U.S. 225 (1957), the necessary mental element for a crime may not be implanted by entrapment; and (5) by analogy to the constitutional defense of estoppel, which bars conviction for actions undertaken upon official advice that such conduct would not violate the law, *Cox v. La.*, 379 U.S. 559 (1965), secret agents may not induce actions in which the defendant was not predisposed to engage.

In *U. S. v. Russell*, supra, the Supreme Court, while noting that the entrapment defense "is not of a constitutional dimension," acknowledged that there might be "a situation in which the conduct of law enforcement agents is so outrageous that due process principles would absolutely bar the government from invoking judicial processes to obtain a conviction."

CHAPTER 4

POLICE INTERROGATION AND CONFESSIONS

---

23. INTRODUCTION

The confession dilemma. No area of constitutional criminal procedure has provoked more debate over the years than that dealing with police interrogation. In large measure, the debate has centered upon the extent of police abuse in seeking confessions and the importance of confessions in obtaining convictions—two matters on which conclusive evidence is lacking.

Because the questioning of suspects has traditionally been undertaken behind station-house doors (for some, a sufficient indication in itself of abuse), there is not sufficient empirical evidence to assert with confidence what always, usually, or often occurs in the course of police interrogation. Attention thus has often turned to celebrated cases of confessions later proved false or to judicial opinions (including many Supreme Court cases, see § 24) revealing outrageous police tactics. Those who assert that police abuses have been widespread contend that these cases are fairly representative, while those of a contrary persuasion claim that these are unusual cases having no relation to day-to-day police work. There is similar disagreement as to what may be logically presumed from the nature of the police and their task: whether it is proper to presume that policemen usually abide by their sworn duty to comply with the law in enforcing the law; or whether the correct assumption is that the police are so caught up in the difficult task of fighting crime that they believe anything goes.

Hard facts about the need for confessions are also lacking. It may be true, as Justice Frankfurter declared in *Culombe v. Conn.*, 367 U.S. 568 (1961), that "despite modern advances in the technology of crime detection, offenses frequently occur about which things cannot be made to speak," but just how frequently they occur is uncertain. Statistics have been offered to establish that confessions are seldom utilized in serious criminal cases and also to show the contrary. The former are challengeable on the ground that they fail to take account of the overwhelming majority of cases disposed of by pleas of guilty, while the latter are contested because they may only demonstrate that the police often fail to use other investigative techniques.

Assuming other techniques are available, there is still disagreement as to whether interrogation is nonetheless desirable. Some hold to the view, as expressed by Justice Goldberg in *Escobedo v.*

Ill., 378 U.S. 478 (1964), that "a system of criminal law enforcement which comes to depend on the 'confession' will, in the long run, be less reliable and more subject to abuses than a system which depends on extrinsic evidence independently secured through skillful investigation." Others question this assumption and suggest that greater use of certain "extrinsic evidence," such as eyewitness identifications (see ch. 5), would result in even less reliability.

The Supreme Court's response. From 1936 to nearly 30 years later, the Court dealt with confessions admitted in state criminal proceedings in terms of the fundamental fairness required by the Fourteenth Amendment due process clause (see § 2). A so-called "voluntariness" test, which depended upon the "totality of the circumstances," was used to determine whether the Constitution required exclusion of a confession (see § 24). Over the years, it became increasingly apparent that this test was most difficult to administer because it required a finding and appraisal of all relevant facts surrounding each challenged confession.

Essentially the same approach was used by the Court during this period on the infrequent occasions when confessions admitted in federal prosecutions were reviewed. In such instances, it might logically be thought that the Court was then relying upon the due process clause of the Fifth Amendment, although the tendency was to refer to earlier holdings in which the basis of exclusion was the Fifth Amendment privilege against self-incrimination or a common law rule of evidence. *U. S. v. Carignan,* 342 U.S. 36 (1951). Beginning in 1943, a confession obtained by federal officers and offered in a federal prosecution could also be excluded on the ground that it was received during a period of "unnecessary delay" in taking the arrested person before a judicial officer. *McNabb v. U. S.,* 318 U.S. 332 (1943); *Mallory v. U. S.,* 354 U.S. 449 (1957). Although these decisions were grounded upon the Court's supervisory power over the federal courts, most commentators viewed them as attempts by the Court to avoid the tremendous problems inherent in the due process voluntariness test, and thus there was some expectation that the *McNabb-Mallory* rule (finally abolished by Title II of the Omnibus Crime Control and Safe Streets Act of 1968) would ultimately be rested upon a constitutional foundation and applied to the states.

This did not come to pass, perhaps because subsequent decisions holding that there was a constitutional right to counsel at certain pretrial "critical stages" provided a better stepping stone. The anticipated move away from sole reliance upon the voluntariness test occurred in *Escobedo v. Ill.,* supra, suppressing the defendant's confession because it was obtained in violation of his right to counsel at the time of interrogation. *Escobedo* was a cautious step, for the holding was carefully limited to the unique facts of the case (see § 25), but it was generally assumed that this newly established right to counsel in the police station would thereafter be expanded on a case-by-case basis. Instead, the Court just two years later decided *Miranda v. Ariz.*, 384 U.S. 436 (1966), which was grounded upon the Fifth Amendment privilege against self-incrimination and proscribed a specific set of warnings as prerequisites to all future custodial interrogations (see § 26).

It is *Miranda* which is of major current significance, and thus the emphasis in this chapter is upon the basis and meaning of that decision. But the voluntariness and right-to-counsel cases also deserve further attention, as: (1) an elaboration of those decisions is essential to an assessment of *Miranda*; (2) neither *Miranda* nor *Escobedo* is retroactive (see § 8), so that many confessions are still subject to collateral attack only on grounds recognized before those decisions; (3) there may be instances in which a post-*Miranda* confession meets the requirements of that case but is nonetheless excludable by resort to these earlier decisions; and (4) limits on the collateral use of the confession and the admission of evidence derived from the confession may be more

stringent where the confession is involuntary as
well as obtained in violation of *Miranda* (see pp.
272, 284–285).

24. THE "VOLUNTARINESS"— "TOTALITY OF CIRCUM- STANCES" TEST

Objectives of the test. Although the Supreme
Court earlier had occasion to review the admissibility of confessions in the federal courts, first
under the common law rule of evidence barring
confessions obtained by threats or promises, *Hopt
v. Utah*, 110 U.S. 574 (1884), and later—at least
in one case—under a voluntariness test apparently derived from the Fifth Amendment privilege
against self-incrimination, *Bram v. U. S.*, 168 U.S.
532 (1897), it was not until *Brown v. Miss.*, 297
U.S. 278 (1936), that the Court barred the use of
a confession in the state courts. It could not, of
course, dispose of the state confession on the
same grounds as were resorted to in the earlier
cases; under our federal system, the Supreme
Court could not proscribe mere rules of evidence
for the states, and the Fifth Amendment privilege
was then not applicable to the states, *Twining v.
N. J.*, 211 U.S. 78 (1908), overruled by *Malloy v.
Hogan*, 378 U.S. 1 (1964). Thus the confessions
in *Brown*, obtained by brutally beating the suspects, were struck down on the notion that inter-

rogation is part of the process by which a state procures a conviction and thus subject to the requirements of the Fourteenth Amendment due process clause.

The interests to be protected under the due process test, and thus the true dimensions of that constitutional protection, remained somewhat obscure in the earlier cases. In *Brown*, the confessions clearly were of doubtful reliability, and thus that case might be read as announcing a due process test for excluding confessions obtained under circumstances presenting a fair risk that the statements are false. Concern with this risk was emphasized in subsequent cases, such as *Chambers v. Fla.*, 309 U.S. 227 (1940); *Ward v. Texas*, 316 U.S. 547 (1942); and *Lyons v. Okla.*, 332 U.S. 596 (1944), and this led many state courts to the conclusion that "unfairness in violation of due process exists when a confession is obtained by means of pressure exerted upon the accused under such circumstances that it affects the testimonial trustworthiness of the confession." *S. v. Schabert*, 15 N.W.2d 585 (Minn.1944).

While it is fair to say that ensuring the reliability of confessions is *a* goal under the due process voluntariness standard, it is incorrect to define the standard in terms of that one objective. In *Rogers v. Richmond*, 365 U.S. 534 (1961), defendant's confession was obtained after the police pretended to order his ailing wife arrested for

[202]

questioning, and the state court had ruled that the statement need not be excluded "if the artifice or deception was not calculated to procure an untrue statement." The Supreme Court disagreed, emphasizing that convictions based upon coerced confessions must be overturned "not because such confessions are unlikely to be true but because the methods used to extract them offend an underlying principle in the enforcement of our criminal law: that ours is an accusatorial and not an inquisitorial system." *Rogers* thus made certain what was strongly intimated in several earlier cases, e. g., *Ashcraft v. Tenn.*, 322 U.S. 143 (1944); *Haley v. Ohio*, 332 U.S. 596 (1948), namely, that the exclusionary rule for confessions (in much the same way as the Fourth Amendment exclusionary rule, see p. 28) is also intended to deter improper police conduct.

In *Townsend v. Sain*, 372 U.S. 293 (1963), the ailing defendant had been given a drug with the properties of a truth serum, after which he gave a confession in response to questioning by police who were unaware of the drug's effect. Although the confession was not obtained by conscious police wrongdoing and apparently was reliable, the Court nonetheless held its use impermissible: "Any questioning by police officers which *in fact* produces a confession which is not the product of free intellect renders that confession inadmissible." *Townsend* thus highlights another theme which runs through many of the earlier cases, e. g., *Lisenba v. Cal.*, 314 U.S. 219 (1941); *Watts v. Ind.*, 338 U.S. 49 (1949): the confession must be a product of the defendant's "free and rational choice." This phrase, however, was not used in an absolute sense, but rather in conjunction with a recognized need to exert some pressure to obtain confessions. As the Court seems to have acknowledged in *Miranda*, the question of whether a confession was "voluntary" had theretofore been determined by a lesser standard than, say, the question of whether a testator's will was his voluntary act.

Viewing the voluntariness test in terms of its objectives, then, it could be said that the test was designed to bar admission of those confessions which: (a) were of doubtful reliability because of the practices used to obtain them; (b) were obtained by offensive police practices, even if reliability was not in question (e. g., where there is strong corroborating evidence); or (c) were obtained under circumstances in which the defendant's free choice was significantly impaired, even if the police did not resort to offensive practices.

The relevant circumstances. Under the voluntariness test, the Supreme Court undertook a continuing re-evaluation on the facts of each case of how much pressure on the suspect was permissible. The rule required examination of the "totality of circumstances" surrounding each confession. *Haynes v. Wash.*, 373 U.S. 503 (1963). The factors deemed most important were: (1) physical abuse, *Lee v. Miss.*, 332 U.S. 742 (1948); (2) threats, *Payne v. Ark.*, 356 U.S. 560 (1958); (3) extensive questioning, *Turner v. Pa.*, 338 U.S. 62 (1949); (4) incommunicado detention, *Davis v. N. C.*, 384 U.S. 737 (1966); (5) denial of the right to consult with counsel, *Fay v. Noia*, 372 U.S. 391 (1963); and (6) the characteristics and status of the suspect, such as his lack of education, *Culombe v. Conn.*, 367 U.S. 568 (1961), emotional instability, *Spano v. N. Y.*, 360 U.S. 315 (1959), youth, *Gallegos v. Colo.*, 370 U.S. 49 (1962), or sickness, *Jackson v. Denno*, 378 U.S. 368 (1964). However, the voluntariness test is by its nature imprecise, and thus it could rarely be said that the presence of any one of these factors or any fixed combination of them clearly required exclusion of a confession.

Administration of the test. Although the *Miranda* dissenters saw the voluntariness test as "a workable and effective means of dealing with confessions in a judicial manner," many critics of the totality-of-circumstances approach had long been of the contrary view. The amorphous character of the test, together with the seeming reluctance of some courts to overturn the conviction of an apparently guilty defendant, led to divergent results in the lower courts. Not infrequent-ly, confessions were upheld although they quite clearly appeared to have been obtained under circumstances previously condemned by the Supreme Court. For example, in *Davis v. N. C.*, supra, it was uncontested that no one other than the police had spoken to the defendant during the 16 days of detention and interrogation which preceded his confessions. The Court reversed, noting it had "never sustained the use of a confession obtained after such a lengthy period of detention and interrogation," but two state courts and two federal courts had previously upheld the confession notwithstanding these objective facts.

Davis was unique in that the relevant circumstances were revealed by police records; usually, an attempt at the trial level to ascertain the "totality of circumstances" has resulted in what has been commonly referred to as a "swearing contest" between the defendant and the police. The ultimate determination of whether the confession should be excluded, therefore, typically had to be made upon the basis of several hotly disputed questions of fact.

25. THE RIGHT TO COUNSEL

Pre-Escobedo developments. Several developments in the late 1950's and early 1960's enhanced the prospect that the Supreme Court might ultimately resolve the confession issue in terms of the right to counsel. In *Crooker v. Cal.*, 357 U.S. 433 (1958), where defendant's confession was obtained following denial of his request to call an attorney, the Court held the confession voluntary and also rejected defendant's separate contention that he had a right to counsel at the police station. Recognition of such a right, asserted the majority, would preclude both fair and unfair questioning, a result not required under the "less rigid" due process concept. *Betts v. Brady* (p. 324), holding that due process did not impose a flat requirement of appointed counsel in all serious state trials, was cited in support. The four dissenters in *Crooker* asserted that under due process "the accused who wants a counsel should have one at any time after the moment of arrest." *Crooker* was followed in *Cicenia v. Lagay*, 357 U.S. 504 (1958), where defendant's requests to see his attorney were refused and his counsel turned away at the station, but again there was a strong dissent. The confession in *Spano v. N. Y.*, 360 U.S. 315 (1959), was found involuntary on traditional grounds, but four concurring justices accepted defendant's contention that his absolute right to counsel in a capital case attached at the time he was indicted (which was prior to his confession).

In *White v. Md.*, 373 U.S. 59 (1963), the absolute right to counsel in a capital case was held applicable to a pretrial "critical stage," a preliminary arraignment at which a guilty plea later introduced into evidence was obtained. Some commentators suggested that if, as in *White*, an uncounseled guilty plea could not be admitted as evidence of guilt at trial, then it followed that the same should be true of an uncounseled confession. *White* took on greater significance when the *Betts* rule (relied upon in *Crooker*) was overruled in *Gideon v. Wainwright*, 372 U.S. 335 (1963), holding that the absolute right to counsel for indigent state defendants existed as to all serious cases and not merely capital cases.

The argument that the right to counsel attaches when the defendant is indicted and his status thereby changes from "suspect" to "accused," not reached by the majority in *Spano*, was accepted in a somewhat different context in *Massiah v. U. S.*, 377 U.S. 201 (1964). After defendant's indictment, he was engaged in an incriminating conversation by a bugged codefendant-turned-informer, about which the overhearing agent testified at trial. Perhaps to avoid a difficult eavesdropping issue (see § 20), the Court held, 6–3, that the Sixth Amendment prohibits extraction of incriminating statements from an indicted person without presence of counsel. The majority indicated this would be equally true had the incriminating statements been obtained by police interrogation. Any thoughts that *Massiah* was limited to federal prosecutions or to cases in which the defendant had already retained counsel were dispelled by the per curiam decision in *Mc-Leod v. Ohio*, 381 U.S. 356 (1965), but most lower courts refused to extend *Massiah* back to the point of earlier tentative charges. *U. S. ex rel. Forella v. Follette*, 405 F.2d 680 (2d Cir. 1969).

The Escobedo case. The confession in *Escobedo v. Ill.*, 378 U.S. 478 (1964), was obtained after defendant's repeated requests to consult with retained counsel were refused and after his attorney had actually been turned away at the station. The Court, 5–4, concluded that this pre-indictment interrogation was just as much a "critical stage" as the preliminary hearing in *White*, in that what happened then could "affect the whole trial," and that *Massiah* was apposite because "no meaningful distinction can be drawn between interrogation of an accused before and after formal indictment."   Yet the Court did not announce a broad right-to-counsel-at-the-station rule, but instead cautiously limited the holding to the facts of the case:

"We hold * * * that where, as here, [1] the investigation is no longer a general inquiry into an unsolved crime but has begun to focus on a particular suspect, [2] the suspect has been taken into police custody, [3] the police carry out a process of interrogations that lends itself to eliciting incriminating statements, [4] the suspect has requested and been denied an opportunity to consult with his lawyer, and [5] the police have not effectively warned him of his absolute constitutional right to remain silent, the accused has been denied 'the Assistance of Counsel' in violation of the Sixth Amendment to the Constitution as 'made obligatory upon the States by the Fourteenth Amendment,' * * * and that no statement elicited by the police during the interrogation may be used against him at a criminal trial."

The meaning of Escobedo.   Because the much broader *Miranda* decision is not retroactive (see § 8), the precise meaning of *Escobedo* is still a matter of significance as to confessions admitted at trials occurring between the two decisions. This matter of interpretation has largely fallen upon the lower courts; they have reached diverse results, but (as in the representative cases cited below) have usually attributed significance to each of the five "elements" in the *Escobedo* holding enumerated above.

Thus: (1) While the Court said in *Miranda* that the focus requirement of *Escobedo* was really intended to mean deprivation of freedom in a significant way, this requirement has been utilized to find *Escobedo* inapplicable where the suspect was in custody on another charge and the interrogation was undertaken while the case was in the investigatory rather than accusatory stage, *P. v. Morse*, 452 P.2d 607 (Cal.1969). (2) *Escobedo* does not apply when the suspect is not in police custody, *S. v. Kelter*, 426 P.2d 500 (Wash.1967), although custody may be present without a formal arrest, *C. v. Brown*, 247 A.2d 802 (Pa.Super. 1968). (3) *Escobedo* does not govern volunteered statements, *P. v. Taylor*, 55 Cal.Rptr. 521 (App.1966), or even interrogation undertaken primarily for another purpose, such as to locate a kidnap victim, *P. v. Modesto*, 398 P.2d 753 (Cal. 1965). (4) *Escobedo* does not require a warning of the right to counsel, *S. v. Outten*, 206 So.2d 392 (Fla.1968), but applies only if the suspect makes a clear and unambiguous request for counsel, *Frazier v. Cupp*, 394 U.S. 731 (1969). (5) *Escobedo* is inapplicable if the police have warned the suspect of his right to remain silent, *Ward v. C.*, 138 S.E.2d 293 (Va.1964). Consider also the discussion of *Escobedo* in *Kirby v. Ill.*, as noted at p. 339.

Some issues concerning the meaning of *Escobedo* are more critical, in that *Escobedo* may also provide a basis for challenging post-*Miranda* confessions not excludable under the latter decision. These are considered in more detail later (see § 27F).

26. THE PRIVILEGE AGAINST SELF–INCRIMINATION

The privilege in the police station. The Fifth Amendment provides that no person "shall be compelled in any criminal case to be a witness against himself." Although a literal reading of this language suggests that the privilege against self-incrimination has no application to unsworn statements obtained by station-house interrogation, in *Bram v. U. S.*, 168 U.S. 532 (1897), the Court asserted that "in criminal trials, in the courts of the United States, wherever a question arises whether a confession is incompetent because not voluntary, the issue is controlled by that portion of the Fifth Amendment." The Court's conclusion that there was a historical connection between the privilege and the confession doctrine appears incorrect, and was subsequently challenged by many commentators. The privilege was not expressly relied upon in later cases concerning the admissibility of confessions in federal courts, while the Court dealt with confessions used in state courts solely in terms of the due process voluntariness test (see § 24). But in *Malloy v. Hogan*, 378 U.S. 1 (1964), which did not involve a confession, the Court held the privilege applicable to the states, and in support of this result noted that the admissibility of a confession in a state trial had long been tested by the same standard as applied to federal prosecutions by *Bram*. Promptly thereafter, the Court decided the *Escobedo* case (see § 25), which, while grounded upon the Sixth Amendment right to counsel, spoke of "the right of the accused to be advised by his lawyer of his privilege against self-incrimination."

Any remaining doubts were dispelled by *Miranda v. Ariz.*, 384 U.S. 436 (1966), holding that the privilege against self-incrimination "is fully applicable during a period of custodial interrogation." Although the apparent assumption of the *Miranda* majority that this proposition was "settled" in the precedents is subject to question, this of course does not compel the conclusion that the *Miranda* holding was in error. Even the dissenters in *Miranda* conceded that the Fifth Amendment privilege "embodies basic principles always capable of expansion," although they forcefully argued that those principles would not be served by extending the privilege to the police station.

The Miranda rules. Apart from this reliance upon the Fifth Amendment rather than the Sixth, *Miranda* is striking in its contrast to *Escobedo*. The latter holding was carefully limited to the facts of the case before the Court, while *Miranda* sets forth what the dissenters called a "constitutional code of rules for confessions":

(1) These rules are required to safeguard the privilege against self-incrimination, and thus must be followed in the absence of "other procedures which are at least as effective in apprising accused persons of their right of silence and in assuring a continuous opportunity to exercise it."

[*213*]

(2) These rules apply "when the individual is first subjected to police interrogation while in custody at the station or otherwise deprived of his freedom of action in any significant way," and not to "general on-the-scene questioning as to facts surrounding a crime or other general questioning of citizens in the fact-finding process" or to "volunteered statements of any kind."

(3) Without regard to his prior awareness of his rights, if a person in custody is to be subjected to questioning, "he must first be informed in clear and unequivocal terms that he has the right to remain silent," so that the ignorant may learn of this right and so that the pressures of the interrogation atmosphere will be overcome for those previously aware of the right.

(4) The above warning "must be accompanied by the explanation that anything said can and will be used against the individual in court," so as to ensure that the suspect fully understands the consequences of foregoing the privilege.

(5) Because this is indispensible to protection of the privilege, the individual also "must be clearly informed that he has the right to consult with a lawyer and to have the lawyer with him during interrogation," without regard to whether it appears that he is already aware of this right.

(6) The individual must also be warned "that if he is indigent a lawyer will be appointed to

represent him," for otherwise the above warning would be understood as meaning only that an individual may consult a lawyer if he has the funds to obtain one.

(7) The individual is always free to exercise the privilege, and thus if he "indicates in any manner, at any time prior to or during questioning, that he wishes to remain silent, the interrogation must cease"; and likewise, if he "states that he wants an attorney, the interrogation must cease until an attorney is present."

(8) If a statement is obtained without the presence of an attorney, "a heavy burden rests on the Government to demonstrate that the defendant knowingly and intelligently waived his privilege against self-incrimination and his right to retained or appointed counsel," and such waiver may not be presumed from the individual's silence after the warnings or from the fact that a confession was eventually obtained.

(9) Any statement obtained in violation of these rules may not be admitted into evidence, without regard to whether it is a confession or only an admission of part of an offense or whether it is inculpatory or allegedly exculpatory.

(10) Likewise, exercise of the privilege may not be penalized, and thus the prosecution may not "use at trial the fact that [the defendant] stood mute or claimed his privilege in the face of accusation."

Criticism of Miranda.   Not unexpectedly, the *Miranda* decision was greeted with criticism from many quarters.   It was contended that police abuse was not so widespread as to call for such a far-reaching decision, and that confessions were essential to law enforcement but would be unobtainable under the new rules (see § 23).   Recent empirical studies, however, have concluded that the impact of *Miranda* has been quite different than predicted by the Court's critics.   In most instances, the *Miranda* warnings have not appreciably reduced the amount of talking by a suspect, and the police are now obtaining about as many confessions as before *Miranda*.

These conclusions lend some support to the views of another group of critics, those who find a fundamental inconsistency in the majority's reasoning.   They claim that the heavy emphasis on the inability of an uncounseled defendant to decide whether to incriminate himself when subject to the inherent pressures of custody is inconsistent with the conclusion that the decision whether to dispense with counsel can be voluntary in the same circumstances.   As stated in one of the *Miranda* dissents: "But if the defendant may not answer without a warning a question such as 'Where were you last night?' without having his answer be a compelled one, how can the court ever accept his negative answer to the question of whether he wants to consult his retained counsel or counsel whom the court will appoint?"

The Crime Control Act. Title II of the Omnibus Crime Control and Safe Streets Act of 1968 amends existing legislation by adding 18 U.S.C. § 3501, which purports to "repeal" *Miranda* in federal prosecutions. The Act states that a confession is admissible in the federal courts if voluntarily given, and that whether the defendant was advised of his right to remain silent or his right to counsel and whether he was without counsel when he confessed are merely to be taken into consideration as circumstances bearing on the issue of voluntariness.

If viewed as a total "repeal" of *Miranda*, this statute is quite clearly unconstitutional, for rights derived from the Constitution cannot be repealed by legislation. However, in support of this legislation it has been noted that the *Miranda* Court indicated Congress might devise equally effective safeguards for protecting the privilege, and the argument is made that Title II does this by a less rigid formula than *Miranda*, permitting a confession to be used where a less than perfect warning was given or a less than conclusive waiver was obtained. In response, the contention can be made that compliance with Title II would result in courts returning to the old practice of considering all of the circumstances of the individual case, a procedure which the *Miranda* Court concluded had proven ineffective in protecting a suspect's constitutional rights.

27. THE MEANING OF MIRANDA

A. WHAT OFFENSES ARE COVERED?

Traffic and other minor offenses. A number of courts have held *Miranda* inapplicable to traffic and other minor crimes. Their underlying reasoning has been obscure; there have merely been general references to the volume of these lesser offenses, *S. v. Bliss*, 238 A.2d 848 (Del.1968), or to the "practical" and "historical" differences between them and serious crimes, *S. v. Zucconi*, 226 A.2d 16 (N.J.Super.1967). In *Campbell v. Superior Ct.*, 479 P.2d 685 (Ariz.1971), on the other hand, *Miranda* was applied to a defendant arrested for driving under the influence. In support of *Campbell*, it may be noted that the privilege against self-incrimination *at trial* (unlike the right to counsel or to jury trial) has never been limited to serious crimes. The *Campbell* court correctly noted that the result would be otherwise in the case of a "routine traffic offense where the driver is detained no longer than is necessary to make out the citation," for in such circumstances the interrogation is not "custodial." Cf. *Schneckloth v. Bustamonte*, 412 U.S. 218 (1973).

Tax investigations. In *Mathis v. U. S.*, 391 U.S. 1 (1968), which concerned statements obtained by an internal revenue agent from a defendant incarcerated in jail on another matter, the government contended that the *Miranda* warnings were not required because the questions were asked as "part of a routine tax investigation where no criminal proceedings might even be brought." The Court acknowledged that such an investigation might be initiated for the purpose of a civil action, but ruled that the warnings are required because there is always the possibility that criminal prosecution will result.

B. WHEN IS INTERROGATION "CUSTODIAL"?

"Custody" vs. "focus." In the course of defining that interrogation which is "custodial," the *Miranda* Court dropped a footnote stating that was "what we meant in *Escobedo* when we spoke of an investigation which had focused on an accused." Some have thus suggested that custody and focus are alternative grounds for requiring the warnings. A more likely explanation for this footnote, which probably does not really state what was intended by the focus element when *Escobedo* was written (see § 25), is that the Court was attempting to maintain some continuity between that case and the new approach of *Miran-*

da, while in fact making a fresh start in describing the point at which the constitutional protections begin. *U. S. v. Hall*, 421 F.2d 540 (2d Cir. 1969).

That the Court does not view the focus test as a meaningful device for determining when constitutional rights attach is made clear by *Hoffa v. U. S.* (pp. 185, 238). Defendant's argument was that incriminating statements elicited by an undercover agent were obtained in violation of his right to counsel which attached when there existed grounds for his arrest. The Court summarily dismissed this contention with the observation that such a rule would require police "to guess at their peril the precise moment at which they have probable cause to arrest a suspect."

Purpose of the custody. *Mathis v. U. S.*, supra, posed the question whether *Miranda* applies when the purpose of the custody is unrelated to the purpose of the interrogation, as there the defendant was in jail serving a state sentence when questioned by a revenue agent about his tax returns. The Court, 5–3, answered in the affirmative, asserting that a contrary result would go "against the whole purpose of the *Miranda* decision." The dissenters were unwilling to accept this conclusion, for they read *Miranda* as resting "not on the mere fact of physical restriction but on a conclusion that coercion—pressure to answer questions—usually flows from a certain type of custody, police station interrogation of someone charged with or suspected of a crime."

On-the-scene questioning. The *Miranda* Court stated that interrogation is custodial if it occurs while the individual is "in custody at the station or otherwise deprived of his freedom of action in any significant way." One reason for the latter part of this disjunctive definition is obvious: if *Miranda* governed only station-house interrogations, the police could easily circumvent the warning requirements by conducting interrogations in such places as hotel rooms or squad cars. But what of questions asked when the custody is arguably less coercive, such as just after arrest or during the brief on-the-street detention for investigation apparently permitted by the *Terry* case (see § 17)?

This issue has frequently confronted the lower courts, and they have generally taken the view that *Miranda* is sometimes but not always applicable on the street. However, these courts have utilized a variety of tests to determine the precise moment at which the "significant" deprivation of freedom occurs, including: (1) the subjective intention of the questioning officer to hold the person or to arrest him, *U. S. v. Gibson*, 392 F.2d 373 (4th Cir. 1968); *P. v. Reason*, 276 N.Y.S.2d 196 (Sup.Ct.1966); (2) the degree to which the investigation has focused on the person, *Windsor v. U. S.*, 389 F.2d 530 (5th Cir. 1968); *C. v. Jef-*

ferson, 226 A.2d 765 (Pa.1967); (3) the subjective belief of the person that he is under arrest or otherwise not free to leave, *P. v. Ceccone*, 67 Cal.Rptr. 499 (App.1968); *S. v. Intogna*, 419 P.2d 59 (Ariz.1966); or (4) the person's reasonable belief that he is under arrest or otherwise not free to leave, *P. v. P. (Anonymous)*, 233 N.E.2d 255 (N.Y.1967); *P. v. Hazel*, 60 Cal.Rptr. 437 (App.1967).

There are grounds upon which each of these approaches might be criticized. The intention-of-the-officer test does not mark the point at which there is a change in the "potentiality for compulsion" discussed in *Miranda*, as the uncommunicated intentions of the officer do not change the situation from the suspect's point of view. The focus test presents the difficulties discussed earlier. As for the subjective-belief-of-the-suspect test, it would "place upon the police the burden of anticipating the frailties or idiosyncracies of every person whom they question." *P. v. P. (Anonymous)*, supra. And the reasonable-belief-of-the suspect approach would also present the officer with an uncertain situation, as he would have to know the facts as they reasonably appear to the suspect; moreover, this test fails to recognize that the suspect who unreasonably believes he is not free to leave is under precisely the same pressure. Thus, some commentators have suggested an all-or-nothing approach to on-the-scene questioning. One view is that *Miranda* should never apply on the street, in that the abusive practices detailed in that case are unlikely to occur in that setting. At the other extreme, it has been said that if *Miranda* must sometimes apply on the street, then the custody requirement has lost its significance, and *Miranda* might as well be extended to all police-suspect confrontations on the ground (to take a proposition quoted in *Miranda*) that "there is still a general belief that you must answer all questions put to you by a policeman, or at least that it will be the worse for you if you do not."

In *Orozco v. Texas*, 394 U.S. 324 (1969), where four policemen entered defendant's bedroom at 4 a.m. and questioned him without the *Miranda* warnings, the Court held that *Miranda* applied, not on the ground that these unique facts established a "potentiality for compulsion" equivalent to station-house interrogation, but rather because the officers had testified that defendant was "under arrest and not free to leave" when he was questioned. The dissenters thought this intention-of-the-officer test inappropriate, in that "it is difficult to imagine the police duplicating in a person's home or on the street those conditions and practices which the Court found prevalent in the station house and which were thought so threatening to the right to silence." The test has also been viewed as unworkable in that the custody issue must be "decided by swearing contests in which officers would regularly maintain their lack of intention to assert power over a suspect," and thus some courts use an objective test whereby "in the absence of actual arrest something must be said or done by the authorities, either in their manner of approach or in the tone or extent of their questioning, which indicates that they would not have heeded a refusal to depart or to allow the suspect to do so." *U. S. v. Hall*, 421 F. 2d 540 (2d Cir. 1969).

C.   WHAT CONSTITUTES "INTERROGATION"?

"Volunteered" statements.   The *Miranda* Court emphasized that "there is no requirement that police stop a person who enters a police station and states that he wishes to confess to a crime, or a person who calls the police to offer a confession or any other statement he desires to make. Volunteered statements of any kind are not barred by the Fifth Amendment and their admissibility is not affected by our holding today." Thus, it is clear that a statement not preceded by the *Miranda* warnings will be admissible when, for example, the defendant walks into a station and confesses, *Lung v. S.*, 420 P.2d 158 (Okla. Crim.1966), or he blurts out an admission when approached by an officer near a crime scene, *C. v.*

Boyd, 239 A.2d 853 (Pa.Super.1968). Also, because the *Miranda* Court found custody-plus-interrogation coercive, rather than mere custody, it likewise seems clear that a statement may qualify as "volunteered" even though made by one in custody, *P. v. Mercer*, 64 Cal.Rptr. 861 (App. 1967); *In re Orr*, 231 N.E.2d 424 (Ill.1967).

But, what if the police have done something (other than questioning the suspect) which appears to have prompted his statement, such as showing him incriminating physical evidence or confronting him with a confessing accomplice or the accusing victim? Although the cases are not in agreement, compare *Combs v. Wingo*, 465 F.2d 96 (6th Cir. 1972), with *S. v. Welch*, 476 P.2d 822 (Ore.App.1970), the better view is that any police activity "likely to or expected to elicit a confession" constitutes "interrogation" under *Miranda*. *C. v. Mercier*, 302 A.2d 337 (Pa.1973). Most clearly encompassed within this rule is confrontation of the suspect with an accusing witness or victim, which, under pre-*Miranda* rules of evidence, was thought so likely to produce a response that the suspect's silence under those circumstances could be admitted against him.

Follow-up questioning. Assuming a truly volunteered statement, may the police follow up that statement with some questions? *Miranda* is not entirely clear on this issue; at one point custodial interrogation is defined as "questioning initiated by law enforcement officers," suggesting that police questioning designed to clarify or amplify a volunteered statement is permissible, but elsewhere it is said that the suspect must be warned "prior to any questioning." So far, courts have been quite willing to admit the answers to follow-up questions on the ground that these answers are a continuation of the volunteered statement, *S. v. Intogna,* 419 P.2d 59 (Ariz.1966); *C. v. Eperjesi,* 224 A.2d 216 (Pa.1966). It may well be, however, that a distinction should be drawn between questions designed to clarify an ambiguous statement (e. g., "did what"? in response to "I did it"), and those which seek to enhance the defendant's guilt or raise the offense to a higher degree (e. g., "why did you do it?").

Purpose of the questioning. The Supreme Court has held that the privilege against self-incrimination offers no protection against requiring a suspect to appear in a lineup, to give a handwriting sample, or to speak for identification the words uttered by the offender at the scene of the crime (see § 28). Thus, *Miranda*-type warnings are not a prerequisite to these procedures. Some commentators have suggested that questions asked for purposes of identification (e. g., "what is your name?", "where do you live?") are likewise outside the privilege, and that therefore they may be put to a suspect in custody without first giving him the *Miranda* warnings. Cf. *Cal. v. Byers,* 402

U.S. 424 (1971), holding that a statute requiring a driver of a car involved in an accident to stop and give the driver of the other car his name and address does not violate the privilege.

What if the police engage in routine questioning, perhaps as a part of the booking process, which is not related to the investigation of the case nor designed, expected or likely to elicit information relevant to guilt, but the defendant responds with a remark which turns out to be incriminating? One view is that the intent with which the question is asked is not relevant, in that even an innocent question asked of one in custody may create the impression that he must answer, so that the response is not voluntary in the sense required by *Miranda. Proctor v. U. S.,* 404 F.2d 819 (D.C.Cir. 1968). But, it may be argued that such innocent inquiries do not add to the pressures generated by police custody and that therefore the reply, especially if unresponsive, should be viewed as equivalent to a volunteered statement. Cf. *Parsons v. U. S.,* 387 F.2d 944 (10th Cir. 1968).

What if the purpose of the police was self-protection? In *S. v. Lane,* 467 P.2d 304 (Wash. 1970), where, immediately after the arrest of an armed robber in his apartment, he was asked if he had a gun and replied in the negative, noting he would not be dumb enough to have the gun there, the statement was held admissible on the ground that the question was asked to protect the immediate physical safety of the officers and could not have been delayed until after the warnings were given. On the other hand, it might be contended that, unlike a routine question about employment or residence, such an inquiry does add to the pressures generated by police custody, and that considering the limitations on search incident to arrest imposed by *Chimel* (p. 132) the need for such an inquiry is not great.

What if the purpose of the questioning was to rescue the victim? in *P. v. Dean,* 114 Cal.Rptr. 555 (App.1974), the court held admissible incriminating responses by a kidnapping suspect to questions about the victim's whereabouts, reasoning that the officer's interest in saving the victim's life justified not giving the *Miranda* warnings and thereby impeding the rescue efforts.

Questioning by non-police. In *Miranda*, the Court defined interrogation as "questioning initiated by law enforcement officers." This language has been relied upon by courts in holding *Miranda* inapplicable to questioning by a private investigator, *S. v. Hess*, 449 P.2d 46 (Ariz.App. 1969), a high school principal, *P. v. Shipp*, 239 N. E.2d 296 (Ill.App.1968), and the victim, *S. v. Little*, 439 P.2d 387 (Kan.1969). It has also been held that *Miranda* is not applicable to interrogation by the defendant's parole or probation officer, *S. v. Johnson*, 202 N.W.2d 132 (S.D.1972), although more persuasive is the contrary holding, based upon the fact that a probationer or parolee "is under heavy pressure to cooperate" with such a person, *S. v. Gallagher,* 313 N.E.2d 396 (Ohio 1974), cert. granted, 95 S.Ct. 1445 (1975).

D.   WHAT WARNINGS ARE REQUIRED?

Adequacy of the warnings. Although it is undoubtedly true that *Miranda* does not require slavish adherence to the precise words used therein for the necessary warnings, certainly the warnings given should be found inadequate if they fail to convey the substance of the *Miranda* requirements. Thus, it is not sufficient that the police told the defendant that "he didn't have to make any statement" (instead of that he had a right to remain silent), or that "he could consult an attorney prior to questioning" (instead of that he also had a right to have the attorney present during questioning), *U. S. v. Fox,* 403 F.2d 97 (2d Cir. 1968). Failure to advise the defendant of his right to have counsel appointed is also fatally defective, *Groshart v. U. S.,* 392 F.2d 172 (9th Cir. 1968), as is a warning that counsel will be furnished only at some future time, *U. S. ex rel. Williams v. Twomey,* 467 F.2d 1248 (7th Cir. 1972). A contrary result has been reached where the defendant later had retained counsel at trial and on appeal, *U. S. v. Messina*, 388 F.2d 393 (2d Cir. 1968), which seems inconsistent with footnote 43 in *Miranda*: "While a warning that the indigent may have counsel appointed need not be given to the person who is known to have an attorney or is known to have ample funds to secure one, the expedient of giving a warning is too simple and the rights involved too important to engage in *ex post facto* inquiries into financial ability when there is any doubt at all on that score." Warnings that anything the suspect says "might," "may," "can," or "could" be used against him have been sustained, *Davis v. U. S.*, 425 F.2d 673 (9th Cir. 1970), but a warning that the statement may be used "for or against" the suspect contains an improper inducement to speak, *C. v. Singleton,* 266 A.2d 753 (Pa.1970).

"Cutting off" the warnings. What if the warning officer never completes his task because the suspect cuts him off with the assertion that the warnings are unnecessary because he is fully aware of all of his rights? The prevailing view is that this is no excuse for not completing the warnings, *S. v. Ross*, 157 N.W.2d 860 (Nev.1968); *Brown v. Heyd*, 277 F.Supp. 899 (E.D.La.1967), and this is consistent with the language in *Miranda* which emphasizes that the expedient of giving adequate warnings is so simple that "we will not pause to inquire in individual cases whether the defendant was aware of his rights without a warning being given."

Multiple interrogation sessions. Once the warnings have been completely given and the defendant has given an effective waiver, must the warnings be repeated again at the outset of a subsequent interview? The courts have quite consistently answered in the negative, both when the later interview follows promptly after the first, *P. v. Hill*, 233 N.E.2d 367 (Ill.1968), and when several days have intervened, *Maguire v. U. S.*, 396 F.2d 327 (9th Cir. 1968). It might be argued, however, that the *Miranda* concern with the suspect's continuing right to invoke the privilege means that a substantial interval calls for repetition of the warnings, particularly so that the "warning will show the individual that his interrogators are prepared to recognize his privilege should he choose to exercise it."

Additional admonitions. Is the suspect entitled to notice from the police of the charge against him or, at least, of the nature and seriousness of the crime they are investigating? No, say most of the courts which have confronted this issue. *S. v. Lucero*, 445 P.2d 731 (Mont.1968); *S. v. McKnight*, 243 A.2d 240 (N.J.1968). This result is often justified by distinguishing confessions from guilty pleas. A plea of guilty, which involves a waiver of the privilege against self-incrimination as well as other rights, is constitutionally defective if the defendant is unaware of the precise nature of the charge. *Boykin v. Ala.*, 395 U.S. 238 (1969). But this, it is argued, is because a plea of guilty involves a legal conclusion (e. g., "I admit guilt as to the crime of battery"), while a confession or admission only involves an acknowledgment that certain possibly incriminating facts occurred (e. g., "I am the one who struck the victim"). And thus, while a plea to battery could not be converted into a homicide plea by the subsequent death of the victim, an acknowledgment of certain acts would be admissible whether the crime turns out to be battery or homicide, for (as the *McKnight* court put it) the privilege is not violated merely because the defendant misconceived the inculpatory thrust of the facts he admitted."

However, it is said in *Miranda* that "any evidence that the accused was threatened, tricked, or cajoled into a waiver will, of course, show that the defendant did not voluntarily waive his privilege." Deliberate acts by the police to mislead the suspect as to the seriousness of the situation might be subject to attack on this basis. Thus, in *Schenk v. Ellsworth*, 293 F.Supp. 26 (D.Mont. 1968), where defendant was suspected of murdering his wife but was only told the questioning would be "in connection with the shooting incident of his wife," the court noted he was "very likely misled" by his interrogator and thus had not intelligently waived counsel.

E. WHAT CONSTITUTES WAIVER?

Express or implied. The courts have not required an express, affirmative statement of waiver by the defendant. *U. S. v. Hayes*, 385 F.2d 375 (4th Cir. 1967). Perhaps it is appropriate to permit an implied waiver under unusual facts which establish that the defendant did elect to submit to questioning without counsel, as in *Hayes*. There, defendant was given the warnings and permitted to make a phone call, but was never asked if he understood the warnings or desired counsel, and he did not volunteer this information. He never confessed, but did make some incriminating statements during 30 minutes of questioning, which he suddenly terminated by declaring he would answer no more questions and demanding that he be allowed to see a lawyer. The court concluded that his later assertion of his rights made it clear that he understood the warnings and knew how to exercise his rights. However, to find waiver from the mere fact that the defendant answered questions, as in *Mullaney v. S.*, 246 A.2d 291 (Md.App.1968), clearly appears inconsistent with the *Miranda* caution that "a valid waiver will not be presumed simply from the silence of the accused after warnings are given or simply from the fact that a confession was in fact eventually obtained."

Refusal to execute written waiver or confession. On the question of whether an effective waiver can be established in the face of defendant's refusal to sign a waiver-of-rights form, or to have his confession reduced to writing, the prevailing view is yes. *U. S. v. Frazier*, 476 F.2d 891 (D.C. Cir. 1973); *Hodge v. U. S.*, 392 F.2d 552 (5th Cir. 1968). However, it does seem that under such circumstances no waiver should be found if other indications of the suspect's intentions to waive are at all ambiguous. Thus, in *U. S. v. Nielsen,* 392 F.2d 849 (7th Cir. 1968), where the defendant said he would not sign the waiver or anything else until he consulted an attorney, who he preferred to call later, the court ruled the government had not met its "heavy burden" to establish waiver; the defendant's willingness to talk and unwillingness to sign anything were contradictory, suggesting that he did not fully appreciate that his oral statements could be just as damaging as a signed confession.

Multiple interrogation sessions. Even more difficult is the question whether a suspect who has once refused to waive his *Miranda* rights may execute an effective waiver at a subsequent interrogation session, perhaps after being confronted with new evidence against him. Again the prevailing view is yes, on the ground that the defendant has already learned that the police are prepared to honor his privilege if he chooses to exercise it, and that the defendant should be free to change his mind as the circumstances change. *S. v. Godfrey*, 155 N.W.2d 438 (Neb.1968). To the contrary is *P. v. Fioritto*, 441 P.2d 625 (Cal. 1968), holding that the police may not initiate renewed interrogation—even to the point of seeking a waiver—if counsel is not present. The concern expressed by the *Fioritto* court, that a contrary result might impose upon courts the difficult task of determining whether the police acted improperly in inducing the defendant's change of heart, is a legitimate one. Another way of reflecting this concern and also recognizing the propriety of allowing the suspect to make an informed choice on the basis of new facts, as suggested in *U. S. v. Bird*, 293 F.Supp. 1265 (D.Mont.1968), would be to require a higher standard for waiver subsequent to the suspect's initial claim of the privilege. This question may soon be resolved by the Supreme Court, *P. v. Mosley*, 214 N.W.2d 564 (Mich.App.1974), cert. granted, 95 S.Ct. 801 (1975).

F. DOES THE RIGHT TO COUNSEL OR THE APPOINTMENT OR RETENTION OF COUNSEL HAVE ADDED SIGNIFICANCE?

Counsel's request to see client. What if defendant is arrested and taken to the station, where he receives the *Miranda* warnings and waives his rights, after which his attorney appears at or telephones the station with a request that he be allowed to see his client? The *Miranda* Court appears to have assumed that the request must be granted, for a footnote (n. 35) to a discussion of *Escobedo* reads: "The police also prevented the attorney from consulting with his client. Independent of any other constitutional proscription, this action constitutes a violation of the Sixth Amendment right to the assistance of counsel and excludes any statement obtained in its wake." But it is unclear why this should be so if the defendant has waived his Sixth Amendment rights, for the implication that the lawyer has a separate constitutional right to see his client is certainly questionable. (See *P. v. Zuniga,* 202 N.E.2d 31 (Ill.1964), holding a lawyer cannot challenge the constitutionality of a statute limiting compensation for representation of indigents, as the Sixth Amendment right to effective representation is not his.)

More understandable is the position taken in *C. v. McKenna,* 244 N.E.2d 560 (Mass.1969), that the attorney's request must be communicated to the client so that he may reconsider his waiver of counsel in the light of this new fact. As the court noted, the defendant "might have chosen to go on with the interrogation," but nonetheless "he was entitled to know of his counsel's availability and, with that knowledge, to make the choice with intelligence and understanding." This position is particularly persuasive if, as held in some of the cases discussed earlier, a defendant who has not waived his rights may be confronted with new facts upon which he might change his mind in favor of waiver.

Questioning without retained or appointed counsel's presence or approval. If counsel has made no such request, but the police know that counsel has been retained or appointed, may they obtain an effective waiver from the defendant in custody without also contacting the lawyer and asking whether he wishes his client to be interrogated or whether he wishes to be present for the interrogation? Applying the above analysis here, it could be said that the Sixth Amendment is a right of the client and not the lawyer, and that (assuming the police did not withhold from the defendant the fact counsel had been appointed or retained for him) no new facts have been withheld from the defendant, so that his waiver will suffice. Such was the holding in *Coughlan v. U. S.*, 391 F.2d 371 (9th Cir. 1968), although the dissenting judge argued that "neglect to notify counsel of a planned interrogation is as effective in preventing consultation as the physical barrier which confronted Escobedo's attorney at the jail house door."

Given the reluctance of most courts to extend the *Escobedo* rule beyond the facts of that case (see § 25), it is not surprising that the position taken in the *Coughlan* dissent has not prevailed. Similarly, *Massiah* has been deemed inapplicable to this situation because limited to cases where there were "circumstances preventing an effective exercise or waiver of rights to counsel," *U. S. v. Durham*, 475 F.2d 208 (7th Cir. 1973), as where the defendant was "coerced" or "tricked" into confessing, *S. v. Chabonian*, 185 N.W.2d 289 (Wis.1971).

Use of secret agents. What if the police falsely book an undercover agent into the jail on a fictitious charge and place him in defendant's cell, where he succeeds in eliciting incriminating information from the defendant? The use of secret agents in other contexts has been upheld (see § 20), and it would be difficult to attack this tactic on *Miranda* grounds, for it seems unlikely that a violation of the privilege is involved. As the Court held in *Hoffa v. U. S.*, 385 U.S. 293 (1966), statements elicited by an undercover agent are not "the product of any sort of coercion, legal or factual," so that no right protected by the Fifth

Amendment is violated. It might be argued, of course, that *Hoffa* is distinguishable in that the conversations there were "wholly voluntary" because of Hoffa's freedom to decide whether to speak *and* with whom to speak, while the jailed suspect cannot choose his cellmate and is induced to speak by the very presence of the cellmate. See the dissent by four Justices to the dismissal of the writ of certiorari in *Miller v. Cal.*, 392 U.S. 616 (1968).

But the outcome is more likely to depend upon the continued vitality and scope of *Massiah* and *Escobedo* (see § 25). As *Massiah* has been interpreted, standing alone it would bar such a use of a secret agent on Sixth Amendment grounds only if the defendant had already been indicted. In *Escobedo* the lack of an indictment was said to "make no difference" because "the investigation had ceased to be a general investigation of 'an unsolved crime,'" but that case cannot be viewed simply as an application of *Massiah* prior to indictment, for limitations not expressed in *Massiah* (most noteworthy here, an actual request for counsel) were also imposed. Nevertheless, four members of the Court, dissenting from the dismissal of the writ of certiorari in *Miller v. Cal.*, supra, concluded that *Massiah*, as expanded by *Escobedo*, applied on such facts. But note the discussion of the initiation of the Sixth Amendment right to counsel in *Kirby v. Ill.*, noted at pp. 338–339.

G.   DOES *MIRANDA* APPLY TO A GRAND JURY WITNESS?

Self-incrimination and the grand jury witness. Although this chapter is concerned primarily with police interrogation, note must be taken of the fact that prosecutors also engage in interrogation, typically by subpoenaing witnesses to appear and testify under oath before a grand jury. The prosecutor possesses broad powers in this regard; a subpoena may issue without a prior showing that the witness probably has facts relevant to the matter under inquiry, *U. S. v. Dionisio*, 410 U.S. 1 (1973), and generally a witness may not challenge the jurisdiction of the grand jury or object on grounds of incompetency or irrelevancy to questions put to him, *Blair v. U. S.*, 250 U.S. 273 (1919). But, a witness cannot be required to testify to facts that might tend to incriminate him. *Counselman v. Hitchcock*, 142 U.S. 547 (1892).

The self-incrimination problem may be obviated by a grant of immunity to the grand jury witness. While in a few states immunity is granted automatically when the witness testifies, in most jurisdictions the prosecutor must obtain a court order, often upon a showing that a grant of immunity is "in the public interest" and that the anticipated testimony relates to an offense included in an immunity statute. *In re Vericker*, 416

F.2d 244 (2d Cir. 1971). Some jurisdictions provide "transactional immunity" (immunity from prosecution for the offenses to which the compelled testimony relates), but the others grant only "use immunity" (immunity from use of the compelled testimony and evidence derived therefrom, but not from prosecution for the offenses related upon evidence derived from an independent source). Use immunity is constitutionally satisfactory, for it is "co-extensive" with the privilege against self-incrimination. *Kastigar v. U. S.*, 406 U.S. 441 (1972). The use immunity extends to prosecutions brought in jurisdictions other than that where the grand jury witness appeared. *Murphy v. Waterfront Comm'n*, 378 U.S. 52 (1964).

Under the prevailing view, the subpoenaed grand jury witness may not exercise his privilege against self-incrimination by refusing to appear and be sworn, even if he is the "target of inquiry" and a potential defendant, *U. S. v. Winter*, 348 F.2d 204 (2d Cir. 1965). This view, and the underlying notion that the "option of refusal" need not be fully protected before the grand jury as at trial by giving the person who is the object of the proceedings the right not to be sworn, *U. S. v. Scully*, 225 F.2d 113 (2d Cir. 1955), has been rejected by a few courts. *S. v. Sarcone*, 233 A.2d 406 (N.J.Super. 1967).

Warning of self-incrimination protection. Even before *Miranda*, state and federal courts were divided on the question whether a prospective defendant is entitled to a warning as to his self-incrimination rights when called before a grand jury. One view is that a grand jury witness is no more entitled to such warnings than a witness at trial, *U. S. v. Scully*, supra; another is that the witness' testimony should not be deemed a voluntary and knowing waiver of self-incrimination rights unless the waiver was explicit, *P. v. Schneider*, 292 P.2d 982 (Colo.1956). But most courts which have confronted the issue have concluded that *Miranda* does not impose a constitutional command that the grand jury witness be given the warnings. Sometimes this is explained upon the ground that the interrogation is not custodial, *C. v. Columbia Inv. Corp.*, 325 A.2d 289 (Pa.1974), relying upon the holding in *U. S. v. Dionisio*, supra, that the compulsion exerted by a grand jury subpoena does not amount to a seizure under the Fourth Amendment; and sometimes on the ground that interrogation before the grand jury constitutes "general questioning of citizens in the fact-finding process," excluded in *Miranda* from the requirements set forth in that case. *S. v. Iverson*, 187 N.W.2d 1 (N.D.1971). But compare *U. S. v. Mandujano*, 496 F.2d 1050 (5th Cir. 1974) cert. granted, 95 S.Ct. 1422 (1975) (*Miranda* applicable where witness is "target" of grand jury investigation). Consider also the discussion at p. 345 on the right of a "target" witness to consult with counsel.

CHAPTER 5

LINEUPS AND OTHER PRETRIAL IDENTIFICATION PROCEDURES

28. THE PRIVILEGE AGAINST SELF-INCRIMINATION

The Schmerber case. In *Schmerber v. Cal.*, 384 U.S. 757 (1966), the Court upheld the taking of a blood sample by a physician at police direction from a defendant over his objection after his arrest for drunken driving. Among the grounds upon which the defendant challenged the admission of this sample in evidence against him was that it violated his Fifth Amendment privilege not to "be compelled in any criminal case to be a witness against himself." The Court, in a 5–4 decision, rejected this contention and held that "the privilege protects an accused only from being compelled to testify against himself, or otherwise provide the State with evidence of a testimonial or communicative nature."

In defining the scope of the privilege, the majority noted that many identification procedures were not protected by the Fifth Amendment. *Holt v. U. S.*, 218 U.S. 245 (1910), holding that a defendant could be compelled to model a blouse, was cited as the "leading case," and it was observed that "both federal and state courts have usually held that it offers no protection against compulsion to submit to fingerprinting, photographing, or measurements, to write or speak for identification, to appear in court, to stand, to assume a stance, to walk, or to make a particular gesture."

Application to pre-trial identification. It is thus not surprising that the Court has subsequently relied upon *Schmerber* in holding that several identification practices do not conflict with the privilege: requiring the defendant to appear in a lineup and to speak for identification, *U. S. v. Wade*, 388 U.S. 218 (1967); or to provide handwriting exemplars, *Gilbert v. Cal.*, 388 U.S. 263 (1967). In both cases the Court split 5–4 on this issue. The majority relied upon the *Schmerber* distinction between an accused's "communications" in whatever form, vocal or physical, and "compulsion which makes a suspect or accused the source of 'real or physical evidence.'" The dissenters argued that *Schmerber* was wrongly decided, in that the privilege is designed to bar the government from forcing a person to supply proof of his own crime, and that even assuming the correctness of *Schmerber* the instant cases were distinguishable because each defendant was required "actively to cooperate—to accuse himself by a volitional act." Other courts have followed the majority view and have thus held the privilege inapplicable to such other identification procedures as fingerprinting, *Johnson v. C.*, 158 S.E.2d 725 (Va.1968), or examination by ultraviolet light, *U. S. v. Richardson*, 388 F.2d 842 (6th Cir. 1968).

Consequences of failure to cooperate. Although not protected by the Fifth Amendment, some identification procedures (such as speaking or writing for identification) require the active participation of the suspect. But, what if the suspect will not cooperate? One possibility, feared the dissenters in *Wade*, is that "an accused may be jailed—indefinitely—until he is willing to" cooperate. In *U. S. v. Hammond*, 419 F.2d 166 (4th Cir. 1969), a federal bank robbery defendant was held in criminal contempt for refusing to obey a court order requiring him to participate in line-ups scheduled by the government. Cf. *U. S. v. Doe*, 405 F.2d 436 (2d Cir. 1968), where a federal grand jury witness was held in contempt and committed to custody until he provided handwriting samples. Another possibility is that the prosecution may be permitted to comment at trial on the lack of cooperation, as in *U. S. v. Parknes*, 424 F.2d 152 (9th Cir. 1970). Comment on the defendant's refusal to speak for identification was held improper in *P. v. Ellis*, 421 P.2d 393 (Cal. 1966), but only because it was the direct result of a prior police warning of the right to remain silent and thus not an indication of guilt.

29. THE RIGHT TO COUNSEL AND CONFRONTATION

A. LINEUPS

Procedures required. At least after the accused has been indicted, ruled the Court in *U. S. v. Wade*, 388 U.S. 218 (1967), and *Gilbert v. Cal.*, 388 U.S. 263 (1967), he should not be exhibited to witnesses in a lineup conducted for identification purposes without notice to and in the absence of his counsel. Rather, both the accused and his counsel must be notified of the impending lineup, and the lineup must not be conducted until counsel is present (expressly left open was the possibility that the presence of substitute counsel might suffice where notification and presence of the suspect's own counsel would result in prejudicial delay). In the absence of "legislative or other regulations * * * which eliminate the risks of abuse and unintentional suggestion at lineup proceedings," the Court emphasized in *Wade*, the above procedures are required by virtue of the defendant's constitutional right to confrontation and his right to counsel at a critical stage of the proceedings. (Apparently no court has yet held any set of regulations to be adequate; see e. g., *P. v. Fowler*, 461 P.2d 643 [Cal.1969].)

As explained by the Court, the right to counsel in this context is supportive of another right—

here, the right to confrontation—in much the same way that the *Miranda* counsel requirement rests upon the privilege against self-incrimination. (But see *Kirby v. Ill.*, discussed at p. 254.) Under past lineup practices, the defense was often unable "meaningfully to attack the credibility of the witness' courtroom identification" because of several factors which militate against developing fully the circumstances of a prior lineup identification by that witness: (a) other participants in the lineup are often police officers, or, if not, their names are rarely recorded or divulged at trial; (b) neither witnesses nor lineup participants are apt to be alert for or schooled in the detection of prejudicial conditions; (c) the suspect (often staring into bright lights) may not be in a position to observe prejudicial conditions, and, in any event, might not detect them because of his emotional tension; (d) even if the suspect observes abuse, he may nonetheless be reluctant to take the stand and open up the admission of prior convictions; and (e) even if he takes the stand, his version of what transpired at the lineup is unlikely to be accepted if it conflicts with police testimony. Moreover, the Court pointed out, the need to learn what occurred at the lineup is great; the risk of improper suggestion is substantial, and once the witness has picked out the accused in a lineup, he is unlikely to go back on his word in court.

The three dissenters to this aspect of *Wade* and *Gilbert* saw no need for the imposition of such a "broad prophylactic rule" in the absence of evidence that improper police practices at lineups were widespread. They also expressed concern that the delays required to comply with the procedures prescribed by the majority would make prompt and certain identification impossible.

Although there are cases to the contrary, the better view is that *Wade* and *Gilbert* apply at the moment of actual identification and not merely the moment of viewing, as it is important for counsel to be able to reconstruct the former at trial. *P. v. Williams*, 478 P.2d 942 (Cal.1971). The contrary position is bolstered to some extent by the *Ash* decision (See § 29B).

Waiver of counsel. The Court in *Wade* indicated that there might be an "intelligent waiver" of counsel, in which case notice to and presence of an attorney would not be required. Although this may seem consistent with the waiver permitted in *Miranda* (see § 26), some have questioned whether the right to counsel at the lineup should be subject to waiver. The argument is that while waiver of counsel under *Miranda* serves the legitimate objective of permitting the suspect to bear witness to the truth, no comparable value is served by waiver under *Wade*.

The *Wade* opinion does not dwell upon the question of what is required to show an effective waiver, although it seems likely that the approach in *Miranda* will be followed here. This means the defendant would have to be advised that he has a right to counsel for this particular purpose and that counsel will be provided for him if he is indigent, and "a heavy burden" would rest upon the government to show an express waiver following the warnings. Moreover, it seems clear that waiver of counsel for another purpose would not suffice, and thus a waiver of counsel following the *Miranda* warnings would not carry over to the lineup.

Consequences of violation. If the required lineup procedures are not followed, then testimony as to the fact of identification at the lineup is inadmissible at trial. "Only a *per se* exclusionary rule as to such testimony can be an effective sanction to assure that law enforcement authorities will respect the accused's constitutional right to the presence of his counsel at the critical lineup." If such testimony is admitted, the defendant is entitled to a new trial unless it is determined that the error was harmless beyond a reasonable doubt (see § 36). *Gilbert v. Cal.*, supra.

But, what of subsequent in-court identification by a witness who earlier identified the defendant at an improperly conducted lineup? This presents a "fruit of the poisonous tree" problem, and consistent with the general approach to that kind of issue (see § 32), it must be determined "whether, granting establishment of the primary illegality, the evidence to which instant objection is made has been come at by exploitation of that illegality or instead by means sufficiently distinguishable to be purged of the primary taint." Thus, the government will be afforded the opportunity to establish by clear and convincing evidence that the in-court identifications were based upon observations of the suspect other than the lineup identification. Relevant factors are "the prior opportunity to observe the alleged criminal act, the existence of any discrepancy between any pre-lineup description and the defendant's actual description, any identification prior to lineup of another person, the identification by picture of the defendant prior to the lineup, failure to identify the defendant on a prior occasion, and the lapse of time between the alleged act and the lineup identification," in addition to "those facts which, despite the absence of counsel, are disclosed concerning the conduct of the lineup." *U. S. v. Wade*, supra.

Justice Black, dissenting in part in *Wade*, argued that this "tainted fruit" determination is "practically impossible," in that the witness will be unable "to draw a sharp line between a courtroom identification due exclusively to an earlier lineup and a courtroom identification due to memory not based on the lineup." The majority rejected his contention that therefore all in-court identifications should be admissible, noting that if this were the case then the state could easily circumvent the lineup requirements by resting upon the witnesses' courtroom identification and thus leave the defendant in the same predicament as before. However, some have taken note of the difficulty in making the "tainted fruit" determination in questioning whether the Court went far enough; they fear that trial judges, inevitably left with considerable discretion in making this decision, will readily find an "independent source" for in-court identifications and in that way free the police from the necessity of complying with the *Wade-Gilbert* formula. Several commentators, upon review of lower court decisions, suggest that experience has shown this to be the case.

18 U.S.C.A. § 3502, a part of the Omnibus Crime Control and Safe Streets Act of 1968, provides that the "testimony of a witness that he saw the accused commit * * * the crime" is admissible in a federal court. Some have viewed this as a patently unconstitutional attempt to "repeal" *Wade*, but a Justice Department spokesman has argued that the statute merely makes the witness' statement that he is positive he saw the defendant commit the crime the "initially controlling factor" on the taint issue (instead of one of several, as in *Wade*), and thus is "an appropriate exercise of [Congress'] traditional rulemaking power."

Role of counsel. What, exactly, is the role of defense counsel at the lineup? *Wade* stresses the need to protect the defendant's "right meaningfully to cross-examine the witnesses against him and to have effective assistance of counsel at the trial itself," which most clearly suggests that counsel should function as an observer at the lineup. On the basis of his observations, he would then be in a position at trial to decide whether it is tactically wise to bring out the lineup identification in order to cast doubt upon an in-court identification. And, if he decides to do so, he will better know what questions to ask the witness about the circumstances of the lineup. The observer-counsel may also have to become a witness at the trial, for the Court in *Wade* emphasized that the suspect, other participants in the lineup, and the witnesses at the lineup are unlikely to observe or recognize prejudicial circumstances. Disciplinary Rule 5–102 of the ABA Code of Professional Responsibility, however, provides that if a lawyer learns he will be required to be a witness for his client, except as to merely formal or uncontested matters, he should withdraw from the case unless doing so "would work a substantial hardship on the client because of the distinctive value of the lawyer * * * as counsel in the particular case."

The majority in *Wade* implies that counsel might also take a more active role at the lineup;

they say that "presence of counsel itself can often avert prejudice" and assist law enforcement "by preventing the infiltration of taint in the prosecution's identification evidence."   The dissenters find in *Wade* "an implicit invitation to counsel to suggest rules for the lineup and to manage and produce it as best he can."   Defense counsel obviously cannot compel the police to conduct the lineup in a certain way, although he might point out unfair features of the identification process and even suggest corrective measures.   As a matter of tactics, however, counsel may prefer simply to allow the prejudicial practices so that he might bring them out in cross-examination, which raises the question of whether he should be permitted to stand silent and then challenge the police practices at trial.   *U. S. v. Allen*, 408 F.2d 1287 (D.C. Cir. 1969), recommends that defense counsel be allowed to take an active role in setting up the lineup, in which case "it might well be that, absent plain error or circumstances unknown to counsel at the time of the lineup, no challenges to the physical staging of the lineup could successfully be raised beyond objections raised at the time of the lineup."

Pre-indictment identifications.   Because both *Wade* and *Gilbert* involved lineups held after indictment and appointment of counsel, lower courts were in disagreement as to whether counsel was required at any pre-indictment identifications.　In *Kirby v. Ill.*, 406 U.S. 682 (1972), the Court held that the *Wade-Gilbert* rule applies only to lineups occurring "at or after the initiation of adversary judicial criminal proceedings— whether by way of formal charge, preliminary hearing, indictment, information, or arraignment."　The rationale was that the constitutional right to counsel has traditionally been so limited, and with good reason, in that only after such initiation is a defendant "faced with the prosecutorial forces of organized society, and immersed in the intricacies of substantive and procedural criminal law."　This conclusion, the three dissenters cogently pointed out, is based upon a misreading of *Wade* and *Gilbert* as purely right to counsel cases, rather than cases concerned with protecting the right to confrontation at trial, and ignores the fact that the practices condemned in those cases may just as easily occur during a pre-indictment lineup.

Except for the language quoted above, *Kirby* does not explore what it takes to "initiate" adversary judicial criminal proceedings, a matter now receiving attention in the lower courts.　It is generally agreed that a warrantless arrest is not sufficient, *S. v. Anderson*, 505 P.2d (Kan.1973), but there is some authority that proceedings are initiated by issuance of an arrest warrant upon information and oath, *U. S. ex rel. Robinson v. Zelker*, 468 F.2d 159 (2d Cir. 1972).

B. OTHER IDENTIFICATION PROCEDURES

The use of pictures. Does it follow from *Wade* and *Gilbert* that an accused in custody has a right to have his counsel present while witnesses view still or motion pictures of him for purposes of identification? No, the Court concluded in *U. S. v. Ash*, 413 U.S. 300 (1973). Throughout the expansion of the constitutional right to counsel to certain pretrial proceedings, said the majority, "the function of the lawyer has remained essentially the same as his function at trial," namely, to give the accused "aid in coping with legal problems or assistance in meeting his adversary." This being so, there is no such right at photo-identification, as unlike a lineup, there is no "trial-like confrontation" involving the "presence of the accused." Moreover, even if a broader view were taken of the right to counsel, it need not extend "to a portion of the prosecutor's trial-preparation interviews with witnesses," given "the equal ability of defense counsel to seek and interview witnesses himself." Stewart, J., concurring, while objecting to the majority's distinction of *Wade* as a situation where the lawyer is giving advice or assistance to the defendant at the lineup, concluded that the lawyer's role "as an observer" need not be extended to photo identification, where "there are few possibilities for unfair suggestiveness."

The three dissenters in *Ash* objected that the risk of "impermissible suggestiveness" which led to *Wade* and *Gilbert* was equally present in the case of identification by pictures, and that because the defendant is not personally present for such identification there is less "likelihood that irregularities in the procedure will ever come to light" if counsel has not observed the identification. As for the majority's characterization of the right to counsel, the dissenters argued that historically the right to counsel attached at certain pretrial procedures not because of the assistance the attorney could immediately render at that time, but rather "to protect the fairness of the trial itself."

Scientific methods. In *Wade*, the government argued that a lineup is no different from other identification procedures, such as taking and analyzing "the accused's fingerprints, blood sample, clothing, hair, and the like," apparently in an attempt to bring the instant case within the ruling of *Schmerber v. Cal.*, 384 U.S. 757 (1966). The majority in *Schmerber* held that the taking of a blood sample was not covered by the Fifth Amendment, and thus found "no issue of counsel's ability to assist petitioner in respect of any rights he did possess." The Court in *Wade* distinguished the other procedures listed by the government on the ground that they do not present the risks attendant lineups: "Knowledge of the

[*256*]

techniques of science and technology is sufficiently available, and the variables in techniques few enough, that the accused has the opportunity for a meaningful confrontation of the Government's case at trial through the ordinary processes of cross-examination of the Government's expert witnesses and the presentation of the evidence of his own experts." On this basis, the Court held in *Gilbert* that the taking of handwriting exemplars is not a critical stage entitling the suspect to the assistance of counsel. Thus, while the suspect might benefit from counsel's advice as to whether to give the exemplars or refuse and suffer the consequences (see p. 245), this does not involve a constitutional right to which the right to counsel might be linked.

30. DUE PROCESS: "THE TOTALITY OF THE CIRCUMSTANCES"

An identification made prior to the *Wade* and *Gilbert* decisions (which are not retroactive, see § 8), made thereafter but under circumstances in which counsel is not required, or perhaps even made in the presence of counsel, might be challenged on yet another ground. A "recognized ground of attack upon a conviction independent of any right to counsel claim" is that the defendant's identification was "so unnecessarily suggestive and conducive to irreparable mistaken identi-

fication that he was denied due process of law."
Stovall v. Denno, 388 U.S. 293 (1967).

It appears that unnecessary suggestiveness alone does not require the exclusion of evidence; at least, the Court declined to hold otherwise as to an identification which predated the *Stovall* decision. *Neil v. Biggers,* 409 U.S. 188 (1972). If there has been suggestiveness, a subsequent in-court identification is inadmissible only if there is "a very substantial likelihood of irreparable misidentification," and "with the deletion of 'irreparable', [that test] * * * serves equally well as a standard for the admissibility of testimony concerning the out-of-court identification itself." *Neil v. Biggers,* supra. Claims under either standard must be evaluated in light of the "totality of the circumstances," and "the factors to be considered in evaluating the likelihood of misidentification include the opportunity of the witness to view the criminal at the time of the crime, the witness' degree of attention, the accuracy of the witness' prior description of the criminal, the level of certainty demonstrated by the witness at the confrontation, and the length of time between the crime and the confrontation." *Neil v. Biggers,* supra.

In the *Wade-Gilbert* context, these same factors bear on the question of whether an in-court identification is a "fruit of the poisonous tree," as to which the government has the burden of proof (see § 29A). But in the context of the *Stovall* rule, these factors bear directly upon the question of whether there has been a violation of due process, which apparently means that the burden is on the defendant. Cf. *P. v. Nelson*, 238 N.E.2d 378 (Ill.1968), concerning proof of the suggestive nature of the lineup.

Lineups. An apt illustration of a due process violation in a lineup identification is provided by *Foster v. Cal.*, 394 U.S. 440 (1969). The Court concluded it was "all but inevitable" that the victim of a robbery would identify defendant "whether or not he was in fact" the robber, as: (1) defendant was placed in a lineup with two other men who were half a foot shorter; (2) only he wore a jacket similar to that worn by the robber; (3) when this did not lead to positive identification, the police permitted a one-to-one confrontation; and (4) because the witness' identification was still tentative, some days later another lineup was arranged, but defendant was the only person in this lineup who had also appeared in the first lineup.

The use of pictures. In *Simmons v. U. S.*, 390 U.S. 377 (1968), FBI agents identified a bank robbery suspect on the basis of his use of a car which was similar to that used in the robbery. From a relative of the suspect they obtained six snapshots, mostly group pictures, in which the suspect appeared, from which five bank employees separately identified the suspect the day after the robbery. Balancing the need against the risks, the Court concluded that this procedure was not "unnecessarily suggestive." The use of the photos was justified, in that a serious felony had occurred, the perpetrators were still at large, inconclusive clues led to the suspect, and it was important for the FBI swiftly to determine whether they were on the right track so that they could properly deploy their forces. Also, there was little risk of misidentification, as the employees had all gotten a good look at the robber, they examined the pictures while their memories were still fresh, each witness examined the pictures separately, and the FBI agents disclosed nothing about the progress of the investigation or suggesting which persons in the pictures were under suspicion.

One-man showups. In contrast to a properly conducted lineup, the display of a single suspect to a witness carries with it a considerable risk of misidentification: the witness may well conclude that the individual displayed must be the offender, for otherwise he would not be in custody and singly displayed. In *Stovall v. Denno*, supra, the Court noted that "the practice of showing suspects singly to persons for the purpose of identification, and not as part of a lineup, has been widely condemned," but held that under the unique circumstances of the case the one-man showup was justified. The defendant was arrested because keys found at the scene of the murder were traced to him. The wife of the murder victim, who herself had been repeatedly stabbed while defending her husband, was hospitalized for major surgery to save her life. Two days after the crime, defendant was brought to her hospital room, where she identified him after he spoke a few words. Defendant was handcuffed to one of the five police officers who were present with two members of the prosecutor's staff, and he was the only Negro in the room. The Court concluded that "an immediate hospital confrontation was imperative," as no one knew how long the witness might live, she could not visit the jail, and she was the only person who could have exonerated the defendant.

While *Stovall* thus rests upon a rather unique showing of need for the one-man showup—the fact that the sole eye witness was near death—there may be other reasons why this less reliable procedure is sometimes "imperative." For example, if *Stovall* is considered with *Simmons*, where the recognized need was for the police "swiftly to determine whether they were on the right track," it might be said that an on-the-scene one-man showup of a suspect who has just been arrested or detained for investigation does not violate due process. This is the conclusion which has been reached by the lower courts, who have also stressed the increased reliability of identifications made promptly after the event. *Bates v. U. S.,* 405 F.2d 1104 (D.C.Cir. 1968); *P. v. Moore,* 244 N.E.2d 337 (Ill.App.1968). Similarly, some courts have upheld a one-man showup where it was the suspect who was seriously injured. *Johnson v. P.,* 470 P.2d 37 (Colo.1970). But failure to use a lineup is not excused merely because it would be inconvenient or difficult to assemble a group of persons physically comparable to the suspect. *Neil v. Biggers,* supra.

CHAPTER 6

APPLICATION OF THE EX-
CLUSIONARY RULE

31. INTRODUCTION

The exclusionary rule constitutes the primary means of implementing the constitutional rights discussed in Chapters 2–5. While other remedies for violation of those rights are available (e. g., tort actions, criminal prosecutions and injunctions), exclusion of the illegally obtained evidence is by far the most frequently utilized remedy. The application of the exclusionary remedy may vary according to the nature of the right violated (and, in that respect, we might more appropriately refer to exclusionary "rules"), but the basic issues relating to the scope of the remedy are largely the same whether a physical search, electronic eavesdropping, interrogation, or special identification procedure is involved. Those issues include: (1) whether the remedy extends to all derivative evidence; (2) whether it bars use of evidence for purposes other than direct proof of guilt; (3) whether it can be utilized by defendants who were not the immediate victims of the violation; (4) whether the burden of proof in establishing the admissibility (or inadmissibility) of the evidence should fall upon prosecutor (or defendant) and the extent of that burden; and (5) whether the erroneous admission of excludable evidence may constitute a harmless error. The resolution of these issues has rested largely upon constitutional rulings. Though a few jurisdictions have adopted a more expansive version of the exclusionary remedy than is constitutionally required, the vast majority have not extended the remedy beyond what they consider the constitutional minimum.

In determining the constitutionally required scope of the exclusionary rule, courts have looked to various factors in different settings, but a recurring theme has been the impact of the particular ruling upon the two functions of the exclusionary rule that were stressed in *Mapp v. Ohio* (p. 28)—the deterrence of constitutional violations by eliminating the prosecutorial benefits of such violations, and the "imperative of judicial integrity" that demands that the courts not be made "party to lawless invasions of constitutional rights of citizens by permitting unhindered governmental use of the fruits of such invasions." *Terry v. Ohio*, 392 U.S. 1 (1968). Moreover, as between the two, far greater emphasis has been placed upon the impact of the ruling upon the deterrence function. See e. g. the discussion in §§ 33, 34. But note *Harrison v. U. S.*, 392 U.S. 219, n. 10 (1968).

32. DERIVATIVE EVIDENCE

Fruits of the poisonous tree. In *Silverthorne Lumber Co. v. U. S.*, 251 U.S. 385 (1920), the Court held invalid a subpoena that had been issued on the basis of information acquired through an illegal search. "The essence of a provision forbidding the acquisition of evidence in a certain way," the Court noted, "is not that merely evidence so acquired shall not be used before the court but that it shall not be used at all." Just as the prosecution could not use in court evidence obtained directly from the unconstitutional search, neither could it use evidence obtained indirectly via a subpoena based upon that search. The exclusionary rule extended to all evidence "tainted" by the unconstitutional search, which included evidence subsequently obtained through use of the information acquired during that search.

The *Silverthorne* requirement of exclusion of "secondary" or "derivative" evidence is commonly described as the rule against admission of the "fruits of the poisonous tree." Though the rule was formulated in applying the exclusionary rule to unconstitutional searches, it generally is viewed as equally applicable to evidence derived from other constitutional violations. The Supreme Court has specifically held the "poisonous tree" rule applicable to the evidentiary fruits of unconstitutional arrests, *Wong Sun v. U. S.*, 371 U.S. 471 (1963), and lineup identification procedures, *U. S. v. Wade* (see p. 249), and lower courts have applied it to the various other violations discussed in Chapters 2–5. See e. g., *P. v. Ditson*, 369 P.2d 714 (Cal.1962) (involuntary confessions); *U. S. v. Cassell*, 452 F.2d 533 (7th Cir. 1971) (*Miranda* violation). Indeed, the Supreme Court also has held the poisonous tree rule applicable to secondary evidence derived from violation of non-constitutional limitations that are commonly implemented by the exclusionary rule. See *Harrison v. U. S.*, 392 U.S. 219 (1968) (*McNabb-Mallory* violations); *Nardone v. U. S.*, 308 U.S. 338 (1939) (wiretaps violating § 605 of the Communications Act).

Independent source exception. In applying the poisonous tree rule, *Silverthorne* stressed that "facts" obtained through the constitutional violation were not necessarily "inaccessible" for court use. Thus, the Court noted, "[I]f knowledge of [the facts] is [also] gained from an independent source, they may be proved like any others." However, neither *Silverthorne* nor subsequent Supreme Court opinions contain any extended discussion of this "independent source" exception, and lower court opinions reflect considerable disagreement as to its scope.

Some courts hold that the independent source exception is not limited to evidence that was in fact obtained from an independent source. The same underlying justification, they contend, also supports admission of evidence derived solely from a constitutional violation if such evidence would "inevitably" have been discovered from lawful investigatory activities without regard to the violation. These courts argue that such an "inevitable discovery" exception does not permit the government to gain any special benefits from a constitutional violation and therefore is consistent with the deterrent function of the exclusionary rule. *P. v. Fitzpatrick*, 300 N.E.2d 139 (N.Y. 1973). This rationale has been criticized on the ground that, as applied, inevitable discovery too often is extended to encompass any evidence that "could" rather than "would" have been otherwise discovered. Id., at 146 (dissent). The inevitable discovery exception is also criticized, aside from its loose application, as providing an incentive for unconstitutional action. "Such a rule," the critics argue, "relax[es] the protection of [constitutional] * * * rights in the very case in which, by the government's own admission, there is no reason for [unlawful action]." It thereby encourages the government to take unconstitutional short cuts to acquire evidence that could otherwise be obtained through longer, lawful channels. *U. S. v. Paroutian*, 299 F.2d 486 (2d Cir. 1962).

Such criticism has lead various courts to reject any form of inevitable discovery exception. *U. S.*

v. Castellana, 488 F.2d 65, modified, 500 F.2d 325
(5th Cir. 1974). Some lower courts have refused
to admit illegally obtained evidence even though
the same evidence could still be reacquired from
an independent source without relying in any way
upon the constitutional violation. Thus, in *Bynum v. U. S.*, 262 F.2d 465 (D.C.Cir. 1958), fingerprints obtained from defendant after an illegal
arrest were held inadmissible as the fruits of the
arrest even though the fingerprints were readily
available from another source (the FBI), and the
police had reasonable grounds to seek the prints
prior to the arrest. When Bynum was subsequently reprosecuted, the fingerprints were obtained from the FBI and were admitted in evidence since they had then come from an "independent source." *Bynum v. U. S.*, 274 F.2d 767
(D.C.Cir. 1960).

The "purged taint" exception. Even where the
secondary evidence would not have been discovered except for the constitutional violation (i. e.,
there was no possible independent source), that
evidence need not necessarily be classified as the
fruit of the poisonous tree. The Court has noted
that, if the means of acquiring evidence are substantially removed and distinguishable from the
initial illegality, neither the "deterrence" rationale nor the "judicial integrity" rationale requires
application of the exclusionary rule. *Harrison v.
U. S.*, supra. Accordingly, it has stated that the

controlling question in applying the poisonous tree doctrine is: "[W]hether, granting establishment of the primary illegality, the evidence to which instant objection is made has been come at by exploitation of that illegality or instead by means sufficiently distinguishable to be purged of the primary taint." *Wong Sun v. U. S.*, 371 U.S. 471 (1963).

The application of this "purged taint" limitation is illustrated by the Court's rulings in *Wong Sun*. Narcotics agents there entered a dwelling without probable cause and chased down and arrested A, who almost immediately thereafter made a statement accusing B of having sold narcotics. Narcotics were subsequently seized from B, who in turn, implicated C, who was also arrested illegally. Several days later, after having been arraigned and released on his own recognizance, C voluntarily made an oral confession to a narcotics agent during interrogation. A argued that his statement and the narcotics later seized from B were fruits of the illegal entry into his dwelling and his illegal arrest. The Court agreed and both items were excluded. It rejected, however, C's claim that his statement was the fruit of his illegal arrest. Even though C might never have confessed if he had never been arrested, his voluntary action after having been released and warned of his rights had made the "connection between the arrest and the statement * * * so attenuated as to [have] dissipate[d] the taint."

As *Wong Sun* indicates, the taint of initial illegality may be purged by an "intervening independent act by the defendant or third party which breaks the causal chain linking the illegality and the evidence in such a way that the evidence is not in fact obtained by 'exploitation of that illegality'". *P. v. Sesslin*, 439 P.2d 321 (Cal.1968). Considerable disagreement exists, however, as to the exact nature of the "independent intervening acts" that meet this standard.   Thus, lower courts have divided over the admissibility of testimony of previously unknown witnesses who were discovered through leads obtained from constitutional violations.   Several courts have admitted such testimony on the ground that a critical element in the production of the testimony—the witness' decision to testify—is a sufficiently independent intervening act to "purge" the taint of the initial illegality. *P. v. Eddy*, 85 N.W.2d 117 (Mich.1957). Others have excluded the testimony, arguing that the production of witness testimony should be treated no differently than the production of secondary physical evidence discovered through constitutional violations. *U. S. v. Alston*, 311 F.Supp. 296 (D.D.C. 1970). Still others have indicated that the treatment of the witness' testimony may vary according to several factors.   One such factor may be the nature of

the witness' response to the request to testify.
The fact that the witness was initially reluctant,
but then changed his mind after "reflection," has
been cited as evidence of "significant" independent action that broke the "chain of causation."
Smith v. U. S., 344 F.2d 545 (D.C.Cir. 1965). Another factor may be the objective of the constitutional violation; a witness discovered through an
illegal search designed in large part to discover
potential witnesses may be treated differently
than a witness discovered through an illegal
search that was directed at another offense and
only incidentally produced a lead to that witness.
Compare *P. v. Schaumloffel*, 346 P.2d 393 (Cal.
1959) with *Lockeridge v. Superior Court*, 474 P.
2d 683 (Cal.1970). See also, *Mich. v. Tucker*, infra.

The relevance of the element of "purposiveness"
is suggested, in part, by *Wong Sun's* reference to
the "exploitation" of the initial illegality. That
element has been stressed in various situations
(besides the "witness-lead" cases) in distinguishing between the taint flowing from unconstitutional activity conducted in good faith and incidentally leading to derivative evidence and unconstitutional activity possessing no pretense of legality and undertaken for the very purpose of
acquiring the derivative evidence. See *U. S. v.
Edmons*, 432 F.2d 577 (2d Cir. 1970); *Brown v.
Ill.*, discussed at pp. 274–275.

Another potentially significant factor, closely related to "purposiveness", is the nature of the initial illegality—i. e. whether it is "technical" or goes to the core of a constitutional right. A recent Supreme Court decision suggests that this factor may have special significance as applied to certain types of *Miranda* violations. In *Mich. v. Tucker*, 417 U.S. 433 (1974), police had interrogated defendant before the *Miranda* decision and learned of an eventual prosecution witness. Since the trial occurred after *Miranda,* that decision governed and barred admission of defendant's own statement. *Johnson v. N. J.*, 384 U.S. 719 (1966). The witness' statement, however, was held admissible. In this case, the Court noted, the "deterrent effect on future police conduct" would not be "significantly augmented" by excluding the testimony of the witness. While the *Tucker* ruling was limited to the pre-*Miranda* interrogation considered there, many of the factors cited in the Court's opinion appear to be equally applicable to evidence derived from *Miranda* violations in other situations. Thus, the Court noted that the police action was pursued in "complete good faith" (thereby causing the "deterrence rationale" to lose "much of its force"); the police interrogation did not involve "compulsion sufficient to breach the privilege against self-incrimination," but "departed only from the prophylactic standards" of *Miranda*; there was no reason to believe that the derivative evidence (the witness' testimony) was untrustworthy; and use of the defendant's voluntary statement to find the witness "[did] no violence to such elements of the adversary system as may be embodied in the Fifth, Sixth, and Fourteenth Amendments."

Initiating investigations. Several courts have suggested that the taint of initial illegality may be purged by the very substantial nature of the investigation that followed the illegal acquisition of a general lead. They argue that unconstitutional action that only leads the police to "focus" their investigation on a particular individual should not, in effect, grant him "immunity from prosecution." *Gissendanner v. Wainwright*, 482 F.2d 1293 (5th Cir. 1973). Thus, where the police, upon returning to the scene of an illegal arrest for the purpose of apprehending other parties, noticed a newspaper clipping referring to a completely separate crime and subsequently engaged in a complete investigation that tied the defendant to that crime, the connection between evidence of that crime and the illegal arrest was viewed as "so attenuated as to dissipate the taint." *Gregory v. U. S.*, 231 F.2d 258 (D.C.Cir. 1956). On the other hand, where an illegal wiretap revealed defendant's connections with organized crime, and he was subsequently made the subject of an intensive investigation for possible tax evasion, all of the evidence developed through that investigation was held inadmissible as the fruit of the wiretap. The court noted that the "unique circumstances of an income tax investigation" made the decision to focus upon a particular person of "critical importance" in the enforcement of tax evasion laws. *U. S. v. Schipani*, 289 F.Supp. 43 (E.D.N.Y.1968), aff'd, 414 F.2d 1262 (2d Cir. 1969).

Confessions as the fruit of the poisonous tree. *Wong Sun* (p. 269) excluded from evidence the incriminating statement of one defendant (A) on the ground that it was the fruit of that defendant's illegal arrest. At the same time, the Court also admitted the incriminating statement of another defendant (C) as the product of an "independent act of free will" that purged the taint of his unconstitutional arrest. The two statements considered in *Wong Sun* have been viewed as so completely at "opposite ends of the pole" as to leave open to question a wide range of cases that fall between those extremes. *U. S. v. McGavic*, 337 F.2d 317 (6th Cir. 1964). Prior to *Brown v. Ill.*, —— U.S. —— (1975), lower courts were sharply divided on the application of the poisonous tree rule to such cases. Compare *Lacefield v. S.*, 412 S.W.2d 906 (Tex.Crim.1967); *Bynum v. S.*, 490 P.2d 531 (Okla.Crim.1971). *Brown*, however, provided further guidelines on the exclusion of incriminating statements obtained subsequent to an unconstitutional arrest.

In *Brown* police officers arrested defendant without probable cause in order to interrogate him in connection with a murder investigation. Following the arrest, defendant was taken to the police station, warned of his *Miranda* rights, and questioned. Defendant made an initial incriminating statement within two hours after his arrest. He was interrogated again several hours later (after the *Miranda* warnings were repeated) and made a second incriminating statement. The state supreme court upheld the admission of both statements on the ground that the *Miranda* warnings automatically purged the taint of defendant's illegal arrest. The Supreme Court unanimously rejected the state court's view of the impact of the *Miranda* warnings. A majority also found that, on the facts of the case, both statements were the fruit of the illegal arrest.

With respect to the *Miranda* warnings, the *Brown* opinion noted: "[T]he *Miranda* warnings, *alone* and *per se*, cannot always make the act [of confessing] sufficiently a product of free will to break, for Fourth Amendment purposes, the causal connection between the illegality and the confession. They cannot assure in every case that the Fourth Amendment violation has not been unduly exploited. * * * The question whether a confession is the product of a free will under *Wong Sun* must be answered on the facts of each case. * * * The *Miranda* warnings are an important factor, to be sure, in determining whether the confession is obtained by exploitation of an illegal arrest. But they are not the only factor to be considered. The temporal proximity of the arrest and the confession, the presence of intervening circumstances, and, particularly, the purpose and flagrancy of the official misconduct are all relevant."

After examining the *Brown* fact situation in light of the factors noted above, the majority concluded that the prosecution had failed to meet its burden of establishing the dissipation of the initial taint. Defendant's first statement was made within two hours of his arrest and the later, second statement was the fruit of the first. No intervening acts of significance (such as presentment before a magistrate, consultation with counsel, or release from custody) had occurred between the arrest and the first statement. Moreover, the majority emphasized, the illegality had "a quality of purposefulness." The "impropriety of the arrest was obvious"; it had been undertaken as an "expedition for evidence" and had been executed in a manner which "gave the appearance of having been calculated to cause surprise, fright, and confession." A concurring opinion argued that the case should be remanded for further findings as to whether the illegal arrest had in fact been a "flagrant" violation of the Fourth Amendment. The concurring opinion contended that where a violation of the Fourth Amendment was only "technical" in nature, a subsequent statement, unless given in the "immediate circumstances" of the illegal arrest, should be admissible where *Miranda* warnings were given. Cf. *Mich. v. Tucker* (p. 272).

Where the earlier violation was the improper acquisition of a confession, a subsequent confession is generally presumed to be the fruit of the first unless significant factors clearly show "a break in the causative chain." *P. v. Spencer*, 424 P.2d 715 (Cal.1967); *Harrison v. U. S.*, 392 U.S. 219 (1968). The Supreme Court has recognized that, "after an accused has once let the cat out of the bag by confessing, no matter what the inducement, he is never thereafter free of the psychological and practical disadvantages of having confessed." *U. S. v. Bayer*, 331 U.S. 532 (1947). But note *U. S. v. Trabucco*, 424 F.2d 1311 (5th Cir. 1970 (where first statement, obtained in violation of *Miranda*, was exculpatory, *Bayer* rationale did not apply to second, inculpatory statement obtained in compliance with *Miranda*).

Notwithstanding its recognition of the continuing impact of an initial confession, the Court has refused to adopt a rule automatically excluding all second confessions where the first was obtained unconstitutionally. The facts of each case must be examined to determine if the "coercive influence" of the first confession has been offset by other factors. *Westover v. U. S.*, 384 U.S. 436, 494 (1966). Thus, in *U. S. v. Bayer*, supra, the second confession was held admissible, where the first, obtained in violation of *McNabb-Mallory*, had been given 6 months earlier and the defendant, a soldier, had subsequently been released from the major restrictions of his prior confinement. Where, on the other hand, the confessions are separated only by several hours, the second confession is very likely to be found the fruit of the first, at least when factors such as consultation with counsel, arraignment before a magistrate, and release from custody are not present. Even when those factors are present, their significance has varied with the particular circumstances of the case (e. g., the nature of the prior violation, the extent of the consultation with counsel, the scope of the magistrate's statement as to defendant's rights) and the attitude of the court. Compare *Killough v. U. S.*, 315 F.2d 241 (D.C.Cir. 1962) with *Lyons v. Okla.*, 322 U.S. 596 (1944). Of course, even though such factors might otherwise suggest that the second confession constituted an "act of free will," they may be offset by extensive reliance upon the earlier confession in the production of the second. *Gilpin v. U. S.*, 415 F.2d 638 (5th Cir. 1969). Thus, in an analogous situation, *Harrison v. U. S.*, supra, the defendant's testimony at his initial trial, offered in response to the erroneous admission of confessions obtained in violation of *McNabb-Mallory*, was viewed as the fruit of those confessions even though defendant was represented by counsel at the trial and realized that he was not legally required to testify.

Guilty pleas as the fruit of the poisonous tree. In *Pa. ex rel. Herman v. Claudy*, 350 U.S. 116 (1956), the Court noted that a plea of guilty entered by an uncounseled defendant was "involuntary" (and therefore invalid, see p. 43) if the plea was "based on a confession extorted [from defendant] by violence or mental coercion." This aspect of the law governing guilty pleas is viewed as a special application of the poisonous tree rule since the characterization of the plea as involuntary rests largely on the finding that it is the fruit of the coerced confession. *Dorsciak v. Gladden*, 425 P.2d 177 (Ore.1967). Consistent with this analysis, the fact that the plea might not have been entered "but for" the earlier constitutional violation does not necessarily render it invalid; the taint of the initial violation may have been "purged" by intervening events. Thus, in *McMann v. Richardson*, 397 U.S. 759 (1970), a divided Court held that "a defendant [represented by counsel at the time of the plea] who alleges that he pleaded guilty because of a prior coerced confession" does not, without more, establish the invalidity of the plea. Though defendant pleaded guilty on counsel's mistaken belief that the confession would probably be admissible, that factor alone does not render the plea involuntary. In such a situation, "whether a plea of guilty is unintelligent and therefore vulnerable * * * depends as an initial matter not on whether a court would retrospectively consider counsel's advice to be right or wrong, but on whether that advice was within the range of competence demanded of attorneys in criminal cases." Assuming that the advice was competent, the guilty plea is no less voluntary because based on an erroneous assessment of the confession than it would be when based on an erroneous evaluation of the strength of the evidence generally. In terms of the application of the poisonous tree doctrine, the consultation with counsel and subsequent determination to plead are viewed as independent intervening acts that "purged" the taint. As the Court later noted, in the absence of special circumstances, a "guilty plea represents a break in the chain of events which has preceded it in the criminal process." *Tollet v. Henderson*, 411 U.S. 258 (1973).

The *McMann* analysis recognizes various exceptional circumstances which permit a successful challenge to a guilty plea based upon a prior constitutional error. The *McMann* Court noted that a plea would be open to challenge where the defendant acted without counsel and entered the plea based upon evidence obtained unconstitutionally. See *Pa. ex rel. Herman v. Claudy*, supra.

Similarly, a plea may be challenged where the oppressive circumstances that produced a constitutional violation (e. g., a coerced confession) had an "abiding impact and also taint[ed] the plea." Cf. *Chambers v. Fla.*, 309 U.S. 227 (1940). A challenge will also be sustained where counsel's advice was outside the range of normal competence (although *Tollet v. Henderson*, supra, noted that, at least with respect to an issue such as unconstitutional selection of the grand jury, the fact that counsel advised defendant to plead guilty without first examining that issue does not in itself establish incompetence). *Blackledge v. Perry*, 417 U.S. 21 (1974), also holds *McMann* inapplicable where the underlying constitutional error goes to the state's capacity to initiate proceedings (e. g., violation of double jeopardy) as opposed to its method of conducting otherwise valid proceedings. Finally, *Lefkowitz v. Newsome*, 420 U.S. 283 (1975), holds *McMann* inapplicable where, pursuant to a practice adopted in several states, a defendant entering a guilty plea specifically reserves the right to appeal his conviction on the basis of prior constitutional errors.

33. THE COLLATERAL USE EXCEPTIONS

Grand jury proceedings. In *U. S. v. Calandra*, 414 U.S. 338 (1974), a divided Court held that a grand jury witness could not refuse to answer questions on the ground that the questions were based on evidence obtained from an unlawful search. The majority concluded that the "speculative and undoubtedly minimal advance in the deterrence of police misconduct" that might result from allowing such an objection was outweighed by the likely deleterious impact upon the effective and expeditious discharge of the grand jury's duties. "Permitting witnesses to invoke the exclusionary rule before the grand jury," the majority noted, "would halt the orderly progress of an investigation and might necessitate extended litigation of issues only tangentially related to the grand jury's primary objective." On the other hand, application of the exclusionary rule in grand jury proceedings could only strengthen the rule's deterrent impact in the rather unique situation where an investigation was "consciously directed" toward obtaining a grand jury indictment notwithstanding "the inadmissibility of the illegally seized evidence in a subsequent criminal prosecution of the search victim." (The *Calandra* dissenters argued that the majority placed too much stress upon the exclusionary rule's "possible deterrent effect" as opposed to its "twin goals of enabling the judiciary to avoid the taint of partnership in official lawlessness and of assuring the people * * * that the government would not profit from its lawless behavior").

Impeachment at trial. In *Walder v. U. S.*, 347 U.S. 62 (1954), the defendant, charged with purchasing and possessing heroin, asserted on direct examination that he had never purchased, sold or handled narcotics at any time "in [his] life." On cross-examination, the government questioned defendant about a heroin capsule that had been seized in his presence approximately two years earlier, and when defendant denied the prior possession, introduced police testimony concerning the seizure. Defense objected on the ground that the capsule had been illegally seized and the defendant had secured its suppression in an earlier prosecution. The trial court, however, admitted the evidence, and "carefully charged the jury" that it was to be considered "solely for the purpose of impeaching the defendant's credibility." A divided Supreme Court affirmed on the basis of that limitation. The Court noted that "it is one thing to say that the Government cannot make any affirmative use of evidence unlawfully obtained, [but] * * * quite another to say that the defendant can turn the illegal method by which evidence in the Government's possession was obtained to his own advantage, and provide him with a shield against contradiction of his untruths." The majority reasoned that the defendant "must be free to deny all the elements of the case against him without thereby giving lease to the Government to introduce by way of rebuttal evidence illegally secured to it * * *. Beyond that, however, there is hardly justification for

letting the defendant affirmatively resort to per-
jurious testimony in reliance on the Government's disability to challenge his credibility."
Such an "extension of the [exclusionary] rule," it
concluded, "would be a perversion of the Fourth
Amendment."

In *Harris v. N. Y.*, 401 U.S. 222 (1971), a divided Court relied upon *Walder* to uphold the use
of defendant's prior statement, obtained in violation of *Miranda*, to impeach his trial testimony.
Unlike *Walder*, the illegally obtained evidence in
Harris had been acquired in the investigation of
the offenses currently charged against defendant.
Also, defendant was impeached "as to testimony
bearing more directly on the crimes charged"
than the "collateral" matter included in Walder's
testimony. The majority concluded, however,
that neither distinction suggested any "difference
in principle that warrants a result different from
* * * *Walder*." The majority also rejected the
contention that *Walder* should not apply to *Miranda* violations because of *Miranda*'s Fifth
Amendment foundation. Viewing *Miranda* as
serving a deterrent function similar to *Mapp*, it
concluded that that function was adequately
served by excluding evidence from the prosecution's case in chief and did not require providing
"a license to use perjury." See also *Ore. v. Hass*,
420 U.S. —— (1975) (impeachment use permitted
where officer obtained statement, in violation of

Miranda, by continuing interrogation after defendant asked for a lawyer; "speculative possibility" that this interrogation technique would be employed purposely to gain impeachment evidence was not sufficient to change the "balance * * * struck in *Harris*").

The *Harris* opinion noted that the petitioner there made no claim that his statements were "coerced or involuntary" and that statements must satisfy "legal standards" governing "trustworthiness" to be used for impeachment. These comments have been viewed as indicating that involuntary confessions (see § 24) may not be used for impeachment purposes since their reliability is inherently suspect. *Iverson v. N. D.*, 480 F.2d 414 (8th Cir. 1973). See also *Ore. v. Hass,* supra.

Harris did not discuss the limitation upon the impeachment use of illegally seized evidence established in *Agnello v. U. S.*, 269 U.S. 20 (1925), but *Walder* did distinguish *Agnello*, and lower courts generally have assumed that the *Agnello* limitation is still binding. *U. S. v. Trejo*, 501 F.2d 138 (9th Cir. 1974). In *Agnello*, the defendant, charged with selling bags of cocaine, acknowledged that he received the bags for the purpose of delivering them to another, but claimed he had not known what they contained. On cross-examination, the prosecution asked Agnello whether he had ever seen narcotics before and, after eliciting the expected denial, produced other narcotics illegally seized at defendant's home. The Court rejected the prosecution's use of that evidence, noting that defendant had done "nothing to waive his constitutional protection or to justify cross-examination in respect [to] the evidence." In distinguishing *Agnello*, the *Walder* majority noted that Walder, on his own initiative, gave direct testimony that went beyond "a mere denial of complicity" in the crime to include a "sweeping claim" relating to his past experience. Although based on *Walder*, both *Harris* and *Hass* appear to have rejected this "sweeping claim" distinction. Nevertheless, *Agnello* may have some continuing validity. Read in light of *Harris* and *Hass, Agnello* may still limit impeachment use of illegally obtained evidence to situations in which the evidence contradicts specific statements in defendant's direct testimony. See *U. S. v. Trejo*, supra, (where defendant simply denied committing robbery and relied upon an alibi defense, prosecution could not impeach by reference to his prior possession of illegally seized items allegedly used in the robbery).

Sentencing. The Supreme Court has not yet ruled upon the application of the exclusionary rule to the sentencing process. But cf. *Gilbert v. Cal.*, 388 U.S. 263, 272 (1967) (unconstitutional lineup identification testimony excluded from penalty hearing before jury). Lower courts generally hold that illegally seized evidence is admissible, but recognize certain exceptions to that rule. Thus, *U. S. v. Schipani*, 315 F.Supp. 253 (S.D.N.Y.1970), upholding a sentencing court's consideration of information derived from illegal wiretaps, stressed that "no appreciable increment in deterrence would result from applying a second exclusion at sentencing after the rule has been applied at the trial itself." The Court noted, however, that it was not considering a situation in which the illegal search "was undertaken not to obtain evidence to support an indictment and conviction, but to * * * enhance the possibility of a heavier sentence after the basic investigation has been completed." The court also distinguished cases prohibiting consideration of involuntary confessions in sentencing [e. g., *U. S. ex rel. Brown v. Rundle*, 417 F.2d 282 (3d Cir. 1969)] since the "genesis" of the involuntary confession prohibition was as a means of excluding unreliable evidence (see § 24). Also, the involuntary confession arguably relates to a direct violation of the self-incrimination prohibition rather than a failure to comply with prophylactic rules designed to implement that prohibition. Cf. *Mich. v. Tucker* (p. 272).

A general extension of the exclusionary rule to sentencing has also been questioned on the basis of "practical considerations." *U. S. v. Schipani*, supra. Serious enforcement of the rule would be difficult under current sentencing practices, which do not require that the judge state his reasons for imposing a particular sentence and often deny defendant a right to examine the presentence report. Moreover, it is argued, even if these practices were changed, it would be "almost impossible for a district judge, who had screened proffered evidence on the motion to suppress, to banish it entirely from his mind at sentencing." Id. Proponents of applying the exclusionary rule argue that these objections are not insurmountable and similar problems of enforcement have not prevented the courts from establishing other limitations upon factors that can be considered in sentencing. See *U. S. v. Weston,* 448 F.2d 626 (9th Cir. 1972) (where trial judge relied upon "evidence obtained in violation of constitutional rights [including illegally seized evidence], * * * the case will be remanded for resentencing without considering the evidence so obtained"). Cf. *N. C. v. Pearce* (p. 75).

Probation and parole revocation. The exclusionary rule has been held inapplicable to probation and parole revocation proceedings on grounds similar to those advanced in *Schipani.* Thus, in *U. S. ex rel. Sperling v. Fitzpatrick,* 426 F.2d 1161 (2d Cir. 1970), the court noted:

"[A] parole revocation proceeding is concerned not only with protecting society, but also, and most importantly, with rehabilitating and restoring to useful lives those placed in the custody of the Parole Board. To apply the exclusionary rule to parole revocation proceedings would tend to obstruct the parole system in accomplishing its remedial purposes. [Moreover,] there is no need for double application of the exclusionary rule, using it first as it was used here in preventing criminal prosecution of the parolee and a second time at a parole revocation hearing. The deterrent purpose of the exclusionary rule is adequately served by the exclusion of the unlawfully seized evidence in the criminal prosecution."

See also *In re Martinez*, 463 P.2d 734 (Cal. 1970) (exclusionary rule will not be extended to parole revocation because little additional deterrent effect can be anticipated, but due process may require exclusion of evidence obtained under circumstances that "shocked the conscience"); *P. v. Atencio*, 525 P.2d 461 (Colo.1974) [refusal to apply exclusionary rule to probation revocation proceedings supported in part by Supreme Court's analysis in *Calandra* (p. 281) and *Gagnon* (p. 349)].

Quasi-criminal proceedings. The exclusionary rule has generally been held applicable to "quasi-criminal proceedings." In *One 1958 Plymouth Sedan v. Pa.*, 380 U.S. 693 (1965), the Court held that evidence obtained through an illegal search could not be used in automobile forfeiture proceedings based upon illegal possession of liquor. The Court noted that the "object of the forfeiture proceeding" was to "penalize the commission of an offense against the law" and the potential loss to the defendant could easily exceed the maximum fine in the criminal proceeding. "Under these circumstances," the Court concluded, "it would be anomalous indeed * * * to hold that in the criminal proceeding the illegally seized evidence is excludable while in the forfeiture proceeding, requiring the determination that the criminal law had been violated, the same evidence would be admissible."

In re Gault, 387 U.S. 1 (1967), held several constitutional rights, including the right to counsel and privilege against self-incrimination, applicable to juvenile proceedings that are based on criminal law violations and permit potential institutional commitment. Lower courts generally have viewed *Gault* as characterizing such proceedings as quasi-criminal in nature and have held that evidence obtained in violation of the constitution accordingly should not be considered in the determination of delinquency. *Leach v. S.*, 428 S.W.2d 817 (Tex.Civ.1968) (*Miranda* applicable); *In Matter of Harvey*, 295 A.2d 93 (Pa. 1972) (*Mapp* applicable).

34. STANDING

A. THE PERSONAL INTEREST REQUIREMENT

Source of the limitation. In order to employ the exclusionary rule, a defendant must have "standing" to challenge the constitutional violation which serves as the basis for the rule's application. This requirement of an appropriate interest or "standing" to invoke a constitutional remedy is not unique to the exclusionary rule, but is applicable generally to all constitutional challenges. As a constitutional minimum, standing requires that the party seeking relief have an adversary interest in the "outcome of the controversy". *Flast v. Cohen*, 392 U.S. 83 (1968). That standard presumably is met in the criminal case by the very position of the defendant as the person against whom the challenged evidence will be used. But in most areas of constitutional law, the Court has also required that the adverse interest be based upon a violation of the rights of the individual raising the claim rather than the violation of the rights of a third party which indirectly affects the claimant. *Tileston v. Ullman*, 318 U.S. 44 (1943). As applied to the exclusionary remedy, this principle limits standing to the defendant who is also the victim of the constitutional violation that necessitates the exclusion of evidence. Thus, in *Wong Sun* (p. 269), where the illegal arrest of A led to the seizure of narcotics in the home of B and the subsequent arrest of C at another location, the narcotics could not be introduced in evidence against A, but could be introduced against C. A had standing because the seizure of the narcotics was the fruit of his illegal arrest, but C lacked standing because neither the arrest of A nor the subsequent seizure of narcotics violated his constitutional rights.

Application in state and federal courts. The prohibition against permitting a litigant to assert the rights of third parties "has not been imposed uniformly as a firm constitutional mandate," *Flast v. Cohen*, supra, and several authorities have argued that an exception should be made in the application of the exclusionary rule in order to preserve the deterrent function of that rule. This view was accepted in *P. v. Martin*, 290 P.2d 855 (Cal.1955), holding that a defendant could require exclusion of evidence obtained through an illegal search that violated the constitutional rights of a third party. The court reasoned that the traditional bar against "third-party" or "vicarious" standing "virtually invites law enforcement officers to violate the rights of third parties and to trade the escape of a criminal whose rights are violated for the conviction of others by the use of the evidence illegally obtained against them." It therefore concluded that the defendant's right "to object to the use of evidence must rest, not on a violation of his own constitutional rights, but on the ground that the government must not be allowed to profit by its own wrong and thus encouraged in the lawless enforcement of the law."   [The California court subsequently refused, however, to extend the *Martin* analysis to permit a defendant to exclude evidence derived from statements of third parties that were obtained in violation of *Miranda.   P. v. Varnum*, 427 P.2d 772 (Cal.1967)].

In *Alderman v. U. S.*, 394 U.S. 165 (1969), the Supreme Court rejected the *Martin* analysis in the context of a claim for "third-party" standing to challenge unconstitutional electronic surveillance.   The majority there denied the alternative contentions that (1) all defendants should derive standing to challenge evidence obtained from the violation of the constitutional rights of others; (2) at least co-defendants and co-conspirators should have such standing to suppress evidence obtained in violation of the rights of other co-defendants or co-conspirators, or (3) a special standing rule should be recognized to permit a defendant to exclude evidence obtained unlawfully from another through a search "directed at" the prosecution of the defendant.   Two dissenters supported the latter position, but the majority concluded that there was "no necessity" to depart from "the general rule that Fourth Amendment rights are personal rights which * * * may not be vicariously asserted." It did not follow from the adoption of the exclusionary rule "that anything which deters illegal searches [must] thereby [be] commanded by the Fourth Amendment." The majority was "not convinced that the additional benefits of extending the exclusionary rule to other defendants [i. e., non-victims] would justify further encroachment upon the public interest in prosecuting those accused of crime and having them acquitted or convicted on the basis of all the evidence which exposes the truth." Without "experience showing the contrary," the Court should not assume that the statutory prohibition against illegal electronic eavesdropping would be "cavalierly disregarded" or that criminal provisions would not be enforced against violators.

In rejecting third party standing, *Alderman* did not foreclose its adoption by state courts or even its imposition upon federal courts through Congressional legislation. The Court emphasized that third party standing was neither required nor prohibited by the constitution. On the other hand, neither a state nor federal court may constitutionally deny standing to a defendant properly viewed as the person whose constitutional rights were violated by the illegal acquisition of evidence. In confession cases, the nature of the constitutional prohibitions clearly identify this "victim" as the defendant who is attacking the admission of his own confession or fruits derived therefrom. In the search and seizure area, on the other hand, there are several factors that must be considered in determining whether a defendant was the victim of the constitutional violation.

B. SEARCH AND SEIZURE OBJECTIONS

Presence at the site of the search. In *Jones v. U. S.*, 362 U.S. 257 (1960), an occasional occupant of an apartment was held to have standing to object to a search of that apartment conducted while he was present. *Jones* rejected the view that a party whose privacy was interrupted by an unlawful search only had standing if he had some special dominion over the premises. The Court noted that property distinctions such as those between "lessee, licensee, invitee, and guest, often only of gossamer strength, ought not to be determinative in fashioning procedures ultimately referable to constitutional safeguards." It concluded that "anyone legitimately on the premises where a search occurs may challenge its legality * * * when its fruits are proposed to be used against him."

Although a few lower courts have held to the contrary, the *Jones* rationale suggests that a passenger should have standing to object to the search of the interior of a car while he was present. *Kleinbart v. S.*, 234 A.2d 288 (Md.App. 1967). Whether his presence would also provide standing to challenge a search of the trunk presents a more difficult issue. Cf. *U. S. v. Medina-Flores*, 477 F.2d 225 (10th Cir. 1973). A similar question might be raised when an invitee present during the search of a home objects to the extension of the search to parts of the home (e. g., the basement) to which he ordinarily would not have access. [Of course, if consent to the search were given by a person with a superior interest (e. g., the homeowner), such consent would undermine the substance of the invitee's claim (see § 15) even though he did have standing to object. *Frazier v. Cupp* (p. 150)].

The *Jones* ruling was specifically limited to persons "legitimately" on the premises. The Court noted that standing would not be available for "those who, by virtue of their wrongful presence, cannot invoke the privacy of the premises searched." Thus, standing clearly would be denied "a trespasser or a burglar who entered another's home and is there when the home is searched." *Cotton v. U. S.*, 371 F.2d 385 (9th Cir. 1967). The lower courts are divided, however, over the standing of a driver or passenger to challenge the search of a stolen vehicle. Most courts have ruled that the driver and passenger

may challenge the search of the car as the fruit
of their unlawful arrest, but, if the arrest was
lawful, they lack standing to challenge the search
on other grounds (e. g., the lack of a warrant).
Harper v. S., 440 P.2d 893 (Nev.1968); *Palmer v.
S.*, 286 A.2d 572 (Md.App.1972). Other courts
have argued that the driver or passenger should
not be placed in the same category as the temporary trespasser or burglar. They note that "even
a trespasser, if he has also taken actual possession of the premises, acquires possessory rights
against all the world except the true owner," and
contend that such limited interest should be sufficient to establish standing. *Cotton v. U. S.*, supra. Standing thus is justified not on presence
alone, but also on dominion over the premises.
See the discussion of *U. S. v. Jeffers* at p. 299.
Accordingly, even where courts accept this view,
standing is lost if the defendant disclaims all interest in the property, or the police, knowing that
the property was stolen, take it into custody on
behalf of the owner prior to the search. *Watkins
v. S.*, 262 So.2d 422 (Miss.1972); *U. S. v. Kucin-
ich*, 404 F.2d 262 (6th Cir. 1968).

Possessory interest in the premises or property.
A defendant with a present possessory interest in
the premises searched, such as the owner or lessee of a house, is generally recognized as having
standing to challenge the search even though he
was not present when the search was made.

Chapman v. U. S., 365 U.S. 610 (1965). The violation of that possessory interest in itself makes him a victim of the unlawful search. The "possessory" interest needed to establish standing ordinarily extends to any interest which grants the defendant a general right to occupy the premises. That right need not be exclusive. Occupants of hotel rooms have been held to have a sufficient interest, *Stoner v. Cal.*, 376 U.S. 483 (1964), and a few decisions suggest that a business associate or friend who has a key to the suite of another and regularly uses that suite may also have a sufficient "possessory" interest to establish standing. *Baker v. U. S.*, 401 F.2d 958 (D.C.Cir. 1968). Cf. *Mancusi v. DeForte*, infra. The defendant's interest must relate, however, to current use. Thus, a tenant who has abandoned the premises may not challenge a subsequent search. *Parman v. U. S.*, 399 F.2d 559 (D.C.Cir. 1968). But compare *U. S. v. Wilson*, 472 F.2d 901 (9th Cir. 1972) (arguing that abandonment does not go to standing, but to the reasonableness of the search).

Mancusi v. DeForte, 392 U.S. 364 (1968), although involving a defendant who was present at the time of the search, reflects the Court's general approach in determining whether an interest in the premises searched is a sufficient basis in itself to justify standing. The Court there held that an employee had standing to object to a search of an office which he shared with several other people. The Court noted that defendant clearly would have had standing if the office had been his alone, and the joint use of the office had not so diminished his expectation of privacy as to eliminate standing. Defendant's "capacity to claim the protection of the [Fourth] Amendment," it noted, "depends not upon a property right in the invaded place but upon whether the area was one in which there was a reasonable expectation of freedom from government intrusion [citing *Katz v. U. S.*, p. 88]." See also *Combs v. U. S.*, 408 U.S. 224 (1972).

Even though a defendant lacks a possessory interest in the premises, he still may challenge a search committed outside his presence if he had a possessory interest in the property seized. A requirement that the possessory interest relate to current use, however, may necessitate that the defendant also have ready access to the premises. *C. v. Raymond*, 194 A.2d 150 (Pa.1963). In *U. S. v. Jeffers*, 342 U.S. 48 (1951), the Court recognized defendant's challenge to the search of his Aunts' hotel room and seizure of narcotics he had stored there. The Court emphasized that search and seizure were directed at defendant's property but the opinion also noted that the "[Aunts] had given [defendant] a key to their room, that he had their permission to use the room as well, and that he often entered the room for various purposes." Moreover, where defendant does not re-

tain ready access to the premises, the transfer of
the property to the residence of another party
may evidence defendant's abandonment of his interest in that property. *U. S. v. Bozza*, 365 F.2d
206 (2d Cir. 1966); *C. v. Dirring*, 238 N.E. 508
(Mass.1968).

To serve as a basis for standing, a current possessory interest in the property seized need not
be an interest that would be recognized under the
traditional law of property. In *Jeffers*, supra, the
government argued that defendant's interest in
the narcotics could not provide standing because
narcotics were contraband goods in which Congress had declared "that no property rights shall
exist." The Court responded that the Congressional declaration merely required forfeiture of
the narcotics, but, "for purposes of the exclusionary rule," the narcotics were defendant's "property" and he therefore had standing. Many lower
court opinions take a contrary view with respect
to claims of standing based upon a possessory interest in stolen property. *S. v. Pokini*, 367 P.2d
499 (Hawaii 1961). Compare, *Cotton v. U. S.*,
supra.

The basis for possessory interest standing has
particular significance in determining which parties have standing to object to illegal wiretapping
or eavesdropping. The parties to the overheard
conversation clearly have standing since their
conversation was the subject of the search. In

Alderman v. U. S., supra, the majority held that the owner or lessee of the premises in which the conversation occurred also had standing "whether or not he was present or participated in these conversations". Two dissenting justices argued that the owner of the premises should not have standing to exclude overheard conversations, as he would to exclude a tangible object illegally seized, because he lacked any possessory interest in a conversation in which he did not participate. The majority argued, however, that the householder's standing to object to a physical search does not rest on his possessory interest in the item seized but the "illegal invasion of the premises". An illegal surveillance by wiretap or electronic eavesdropping, they concluded, also constitutes such an invasion because it "invades an area in which the homeowner has a right to expect privacy for himself, his family, and his invitees."

Automatic standing. In *Jones v. U. S.*, supra, the defendant was charged with sale and distribution of narcotics under two statutes which permitted conviction largely on proof of unexplained possession of narcotics. The lower court denied standing on the ground that the defendant failed to allege ownership or possession of the narcotics, although meeting this requirement would have "forced [him] to allege facts the proof of which would tend, if indeed not be sufficient, to convict him." The Supreme Court held that the standing requirement could not be employed to place the defendant in such a dilemma. Under the lower court ruling, the government improperly gained the "advantage of contradictory positions as a basis for conviction"—it "subjected the defendant to the penalties meted out to one in lawless possession while refusing him the remedies designed for one in that situation." The Court ruled that, where "possession both convicts and confers standing", standing would be assumed without "a preliminary showing of an interest in the premises searched or the property seized."

Although *Jones* was based on an interpretation of the Federal Rules of Criminal Procedure, it generally is viewed as establishing a constitutional guideline applicable to state as well as federal cases. *U. S. ex rel. Coffey v. Fay*, 344 F.2d 625 (2d Cir. 1965). The offense in *Jones* was established almost entirely by the factor of possession, but the Supreme Court has noted that *Jones* applies to any offense in which possession is "an essential element." *Simmons v. U. S.*, 390 U.S. 377 (1968). Thus, *Jones* has been held applicable to offenses involving possession of items that are not contraband per se, and therefore also require proof of defendant's knowledge of the illicit character of the item. *Niro v. U. S.*, 388 F.2d 535 (1st Cir. 1968). Automatic standing is not provided, however, where possession raises an inference that may support conviction, but is not utilized by the government as an element of proof. Thus, *Brown v. U. S.*, 411 U.S. 223 (1973), rejected automatic standing on a charge of transporting and conspiring to transport stolen goods. The goods had been found on the premises of a co-conspirator, but the government's case against the petitioners was based on their transportation and sale of the goods to the co-conspirator two months before the challenged search. Here, unlike *Jones*, there was no "prosecutorial self-contradiction" since proof of the offense did not depend "on petitioner's possession of the seized evidence at the time of the contested search."

The automatic standing rule of *Jones* was established before *Simmons v. U. S.* (discussed infra) held that defendant's pretrial testimony to establish standing could not be used against him at trial. In *Brown v. U. S.*, supra, the Court stated that the "automatic standing" rule now is subject to reconsideration in light of *Simmons*. The Court noted that the "self-incrimination dilemma, so central to the *Jones* decision, can no longer occur" under *Simmons*. The defendant is permitted to establish standing by acknowledging possession of incriminating evidence, and whether he succeeds or fails in excluding the evidence, his testimony is not "directly admissible against him at trial." The *Brown* opinion noted, however, that since the *Jones* rule was not applicable to the

Brown facts, there was no need to decide in that case whether automatic standing would still be required in the *Jones* situation.

Establishing standing. In *Simmons v. U. S.,* 390 U.S. 377 (1968), the defendant, seeking to establish standing to challenge the search of a suitcase, testified that he was the owner of the suitcase. His motion to suppress was subsequently denied, and the government used his testimony at trial in establishing guilt. In finding the use of the testimony unconstitutional, the Supreme Court noted that, at least in marginal cases where the defendant is uncertain as to the probable outcome of his motion, the potential use of such testimony at trial obviously would have a deterrent impact upon the assertion of Fourth Amendment rights. Moreover, the placement of this condition upon the assertion of those rights raised self-incrimination difficulties since "the defendant who wishes to establish standing must do so at the risk that the words which he utters may later be used to incriminate him." The Court acknowledged that, as an "abstract matter," such incrimination might be viewed as entirely "voluntary"—compulsion existed only in the sense that the defendant would forgo a "benefit" if he refrained from testifying. However, where that lost "benefit" is a remedy afforded by another provision of the Bill of Rights, an "undeniable tension" is created, and the state can no more impose that dilemma on the defendant than it could the "Hobson's choice eliminated in *Jones*." Accordingly, the Court held "that when a defendant testifies in support of a motion to suppress evidence on Fourth Amendment grounds, his testimony may not thereafter be admitted against him at trial on the issue of guilt unless he makes no objection."

Although the *Simmons* ruling concerned Fourth Amendment claims, a similar restriction has been applied to defendant's testimony on motions to suppress based upon other constitutional grounds. *P. v. Walker*, 132 N.W.2d 87 (Mich. 1965). The dilemma that *Simmons* sought to avoid is equally present whether defendant is objecting on the basis of an illegal search, confession, or lineup identification. Other extensions of the *Simmons* ruling, however, are not so easily resolved. In particular, the *Simmons* ruling referred only to use of defendant's testimony on the issue of guilt, and there remains the possibility that his testimony could be used for impeachment purposes in light of *Harris* (p. 284) and *Walder* (p. 282). *P. v. Sturgis*, 317 N.E.2d 545 (Ill.1974) (permitting impeachment use).

35. BURDEN OF PROOF

Allocation of burden. The Supreme Court has held that the prosecution must bear the burden of proving several elements that relate to the possible application of the exclusionary remedy. *Miranda v. Ariz.*, supra (waiver of privilege against self-incrimination and right to counsel); *Bumper v. N. C.* (p. 146) (consent to a search); *U. S. v. Wade* (pp. 249–251) (in-court identification not based upon unconstitutional lineup identification). Supreme Court opinions do not, however, clearly allocate the burden on many other equally significant elements. In some areas, the Court's opinions do point in a particular direction, and lower courts largely have agreed on the proper allocation. Thus, lower courts generally hold that the burden of establishing the constitutional admissibility of a confession rests upon the prosecution, *Pea v. U. S.*, 397 F.2d 627 (D.C.Cir. 1968). Cf. *Lego v. Twomey* (discussed infra). The lower courts are sharply divided, however, in other areas, most notably search and seizure.

A few jurisdictions place upon the prosecution the burden of proving the lawfulness of a search and seizure. *S. v. Voit*, 485 P.2d 1306 (Kan. 1971). They take the view that no sufficient basis exists for distinguishing search issues from other constitutional issues (e. g., voluntariness of a confession) on which the prosecution traditionally carries that burden. A significant number of state courts, however, take the position that the defendant, as the party seeking to suppress the evidence, should bear the burden of proving the illegality of a search. *S. v. Holt*, 415 S.W.2d 761 (Mo.1967). Cf. *P. v. Berrios*, 270 N.E.2d 709 (N.Y.1971) (ultimate burden of persuasion is on defendant, but prosecution must initially present evidence showing legality). States placing the burden on the defendant do recognize, as required by *Bumper*, supra, that the burden shifts to the prosecution when it relies on consent as the justification for the search. Some also shift the burden when the prosecution relies on information obtained from informers to establish probable cause. In *Beck v. Ohio*, 379 U.S. 89 (1964), the Court noted that, where the defense challenged the validity of an arrest based upon an informer's tip, it was "incumbent upon the prosecutor to show * * * what the informer actually said, and why the officer thought the information was credible." The relation of this prosecutorial showing to the ultimate burden of proof is not entirely clear, but it has been suggested that, even if the burden generally may be placed upon defense, a special exception must be created in "informer cases" because the informer privilege (see p. 105) places a severe handicap upon the defendant in showing a lack of probable cause.

Various jurisdictions follow the federal court pattern in allocating the burden of proof; the prosecution bears the burden where the search was made without a warrant, while the defendant bears the burden on searches made with a war-

rant. *U. S. v. Pearson*, 448 F.2d 1207 (5th Cir.
1971); *S. v. Smithers*, 269 N.E.2d 874 (Ind.
1971). Compare *Rogers v. U. S.*, 330 F.2d 535
(5th Cir. 1964) (burden of persuasion always is
on the defendant, but the burden of producing evidence is on the prosecution when the search was
warrantless). Tying allocation of the burden to
the presence of a warrant authorization is justified as a logical extension of Supreme Court rulings noting a Fourth Amendment presumption in
favor of the use of warrants (see p. 98). *U. S.
v. Pearson*, supra. Indeed, some courts reason
that a defense showing of the lack of a warrant
constitutes "prima facie" evidence of illegality
that shifts the burden to the prosecution. *Badillo
v. Superior Court*, 294 P.2d 23 (Cal.1956). Placing the burden on the defendant where a warrant
was used has been justified on related grounds.
Thus, the argument has been advanced that the
presence of the warrant, setting forth the government's basis for finding probable cause, makes it
considerably easier for the defendant to prepare
his attack on the probable cause determination
than in the instance of a warrantless search.
Moreover, the burden of proof arguably has less
significance in attacking a warrant since most jurisdictions will not permit the defendant to challenge the accuracy of the factual allegations contained in the sworn affidavits supporting the warrant—i. e., probable cause to issue the warrant is

tested solely by the evidence originally presented to the magistrate. *P. v. Bak*, 258 N.E.2d 341 (Ill.1970). (See p. 99).

In *Jones v. U. S.* (p. 295), the Supreme Court noted that it was "entirely proper" to require the defendant to "establish" his standing to raise a Fourth Amendment claim, and most jurisdictions place that burden on the defendant. *Draper v. Md.*, 265 F.Supp. 718 (D.Md.1967). The defendant, of course, is in the most appropriate position to allege and establish that he was the victim of the search. (See § 34A).

Quantum of proof. In a few areas, the Supreme Court has spoken on both the allocation of the burden of proof and the level of that burden. Thus, *Miranda v. Ariz.*, supra, noted that the prosecution bears a "heavy burden" in showing a valid waiver of the rights recognized in that decision. Similarly, *U. S. v. Wade*, supra, noted that the prosecution must show by "clear and convincing evidence" that an in-court identification is not the product of an unconstitutional lineup identification. The Court's opinions usually have specified the appropriate level of the burden with little supporting discussion. In *Lego v. Twomey*, 404 U.S. 477 (1972), however, the Court discussed at length the appropriate standard to be applied in determining the admissibility of allegedly involuntary confessions.

The majority in *Lego* concluded that the Constitution requires no greater proof of admissibility of a confession than by a preponderance of the evidence. It distinguished *In re Winship* (p. 68), requiring proof of guilt beyond a reasonable doubt; the standard of proof for admissibility of evidence need not reach the high level applied to proof of the offense itself in order to ensure against unreliable verdicts. Similarly, it rejected the contention that a higher standard of proof was suggested by *Jackson v. Denno*, 378 U.S. 368 (1974), which held unconstitutional a state practice of submitting the voluntariness issue to the jury without a prior judicial ruling that the confession was constitutionally admissible; *Jackson* did not reflect any need to provide additional safeguards respecting the jury's evaluation of the reliability of a confession in determining guilt or innocence, but only reflected concern as to the jury's ability to apply admissibility standards unrelated to reliability. Finally, the *Lego* majority also rejected the contention, advanced in the dissent, that proof of admissibility beyond a reasonable doubt was needed "to give adequate protection to these values that the exclusionary rules are designed to serve." The majority found it "very doubtful that escalating the prosecution's burden of proof in Fourth and Fifth Amendment suppression hearings would be sufficiently productive [in implementing the deterrent impact of

[*310*]

the exclusionary rule] to outweigh the public interest in placing probative evidence before juries for the purpose of arriving at truthful decisions about guilt or innocence." Moreover, the defendant had "offer[ed] nothing to suggest that admissibility rulings [based upon a preponderance of the evidence standard] have been unreliable or otherwise wanting in quality because not based on some higher standard." *Lego*, of course, left the states free to apply a higher standard of proof if they so desired, and several have adopted a reasonable doubt standard. *S. v. Collins*, 297 A.2d 620 (Me.1972).

36. HARMLESS ERROR

Application to constitutional errors. All fifty states and the federal government have "harmless error" provisions that prohibit appellate reversals based upon errors which do not "affect the substantial rights" of the defendant. Fed.R.Crim.P. 52(b). Prior to 1967, it frequently was assumed that the harmless error principle did not apply to review of constitutional errors because such errors were "per se injurious to the defendant". *Allen v. S.*, 137 S.E.2d 711 (Ga.App.1964). While there were no explicit Supreme Court rulings to that effect, the Court had regularly reversed convictions upon a finding of constitutional error without discussing the possibility that the error might be harmless. In 1967, however, the issue was squarely presented in *Chapman v. Cal.*, 386 U.S. 18 (1967), and the Court held the harmless error principle applicable to at least some constitutional errors. The *Chapman* opinion acknowledged that "prior cases have indicated that there are some constitutional rights so basic to a fair trial that their infraction can never be treated as harmless error", but noted that other precedent "beli[ed] any belief that all trial errors which violate the constitution automatically call for reversal". The opinion concluded "that there may be some constitutional errors which in the setting of a particular case are so unimportant and insignificant that they may, consistent with the Federal Constitution be deemed harmless". The majority indicated that a violation of the *Griffin* ruling (prohibiting prosecutorial comment upon defendant's failure to take the stand, see p. 64) could fall within that category, but found that the particular *Griffin* violation in *Chapman* was not harmless and therefore required reversal.

The applicable federal standard. *Chapman* also held that the substantive standard for determining whether an error was harmless, as applied to constitutional errors, was a matter of federal rather than state law: "Whether a conviction for crime should stand when a state has failed to accord federal constitutionally guaranteed rights is every bit as much a matter of a federal question

as what particular constitutional provisions themselves mean, what they guarantee and whether
they had been denied." The state court in *Chapman* had applied a harmless error standard that
placed primary emphasis upon the "presence of
other substantive evidence that proof of guilt was
overwhelming," but the Supreme Court stressed
that the standard should emphasize the impact of
the error upon the "substantial rights" of the defendants. Accordingly, the Court ruled that a
constitutional error could be viewed as harmless
only if the "beneficiary" of the error (i. e., the
prosecution) could "prove beyond a reasonable
doubt that the error * * * did not contribute to
the verdict obtained."

Harrington v. Cal., 395 U.S. 250 (1969), provided further amplification of the federal standard. The Court there held that the determination as to whether the unconstitutional admission
of evidence constituted harmless error was to be
based upon the "probable impact of the [evi-
dence] in the minds of an average jury" in the
context of the particular case. The majority noted that this evaluation was to be applied to the
jury as a whole; a conviction need not be reversed simply because the reviewing court could
"imagine a single juror whose mind might have
been made up because of [the illegally admitted
evidence]." Moreover, while the *Chapman* definition was designed to avoid giving "too much

emphasis to overwhelming evidence of guilt," the nature of the other evidence in the case remained an important factor in evaluating the impact of the illegally admitted evidence. Thus, the majority stressed that the illegally admitted evidence in that case, confessions of co-defendants admitted in violation of the *Bruton* ruling (p. 37), only supplied evidence relating to a single element that was well established by other testimony, including defendant's own admission. The majority concluded: "The case against [the defendant] is so overwhelming that unless we say that no violation of *Bruton* can constitute harmless error, we must leave this state conviction undisturbed." A dissenting opinion contended that this conclusion departed from *Chapman* by shifting the relevant inquiry from the impact of the tainted evidence to the weight of the untainted evidence, but the majority responded that it was only reaffirming *Chapman*. The majority noted in this regard that it was "not suggesting that, if evidence bearing on all ingredients of the crime is tendered," the unconstitutional admission of "cumulative evidence" necessarily constitutes harmless error. Its decision was based only on the "evidence in this record."

The *Harrington* analysis was also applied in *Milton v. Wainwright*, 407 U.S. 371 (1972). The Court there held that, assuming arguendo that admission of defendant's post-indictment confession violated his Sixth Amendment rights under *Massiah v. U. S.* (p. 208), that error nevertheless "was, beyond a reasonable doubt, harmless." The majority stressed that the jury had been presented with "overwhelming evidence, including no less than three full confessions that were made by petitioner prior to his indictment" and found not to violate constitutional standards. The dissent argued that at least a reasonable doubt was raised under the *Chapman* standard because the pre-indictment confessions were given under circumstances that might have led the jury to give them much less weight if not for the strong corroboration supplied by the post-indictment confession.

Automatic reversals. While the *Chapman* opinion acknowledged that earlier cases, such as *Gideon v. Wainwright*, had "indicated that there are some constitutional rights so basic to a fair trial that their infraction can never be treated as harmless error," the Court never explicitly accepted the validity of that position. Neither the *Chapman* holding nor the Court's discussion of harmless error necessarily forecloses a subsequent ruling that all types of constitutional violations may constitute harmless errors in particular situations (although some are more likely to be harmless errors than others). Nevertheless, the Court's reference to its earlier decisions suggests that certain classes of constitutional error are classified as harmful per se and therefore require automatic reversal in all cases. (See, e. g., the discussion of *Hamilton v. Ala.* at p. 348).

Neither *Chapman* nor the earlier opinions cited there suggest any clear line for distinguishing between those errors that might require automatic reversal and those to which the *Chapman* harmless error standard should be applied. Justice Harlan, dissenting in *Chapman,* suggested that two factors are relevant in making such a distinction—certain errors "have an effect which is so devastating or inherently unreliable" as to require automatic reversals while others involve those "types of official misbehavior [that] require [automatic] reversal because society cannot tolerate giving final effect to a judgment tainted with such intentional misconduct." *Chapman v. Cal.*, supra (dis.). As an illustration of the former category, Justice Harlan cited the admission of a coerced confession and the failure to appoint counsel at trial. As an illustration of the second type, he cited a prosecutor's use of improper assertions and insinuations calculated to mislead a jury, *Berger v. U. S.*, 295 U.S. 78 (1935), and the trial of a defendant before a judge with a direct pecuniary interest in the outcome of the case, *Tumey v. Ohio*, 273 U.S. 510 (1927). Considerable question exists, however, as to whether either *Chapman* or post-*Chapman* decisions are entirely consistent with the distinctions advanced by Justice Harlan. *Chapman* and subsequent decisions have held the *Chapman* standard applicable on a case-by-case basis to violations of (1) the self-incrimination prohibition against prosecutorial comment on the defendant's failure to testify (*Chapman*); (2) the confrontation clause limitations upon the use of a co-defendant's confession (*Harrington*); (3) the prohibition against admission of eye-witness identification derived from a lineup at which the right to counsel was denied (*U. S. v. Wade*, p. 249); (4) the denial of right to counsel at a preliminary examination (*Coleman v. Ala.*, p. 342); (5) the prohibition against admission of incriminating statements obtained in violation of defendant's right to counsel (*Milton*); and (6) the prohibition against the admission of evidence obtained by an unconstitutional search and seizure (*Chambers v. Maroney,* infra).

Unconstitutional search and seizure. *Chambers v. Maroney*, 399 U.S. 42 (1970), held that the admission of evidence in violation of *Mapp* could constitute harmless error under *Chapman*. In *Chambers*, two lower courts "found that if there was error in admitting the ammunition [seized in the course of a search of petitioner's house], the error was harmless beyond a reasonable doubt." The Supreme Court also rejected petitioner's Fourth Amendment claim on that ground, noting that it was "not prepared to differ with the two courts below," and citing *Harrington* as support.

While the *Chambers* opinion offered no explanation as to why *Mapp* violations should be subject to a harmless error standard rather than an automatic reversal requirement, several separate opinions of individual justices explored that issue prior to *Chambers*. Those opinions noted that neither the nature of illegally seized evidence nor the function of the exclusionary rule required automatic reversal. "There is no necessary connection between the fact that evidence was unconstitutionally seized and the degree of harm caused by its admission." *Fahy v. Conn.*, 375 U.S. 85, 92 (1963) (Harlan, J., dis.). Illegally seized evidence may, in a particular case, relate only to a minor, otherwise well established element of the offense. Moreover, since the harmless error rule applies only when the conviction is sustained by other evidence and the illegally seized evidence has no significant impact, application of the rule will not "lessen police sensitivity to the exclusionary rule" or otherwise "undermine the prophylactic function" of that rule. "Obviously at the time a search is carried out the police are not going to know whether the evidence they hope to obtain is going to be necessary for the prosecution's case, and, of course, if they know it will not be necessary, no search is needed." *Bumper v. N. C.*, 391 U.S. 543, 551 (1968) (Black, J., dis.).

Confessions. In *Payne v. Ark.*, 356 U.S. 560 (1958) the Court rejected a contention that the admission of an involuntary confession constituted harmless error:

> "[W]here, as here, a coerced confession constitutes a part of the evidence before the jury and a general verdict is returned, no one can say what credit and weight the jury gave to the confession. And in these circumstances, this Court has uniformly held that even though there may have been sufficient evidence, apart from the coerced confession, to support a * * * conviction, the admission in evidence * * * of the coerced confession vitiates the judgment * * *."

The scope of the ruling in *Payne* is not clear; the Court's refusal to sustain a conviction when there was other "sufficient evidence" does not necessarily indicate it would also refuse to affirm where the inadmissible confession meets the harmless error standard of *Chapman*. However, *Payne* was cited in *Chapman* as one of those earlier cases that "indicated that there are some constitutional rights so basic to a fair trial that their infraction can never be treated as harmless error," and most lower courts have viewed *Payne* and similar rulings [e. g., *Haynes v. Wash.*, 373 U.S. 503 (1963)] as requiring an automatic reversal whenever an involuntary confession is admitted in evidence. *C. v. Coyle*, 233 A.2d 542 (Pa.1967). But note, *P. v. Haydel*, 524 P.2d 866

(Cal.1974) (distinguishing between confessions and admissions).

The application of an automatic reversal requirement has been justified on the ground that the involuntary confession is a "kind of evidentiary bombshell" that almost invariably has such a dramatic impact upon the jury that a reviewing court could not appropriately conclude under *Chapman* that it "did not contribute to the verdict." *P. v. Schader*, 401 P.2d 665 (Cal.1965). This justification, however, appears to have been rejected in *Milton v. Wainwright*, supra, at least where admissible confessions covering the same ground were also before the jury. Although the confession in *Milton* had not been coerced, the dramatic impact of a confession obtained in violation of *Massiah* would not appear to be any less than that of an involuntary confession. Application of the automatic reversal standard also has been justified on the ground that involuntary confessions are "inherently unreliable," but the presence of similar, admissible confessions, as in *Milton*, may also negate that premise. Thus, current acceptance of an automatic reversal requirement is most likely to be based on the ground that the particular "values" underlying the prohibition against admission of involuntary confessions (see § 24) are "too fundamental" to permit application of a harmless error rule. *Chapman v. Cal.* (Stewart, J., con.).

Lower courts generally have not applied an automatic reversal requirement to confessions or admissions that violate the *Miranda* requirements, but are not "coerced" under traditional involuntariness standards. They reason that the *Miranda* standard is not as closely related to preserving the "very integrity of the fact finding process" as the prohibition against admitting involuntary confessions, and, accordingly, a harmless error standard is more appropriately applied to *Miranda* violations. *Guyette v. S.*, 438 P.2d 244 (Nev.1968). Support for this rationale is found in the Supreme Court's application of the *Chapman* standard to violations of both *Massiah* and *Wade* (see p. 317), decisions which are viewed as similar in nature to *Miranda*. *C. v. Padgett*, 237 A.2d 209 (Pa.1968). But see *U. S. v. Blair*, 470 F.2d 331 (5th Cir. 1972).

CHAPTER 7

RIGHT TO COUNSEL

Introduction. The Sixth Amendment provides that, "in all criminal prosecutions, the accused shall enjoy the right * * * to have the Assistance of Counsel for his defense." This right was held fully applicable to the states, via the Fourteenth Amendment, in *Gideon v. Wainwright* (p. 20). Most of the decisions dealing with the right to counsel have been concerned with the state's failure to appoint counsel, at its expense, to assist the indigent defendant, rather than the right of the more affluent defendant to utilize the assistance of privately retained counsel. The latter right is so clearly established by the Sixth Amendment's language and history that it rarely has been the subject of litigation, at least as applied to the formal stages of the criminal prosecution. The Supreme Court has characterized that right as "unqualified," and early established that it included, as a "necessary corollary," the right to a reasonable delay in the proceedings to permit the defendant to employ and consult with counsel. *Powell v. Ala.*, 287 U.S. 45 (1932); *Chandler v. Fretag*, 348 U.S. 3 (1954).

37. THE RIGHT TO APPOINTED COUNSEL

A Sixth Amendment requirement. The constitutional right of an indigent defendant to the assistance of court appointed counsel was first recognized by the Supreme Court in *Powell v. Ala.*, supra, but that decision was carefully limited to situations similar to that before the Court—"a capital case" in which the defendant was "incapable adequately of making his own defense because of ignorance, feeble mindedness, illiteracy or the like." The *Powell* Court concluded that, at least under those circumstances, the appointment of counsel to assist the indigent was a "logical corollary" of the right to a fair hearing. Despite its limited holding, the *Powell* opinion suggested the need for the appointment of counsel generally. The opinion stressed the inability of even the "intelligent and educated layman" to properly represent himself, and concluded that there was a need for "the guiding hand of counsel at every step of the proceedings." The Court noted, for example, that the defendant ordinarily would be incapable of determining the validity of an indictment, applying the rules of evidence or preparing his defense. "Left without the aid of counsel he may be put on trial without a proper charge, and convicted upon incompetent evidence, or evidence irrelevant to the issue or otherwise inadmissible."

In *Johnson v. Zerbst*, 304 U.S. 458 (1938), the Court relied heavily upon *Powell's* statement as to the general need for counsel in holding that the Sixth Amendment required federal courts to appoint counsel in all felony cases. But in *Betts v. Brady*, 316 U.S. 455 (1942), the Court refused to apply the *Johnson* ruling to the states via the Fourteenth Amendment. The majority held that due process did not necessarily require appointment of counsel in all criminal cases, but only in those cases where the particular circumstances indicated that the absence of counsel would result in a trial lacking "fundamental fairness." The Court ruled that these circumstances were not present in the case before it since the trial rested upon the "simple issue" of evaluating conflicting testimony, and the defendant, a man of ordinary intelligence and some familiarity with the courts, had been able to present adequately his case. Over the next twenty years, the Court decided over thirty cases involving application of the *Betts* standard. In all except a few, it found that "special circumstances," such as the complexity of the legal issues presented, the youth or mental incapacity of the defendant, or the fact that the offense charged was punishable by death, required the appointment of counsel to ensure fundamental fairness.

Gideon v. Wainwright, 372 U.S. 335 (1963), overruled *Betts*. *Gideon* held that the Fourteenth Amendment fully incorporated the Sixth Amendment right and accordingly required the state to make appointed counsel available to indigent defendants in all criminal cases. The opinion for the Court relied essentially upon *Johnson's* application of the *Powell* rationale and argued that *Betts'* case-by-case approach had departed from the basic thrust of that rationale. It concluded that "in our adversary system of criminal justice, any person hauled into court, who is too poor to hire a lawyer cannot be assured a fair trial unless counsel is provided for him." The "obvious truth" of this conclusion, the Court noted, was evidenced by the fact that "lawyers to prosecute are everywhere deemed essential" and "there are few defendants charged with crime * * * who fail to hire the best lawyers they can get." A concurring opinion suggested that decisions applying *Betts* had so frequently found "special circumstances" requiring appointment of counsel that the *Betts* rule was no longer a reality, and retention of a rule emphasizing a case-by-case analysis would only lead astray the state courts "charged with the front line responsibility for the enforcement of constitutional rights."

An equal protection requirement. Both Supreme Court and lower court opinions have suggested that, aside from the Sixth Amendment requirements of *Gideon*, appointment of counsel to

assist the indigent may be required by the equal
protection clause of the Fourteenth Amendment
and the equal protection concept incorporated
within the Fifth Amendment due process clause.
Primary support for this position is found in
Griffin v. Ill., 351 U.S. 12 (1956), and *Douglas v.
Cal.*, 372 U.S. 353 (1963). *Griffin* did not deal
directly with appointment of counsel, but was
based on a principle that was later applied to
counsel in *Douglas*. *Griffin* held that where state
law conditioned appellate review upon the availability of a stenographic transcript or report of
the trial proceedings, the state must make such a
transcript or report available without charge to
indigent defendants so they would have equal access to appellate review. The plurality opinion
stressed that, although the state was not required
by due process to afford appellate review, once it
did so, it could not condition such review "in a
way that discriminates against some convicted
defendants on account of their poverty." "There
can be no equal justice," the opinion noted,
"where the kind of trial a man gets depends on
the amount of money he has." In *Douglas*, the
Court relied upon the "*Griffin* principle" to hold
invalid the California practice of refusing to appoint counsel on an appeal by an indigent when
the appellate court, after reviewing the trial record, concluded that "no good whatever could be
served" by appointment. The Court noted that

the more affluent defendant was not required to run the "gauntlet of a preliminary showing of merit" to have his appeal presented by counsel. The indigent defendant, it concluded, was entitled to equal treatment, at least on a first appeal granted by the state as a matter of right. The state therefore was required to appoint counsel for all indigent defendants on first appeal, just as it was required by *Gideon* to provide counsel at the trial level.

Construed broadly, the *Griffin-Douglas* concept of equal protection could require the appointment of counsel to assist the indigent at every stage in the administration of criminal justice at which the more affuent defendant is allowed by state law to be represented by privately retained counsel. The question of appointment would rest on the need for providing equal treatment rather than the need for a lawyer's assistance to assure a fair hearing. Thus, even though due process might not require appointment of counsel at a parole proceeding or at a trial of a misdemeanor punishable only by a fine, equal protection would require appointment if the more affluent defendant had a right under state law to be represented by counsel at those proceedings. This view of *Griffin-Douglas* was suggested in several lower court opinions decided before *Ross v. Moffit*, 417 U.S. 600 (1974). See, e. g., *Earnest v. Willingham*, 406 F.2d 681 (10th Cir. 1969). In *Ross*, however, the Supreme Court appears to have adopted a considerably narrower view of *Griffin-Douglas*.

Ross involved a state practice of appointing counsel to assist indigent appellants on their appeals to the state intermediate appellate court, but not on their applications for review by the State Supreme Court or their petitions for certiorari to the United States Supreme Court. A divided Court (6–3) held that the failure to appoint counsel at these later stages of the appellate process did not deprive the appellants of equal protection. The Court stressed that the indigent defendant did not need counsel to have "meaningful access" to the higher appellate courts. On application for review, the State Supreme Court would have before it a transcript, the lower court brief, and, in many cases, an opinion of the state intermediate court. These materials, supplemented by any personal statement of appellant, provided an "adequate basis" for the state court to determine whether to grant review—especially since the "critical issue" for that decision was not whether there had been "a correct adjudication of guilt in every individual case," but whether the appeal presented issues of general legal significance. The same factors, the Court noted, also applied to its own consideration of petitions for writ of certiorari.

The *Ross* majority acknowledged that a lawyer skilled in preparing petitions for review "would * * * prove helpful" to an appellant (a point emphasized by the dissenters). But, it noted, "the fact that a particular service might be of benefit to an indigent defendant does not mean that service is constitutionally required." Equal protection "does not require absolute equality or precisely equal advantages". "The duty of the state * * * is not to duplicate the legal arsenal that may be privately retained by a criminal defendant in a continuing effort to reverse his conviction, but only to assure the indigent defendant an adequate opportunity to present his claims fairly in the context of the State's appellate process."

Determining indigency. Supreme Court opinions have referred generally to the "indigent defendant" without offering any specific definition of "indigency." Although it has described indigent defendants as persons "lack[ing] funds to hire a lawyer," the Court has not indicated what sources of funds and what alternative expenditures are to be considered in determining whether a particular defendant falls in this category. Lower courts considering these issues generally have held that the separate financial resources of a spouse or relatives will not be considered in determining indigency. *P. v. Gustavson*, 269 N.E. 2d 517 (Ill.App.1971). Lower courts also have ruled that a defendant should be classified as indigent if his available resources are not sufficient to both retain counsel and post bond—i. e., that he cannot be made to choose between personal liberty and representation at trial. *P. v. Eggers*, 188 N.E.2d 30 (Ill.1963). Finally, the owner of some assets does not have to become destitute before he can be classified as an indigent. *McCraw v. S.*, 476 P.2d 370 (Okla.Crim.1970); *U. S. v. Cohen*, 419 F.2d 1124 (8th Cir. 1969).

Many states have "recoupment programs" requiring indigent defendants to reimburse the state for the costs of their legal defense if the defendant subsequently becomes financially able to make such reimbursement. The Court has upheld such programs in principle, but has insisted that they not discriminate arbitrarily against indigent defendants generally or particular groups of defendants. Thus, *Rinaldi v. Yeager*, 384 U.S. 305 (1966), invalidated a state law that required only those indigent defendants sentenced to prison to reimburse the state; the statute invidiously discriminated between those imprisoned defendants and other convicted defendants sentenced only to probation or the payment of a fine. *James v. Strange*, 407 U.S. 128 (1972), similarly held invalid a state recoupment statute because it failed to permit the indigent defendant to avail himself of the restrictions on wage garnishment and other protective exemptions afforded to other civil judgment debtors (including debtors under recoupment laws relating to other forms of public assistance). *Fuller v. Ore.*, 417 U.S. 40 (1974), on the other hand, upheld a recoupment program that applied only to convicted indigent defendants. In the particular case, required repayment had been imposed as a condition of probation following a work release program, but the defendant could be relieved of that condition if repayment would impose "manifest hardship." The Court noted initially that the distinction drawn between those defendants convicted and those acquitted "reflect[ed] no more than an effort to achieve elemental fairness and is a far cry from * * * invidious discrimination." It also rejected a contention that recoupment imposed an improper burden on the indigent's right to appointed counsel that would "chill" his exercise of that right. A defendant "who is just above the line separating the indigent from the nonindigent," the Court noted, is subjected to considerable financial hardship to retain a lawyer. The Constitution does not "require that those only slightly poorer must remain forever immune from any [similar] obligation to shoulder the expenses of their legal defense."

38. THE SCOPE OF THE RIGHT TO COUNSEL

A. INTRODUCTION

Perhaps the two most significant problems involving the right to counsel are the determination of (1) the level of the charge to which it applies and (2) those stages in the proceedings based upon the charge to which it applies. These determinations usually have been presented to the courts in the context of an indigent's demand for appointed counsel, and the decisions generally have referred only to that element of the right to counsel. Depending upon outcome and analysis, the decisions may or may not be controlling as to the defendant's right to be represented by privately retained counsel. As noted at p. 322, the Court has given special recognition to that aspect of the Sixth Amendment right. Moreover, it has suggested that the right to be heard by retained counsel has an independent due process foundation that extends beyond the criminal prosecution. *Powell v. Ala.*, supra at 69; *Manness v. Meyers*, 419 U.S. 449, 470 (1975) (Stewart, J., con.).

A decision finding a constitutional right to appointed counsel at a particular proceeding should *a fortiori* support the right of a defendant to be represented by a retained counsel at the same proceeding. On the other hand, decisions finding no right to appointed counsel ordinarily should not be read to suggest that the state could constitutionally exclude retained counsel for that proceeding. Thus, a court may find no constitutional right to the assistance of appointed counsel in the trial of a misdemeanor punishable only by fine, but recognize a constitutional right to be assisted by retained counsel at the same trial. Cf. *Hendrix v. Seattle*, 456 P.2d 696, 703 (Wash. 1969); *Ross v. Moffit*, supra. In some instances, however, a finding that the special functions of the proceeding eliminates the need for appointed counsel may at least raise the possibility that the state could exclude counsel altogether. *Gagnon v. Scarpelli*, discussed at p. 349, is illustrative. The Court there held that, in light of various factors, including the impact of counsel upon the "nature of the proceeding," due process did not require the appointment of counsel in all probation revocation proceedings. It added that, since the particular case did not present the issue, there was no need to decide whether a probationer has "a right to be represented * * * by retained counsel" in those revocation proceedings that would not require appointed counsel for the indigent. See also *Morrissey v. Brewer*, (p. 72) (a pre-*Gagnon* ruling establishing the right to a parole revocation hearing, but leaving open the question "whether the parolee is entitled to the

assistance of [either] retained counsel or * * *
appointed counsel").

B. THE LEVEL OF THE CHARGE

Misdemeanors. Prior to *Argersinger v. Hamlin*,
407 U.S. 25 (1972), some doubt existed as to
whether the constitutional right to appointed
counsel applied to misdemeanor prosecutions.
Gideon v. Wainwright (p. 324) itself involved a
felony prosecution, and later cases referred to
Gideon as establishing a right to counsel in "felony prosecutions." *Mempa v. Rhay*, 389 U.S. 128,
134 (1967). *Argersinger*, however, held *Gideon*
applicable to all indigent misdemeanor defendants
who are sentenced to a jail term. The Court rejected the State's contention that the Sixth
Amendment right to counsel, like the Sixth
Amendment right to a jury trial (see p. 52),
should not apply to "petty offenses" even where
a jail sentence was imposed. While there was
"historical support" for the jury trial limitation, "nothing in the history of the right to counsel" suggested a "retraction of the right in petty
offenses wherein the common law previously did
require that counsel be provided." Moreover,
there was no functional basis for drawing the line
at petty offenses. The "problems associated with
* * * petty offenses," the Court noted, "often
require the presence of counsel to insure the ac-

cused a fair trial." It could not be said that the legal questions involved in a misdemeanor trial were likely to be less complex because the jail sentence did not exceed six months. Neither is there less need for advice of counsel prior to entering a plea of guilty to a petty offense. Indeed, petty misdemeanors may create a special need for counsel because their great volume "may create an obsession for speedy dispositions, regardless of the fairness of the result."

Argersinger noted that by tying its ruling to the actual imposition of imprisonment, it placed upon the trial judge the burden of determining in advance whether a sentence of imprisonment was possible, as a practical matter, in the particular case. If the judge concluded that it was not, and therefore failed to appoint counsel, "no imprisonment may be imposed, even though local law permits it." *Argersinger* left open, however, the possible extension of the right to appointed counsel to certain misdemeanor charges even where imprisonment was not imposed. In response to a concurring opinion's suggestion that the need for counsel may exist without regard to the punishment imposed, the Court noted: "We need not consider the requirements of the Sixth Amendment as regards the right to counsel where loss of liberty is not involved, however, for here petitioner was in fact sentenced to jail. And, as we said in *Baldwin v. N. Y.* (p. 52 supra), the prospect of imprisonment, for however short a time, will seldom be viewed by the accused as a 'trivial' or 'petty' matter and may well result in quite serious repercussions affecting his career and his reputation."

A possible basis for the future extension of *Argersinger* to non-imprisonment cases may be found in *Mayer v. Chicago*, 404 U.S. 189 (1971). The Court there extended the *Griffin-Douglas* equal protection analysis to an appeal from a non-imprisonment misdemeanor conviction. *Mayer* found that an indigent defendant, fined $500.00 upon ordinance convictions for disorderly conduct and interference with a police officer, was entitled to a free transcript needed to present an appeal. The Court stressed, *inter alia*, the potential significance of conviction for "even petty offenses" of the "kind involved here." "A fine," it noted, "may bear as heavily upon an indigent accused as forced confinement," and "the collateral consequences may be even more severe, as when (as was apparently a possibility in this case) the impecunious medical student finds himself barred from the practice of medicine because of [the] conviction * * *." Although providing a transcript may be distinguished from providing a lawyer, and the equal protection clause may require assistance apart from Sixth Amendment requirements, the *Mayer* analysis suggests the possible extension of *Argersinger* to require counsel in those non-imprisonment misdemeanor cases where the consequences of conviction are nevertheless particularly severe. See *Wood v. Superintendent*, 355 F.Supp. 338 (E.D.Va.1973) (noting that *Argersinger* "applies to those non-imprisonment [misdemeanor] cases in which fundamental fairness * * * mandates the appointment of attorneys").

Quasi-criminal proceedings. *In re Gault*, 387 U.S. 1 (1967), held that "the Due Process Clause of the Fourteenth Amendment requires that in respect to proceedings to determine [juvenile] delinquency which may result in commitment to an institution in which the juvenile's freedom is curtailed, the child and his parent must be notified of the child's right to be represented by counsel retained by them, or if they are unable to afford counsel, that counsel will be appointed to represent the child." The Court stressed the need for counsel to assure a fair hearing in a proceeding which "was comparable in seriousness to a felony prosecution." The *Gault* ruling appears equally applicable to other proceedings, such as sexual psychopath, that are also based upon activities that violate the criminal code and may result in lengthy incarceration. Indeed, *Gault* has been extended by several courts to commitment proceedings that are based on non-criminal activities. *Heryford v. Parker*, 396 F.2d 393 (10th Cir. 1968).

C.   THE STAGE OF THE PROCEEDING

The Sixth Amendment recognizes the right of an "accused" to the assistance of counsel in "all criminal prosecutions." The Court has held that this right "attaches only at or after the time that adversary judicial proceedings have been initiated." *Kirby v. Ill.* (p. 254). That point marks the "commencement of the 'criminal prosecutions' to which alone the explicit guarantees of the Sixth Amendment are applicable." Id. Once adversary judicial proceedings have been initiated, the indigent defendant's right to appointed counsel extends to every "critical stage" of the prosecution—i. e. every stage "where substantial rights of the accused may be affected," and the "guiding hand" of counsel is therefore necessary. *Mempa v. Rhay*, supra.

The Sixth Amendment is not the only potential source of a constitutional right to appointed counsel at a particular proceeding. *Douglas v. Ala.* (p. 326) required appointment of counsel at the appellate level on equal protection grounds. Other cases have noted that, even though a proceeding is not part of a criminal prosecution, the right to appointed counsel may be necessary to protect the exercise of another constitutional right, *Miranda v. Ariz.* (p. 213), or to provide a fair hearing as required by due process, *Gagnon v. Scarpelli* (p. 72).

Police investigation. As noted in the discussion of *Kirby* at p. 254, some uncertainty exists as to exactly what constitutes the initiation of adversary judicial proceedings. Once such proceedings have been initiated (e. g., by the filing of a formal charge), police investigatory operations are subject to the Sixth Amendment right to appointed counsel if they constitute a critical stage in the criminal proceedings (e. g., lineup identification). See § 29A. However, many police investigatory operations, though involving the accused's personal participation, are not viewed as critical stages in the criminal prosecution. See § 29B.

The investigatory process also may be subjected through other constitutional rights to restrictions relating to counsel. Such restrictions may apply even prior to the commencement of the criminal prosecution. Thus, *Miranda v. Ariz.* (p. 213) determined that assistance of counsel should be available to protect a suspect's self-incrimination rights during custodial interrogation, and consequently required exclusion of statements obtained from the suspect without properly affording him such assistance. *Escobedo v. Ill.* (p. 209) required exclusion of similar pre-charge statements on Sixth Amendment grounds, but that ruling subsequently has been viewed as a decision designed primarily to "vindicate" self-incrimination rights, and hence largely supplanted by the *Miranda* analysis. *Kirby v. Ill.* (p. 338) (noting

[*339*]

Escobedo is now limited in its "holding * * * to its own facts"). See also *Kirby v. Ill.* (p. 254), where the majority rejected a *Miranda*-type argument that counsel was needed at a pre-charge lineup to support the defendant's constitutional right to confront adverse witnesses at trial.

Initial appearance. One of the first formal steps in the criminal case is the defendant's initial appearance before the magistrate, which ordinarily follows defendant's arrest. At that point, the defendant is informed of the charges against him (as stated in the complaint) and his rights to the assistance of counsel, to remain silent, and to a preliminary examination (in felony cases). In addition, the magistrate usually will set bail.

White v. Md., 373 U.S. 59 (1963), establishes that the initial appearance constitutes a critical stage, requiring the appointment of counsel, if the state requires the defendant to make an election at that point that is subsequently used against him at trial. In *White* the state followed a practice, utilized in several jurisdictions, of requesting a felony defendant to enter an initial, non-binding plea before the magistrate. The defendant there, without the assistance of counsel, entered a plea of guilty. Subsequently, at the formal arraignment before the trial judge, defendant was assisted by appointed counsel and entered a plea of not guilty. The initial plea of guilty was nevertheless introduced as evidence against him at trial. The Supreme Court reversed the conviction holding that the use of the plea rendered defendant's appearance before the magistrate a critical stage where counsel should have been made available to assist the "accused to * * * plead intelligently."

The combination of *White* and *Coleman v. Ala.,* (discussed at p. 342) also brings into question the constitutionality of a magistrate permitting an accused to waive his right to a preliminary examination without first making available the assistance of counsel. *Coleman* found the preliminary examination to be a critical stage because, *inter alia,* the examination could have a significant impact upon the accused's presentation of a defense at trial. Arguably, unless the State offers appointed counsel to assist the indigent defendant in making his decision, it can no more hold him to a waiver of a right of significance in preparing for trial than it could utilize against him at trial the initial plea election in *White.* Compare, however, *S. v. Simones,* 272 N.E.2d 146 (Ohio App.1971), aff'd, 282 N.E. 573 (1972), (suggesting that full advice by the court as to nature of the preliminary examination "supplants" the need for counsel).

Coleman v. Ala., supra, also provides grounds for arguing that the first appearance is a "critical stage" even when defendant makes no significant decisions such as waiving an examination or entering an informal plea of guilty. In holding that the preliminary examination was a "critical stage," *Coleman* noted the value of counsel in making effective arguments on bail. The setting of bail is also a major element in the first appearance. However, since *Coleman* pointed to several functions requiring counsel's assistance at the preliminary examination, the bail function alone may not be sufficient to require appointment of counsel at the first appearance. Cf. *Gerstein v. Pugh* (discussed at p. 120) (initial judicial determination of probable cause following arrest is not critical stage because of "its limited function and its nonadversary character").

Preliminary examination. The preliminary "examination" or "hearing," also conducted by the magistrate, is usually held at least several days after the defendant's initial appearance. In most jurisdictions, the basic function of the preliminary examination is to determine whether there is probable cause to "hold" the accused for possible prosecution. (The final decision as to prosecution ordinarily rests with the prosecutor or grand jury). If the accused is "boundover" for prosecution, the magistrate also may reconsider the appropriate level of bail.

Coleman v. Ala., 399 U.S. 1 (1970), held that the preliminary examination was a "critical stage" under the Sixth Amendment. While there was no opinion for the Court, a majority agreed that the failure to appoint counsel at a typical state preliminary examination resulted in a constitutional violation, though not necessarily requiring reversal of a subsequent conviction. The majority stressed the practical importance of the preliminary examination and noted various advantages that could result from assistance of counsel:

> "First, the lawyer's skilled examination and cross-examination of witness may expose fatal weaknesses in the State's case that may lead the magistrate to refuse to bind the accused over. Second, in any event, the skilled interrogation * * * by an experienced lawyer can fashion a valuable impeachment tool for use in cross-examination of the State's witnesses at the trial, or preserve [favorable] testimony * * * of a witness who does not appear at trial. Third, trained counsel can more effectively discover the case the state has against his client and make possible [better] preparation * * * [for] trial. Fourth, counsel can also be influential at the preliminary hearing in making effective arguments for the accused on such matters as the necessity for an early psychiatric examination or bail."

Though finding that these "advantages of a lawyer's assistance" were sufficient to require appointment of counsel, the majority also recognized that the loss of these advantages might not have a significant bearing on a particular trial. Accordingly, it remanded the case to the lower court to determine whether "the denial of counsel * * * was harmless error under *Chapman v. Cal.* (p. 312)." Four members of the majority made no effort to explore the application of the harmless error concept beyond citing *Chapman.* Two members, however, suggested that the denial of counsel would constitute harmless error unless the defendant could point to a specific omission or action at the preliminary examination that had a direct impact on his trial—e. g., that "important testimony of a witness unavailable at trial could have been preserved had counsel been present." Other, more general advantages of counsel—e. g., that counsel may have persuaded the magistrate to dismiss the case, may have known more about the state's case before trial, or may have obtained defendant's release on bail—were viewed as too speculative in their bearing upon the trial itself to require reversal of an otherwise valid conviction. The harmless error issue is now largely mooted in the *Coleman* situation since the *Coleman* ruling on the right to counsel was held not to have retroactive application in *Adams v. Ill.*, 405 U.S. 278 (1972), and states now

· regularly provide counsel at preliminary examinations.

Grand jury proceedings. A person against whom charges are being considered by the grand jury has no constitutional right to present his case, either by himself or by counsel, before that body. Grand jury sessions are protected by secrecy restrictions and the target of an investigation need not even be informed of the ongoing investigation. The grand jury is viewed as performing an essentially discretionary function, similar to that performed by the prosecutor (whose decision it screens), rather than an adjudicative function requiring representation of the prospective defendant.

A person who is the subject of a grand jury investigation may be called before the grand jury in most jurisdictions. See *U. S. v. Dionisio,* 410 U.S. 1, 10 (1973). Compare *S. v. Sarcone,* 233 A.2d 406 (N.J.Super.1967). He retains the right, of course, to refuse to answer questions pursuant to his privilege against self-incrimination (see § 27G), but courts traditionally have held that representation by counsel is not necessary to protect the exercise of that right. *In re Groban,* 352 U.S. 330 (1957). A few recent decisions suggest, however, that *Miranda* (p. 213) requires a partial alteration of this rule. *U. S. v. Mandujano,* (p. 242). They argue that the witness who is

the "target" of the grand jury investigation
is placed in a situation akin to custodial
interrogation and is therefore entitled to the
assistance of counsel while testifying, although not necessarily through counsel present
during the testimony. [Because of grand jury secrecy requirements, jurisdictions permitting assistance of counsel usually exclude counsel from
the grand jury room, but permit the witness to
leave the room and consult with counsel, located
in an adjoining room, before answering any question that may raise a potential self-incrimination
issue. *P. v. Ianniello*, 235 N.E.2d 439 (N.Y.1968)].
Other courts have viewed *Miranda* as completely
inapposite. See *C. v. Columbia Investment*, 325
A.2d 289 (Pa.1974) (collecting cases). They
note that in *In re Groban*, supra, four justices
who later joined in the *Miranda* decision argued
that interrogation before the grand jury was
quite different from interrogation in a closed investigatory proceeding. In the latter situation,
they argued, there was a potential for coercion,
trickery, and uninformed waiver, but the grand
jury interrogation was conducted in the presence
of lay jurors who "had no axes to grind, and
* * * tend to bring to the grand jury room the
experience, knowledge, and viewpoints of all sections of the community." Under such circumstances, they concluded, it would be "very difficult for officers of the state seriously to abuse or

deceive a witness." Consider also pp. 240–242 noting other grounds on which *Miranda* has been
held inapplicable to grand jury proceedings.

Arraignment. The formal arraignment occurs
after the information or indictment is issued, and
involves a reading of the charges contained therein and the entry of a plea (guilty, not-guilty, or
nolo contendere) in response to those charges.
Although the defendant is entitled to consultation
with counsel before entering a guilty plea, the denial of counsel has been viewed as harmless error
where the defendant was later allowed to withdraw the guilty plea and the fact that he originally entered such a plea could not be used against
him in evidence. *Vitoratos v. Maxwell*, 351 F.2d
217 (6th Cir. 1965); cf. *White v. Md.,* supra.
Similarly, failure to appoint counsel at arraignment will not constitute grounds for reversal
where the defendant entered a not-guilty plea,
unless the jurisdiction is one that views entry of
the plea as barring the defendant from subsequently raising objections (e. g., attacks on the indictment) or defenses (e. g., insanity). In that
case, *Hamilton v. Ala.*, 368 U.S. 52 (1961), holds
that the arraignment is a critical stage of a
state's criminal process. In *Hamilton*, local law
treated certain defenses, such as insanity, as "ir-
retrievably lost" if not raised at arraignment.
The Court rejected the contention that the critical nature of the proceeding should depend upon

a showing of actual prejudice—i. e., a showing
that defendant would have raised one of the "lost"
defenses if he had been assisted by counsel.   It
concluded that the degree of prejudice "can never
be known" because only counsel present at the
time "could have enabled the accused to know all
the defenses available to him and to plead intelligently."   Compare *Coleman v. Ala.* (p. 342).

Trial.   The earliest right to counsel cases dealt
primarily with assistance of counsel at trial, and
such assistance is clearly recognized as the "core"
of the Sixth Amendment right.   See *Powell v.
Ala.* (p. 323); *Gideon v. Wainwright* (p. 324).

Sentencing, probation and parole.   *Mempa v.
Rhay*, 389 U.S. 128 (1968), confirmed the impli-
cations of prior decisions in holding that sentencing was a "critical stage" of a criminal prosecution requiring the assistance of appointed counsel.
Mempa held, moreover, that sentencing remained
a "critical stage" even though deferred to a probation revocation proceeding.   In *Mempa*, the
trial judge placed the defendant on probation
without fixing the term of imprisonment that
would be imposed if probation was later revoked.
The Court concluded that the subsequent determination and imposition of the prison sentence at
the probation revocation proceeding was as much
a part of the "criminal prosecution" as sentencing
imposed immediately after trial.   The Court re-

jected the state's contention that counsel was not needed since the term of the prison sentence was set by state law. The trial judge was required to submit a recommendation as to the portion of the sentence to be served, and counsel could assist the defendant in presenting his case on that matter. Also, as in most states, certain legal rights (e. g., withdrawal of a guilty plea) could be lost if not raised at the time the sentence was initially imposed, and counsel also was needed to protect those rights. Cf. *Hamilton v. Ala.* (p. 347).

In *Gagnon v. Scarpelli*, 411 U.S. 778 (1973), the Court held that *Mempa* did not extend to a probation revocation proceeding that involved only determination of revocation, a prison sentence previously having been imposed and suspended in favor of probation. The probation revocation determination is not based on the commission of the original offense and accordingly is not part of the "criminal prosecution" governed by the Sixth Amendment. The Court noted, however, that the "loss of liberty entailed [in a probation revocation] is a serious deprivation requiring that [the probationer] be accorded due process." Under *Morrissey v. Brewer* (p. 72), the probationer has a due process right to a preliminary and a final revocation hearing that includes the right to present evidence, confront witnesses, etc. *Gagnon* concluded that due process also requires that the state provide appointed counsel where, under the facts of the particular case, counsel is needed to assure the "effectiveness of the [hearing] rights guaranteed by *Morrissey*."

The *Gagnon* Court considered, but refused to impose, a flat requirement of counsel in all cases. While such a requirement had the "appeal of simplicity, it would impose direct costs and serious collateral disadvantages" without regard to the need for counsel. In most cases, the Court noted, the probationer has been convicted of committing another crime or admits the probation violation. Mitigating circumstances, if advanced, often are "not susceptible of proof" or are "so simple as not to require either investigation or exposition by counsel." Moreover, the introduction of counsel would "alter significantly the nature of the [probation-revocation] proceeding." The state would, in turn, retain its own counsel, and the role of the hearing body would become "more akin to that of a judge at trial and less attuned to the rehabilitative needs of the individual probationer." The Court acknowledged that a case-by-case evaluation of the need for counsel departed from the approach taken in *Gideon* (p. 324) and *Argersinger* (p. 334), but that departure was justified by "critical" distinctions between the functions and nature of criminal trials and revocation hearings. Indeed, in light of those distinctions, the Court left open the issue as to whether the probationer must be afforded the right to have retained counsel in hearings where appointed counsel would not be required (see p. 333).

The *Gagnon* opinion refused to attempt to formulate "a precise and detailed set of guidelines" to be followed in individual cases. It did note that "presumptively" counsel should be provided where, after being informed of his right, the indigent probationer requests counsel on the basis of a "timely and colorable claim" that (1) he has not committed the alleged violation or (2) that there are "substantial reasons which justified or mitigated the violation and made revocation inappropriate, and that the reasons are complex or otherwise difficult to develop or present." The opinion further noted that, "especially in doubtful cases," consideration should be given as to "whether the probationer appears to be capable of speaking effectively for himself." Finally, where a request for counsel was refused, grounds for refusal must be succinctly stated in the record.

While *Gagnon* itself involved a probation revocation proceeding, the opinion made clear that the same standards also applied to parole revocation hearings under *Morrissey v. Brewer*, supra. See *Russel v. Douthitt*, 304 N.E.2d 793 (Ind. 1973).

Appeals. As discussed at p. 326, *Douglas v. Cal.* requires appointment of counsel to assist the indigent defendant at the first level of appellate review granted as a matter of right. *Ross v. Moffit* (p. 328) held, however, that appointed counsel need not also be provided to prepare an application for review at subsequent levels of the appellate process, where review is discretionary. *Ross* did not involve appointment of counsel where discretionary review is granted by a higher appellate court, but counsel regularly is provided at that point as a matter of local practice.

In finding no constitutional right to the assistance of appointed counsel, *Ross* considered the applicability of due process as well as equal protection. In that connection, the Court emphasized the different constitutional status of the trial and the appellate process. While a state could not dispense with the trial stage of criminal proceedings, it could refuse to provide "any appeal at all." *McKane v. Durston* (p. 74). Similarly, while due process requires that the state provide an attorney to serve as a "shield to protect [defendant] against being 'hauled into court' by the State and stripped of his presumption of innocence," it does not require, absent discrimination, that the state also provide an attorney to "serve as a sword to upset the prior determination of guilt."

Where *Douglas* requires appointment of counsel, it also bars the state from adopting a procedure that invites counsel to evade his obligation of advocacy on his client's behalf. Thus, *Anders v. Cal.*, 386 U.S. 738 (1967), found a denial of defendant's rights under *Douglas* when appointed counsel filed a statement simply noting that the appeal had no merit, and the appellate court, without further briefing, then examined the record and affirmed the judgment. The Court held that, while appointed counsel may request the right to withdraw when he finds a case to be "wholly frivolous," he cannot do so by simply stating his conclusion that the appeal lacks merit. His request must be accompanied by a brief discussing all points in the record "that might arguably support the appeal." The appellate court may then dismiss the appeal (or affirm the conviction) if it finds that none of the legal points are "arguable." Otherwise, the appellate court "must, prior to its decision, afford the indigent the assistance of counsel to argue the appeal."

Collateral proceedings. The Supreme Court has not yet had occasion to decide whether the constitutional right to assistance of appointed counsel extends to collateral proceedings (e. g., coram nobis, habeas corpus) that may be available to challenge a prior conviction. (See §§ 44–46). *Johnson v. Avery*, 393 U.S. 483 (1969), held only that a state regulation prohibiting prisoners from assisting each other in preparing federal habeas corpus petitions violated the prisoner's right of access to federal habeas corpus. The majority opinion noted that federal courts generally do not appoint lawyers to assist prisoners in preparing habeas petitions, but it did not rule on the constitutionality of that practice. Three justices suggested, in separate opinions, that it was "neither practical nor necessary to require the help of lawyers" in the preparation of habeas corpus petitions.

Several lower courts have argued that there is no constitutional right to appointed counsel at any stage of a collateral proceeding. *Honore v. Wash. S. Bd.*, 466 P.2d 485 (Wash.1970) (collecting cases). Support for this position is based on several arguments. First, collateral proceedings are deemed not to be part of the "criminal prosecution" encompassed by the Sixth Amendment. Those proceedings have traditionally been designated as civil, and, in any event, are not a part of the process of conviction. Equal protection is also rejected as a basis for appointing counsel, although the *Griffin-Douglas* (p. 326) analysis has been applied by the Supreme Court to require that the state furnish indigents other assistance (transcripts) in post-conviction proceedings. *Long v. Dist. Ct.*, 385 U.S. 192 (1966). Assistance of counsel, it is contended, is no more essential in collateral proceedings, at least with respect to the preparation of the petition, than it is on the second level of appellate review, where equal protection claims also have been rejected. See

Ross v. Moffit (p. 328). A due process justification is rejected on a similar analysis. Cf. *Ross v. Moffit* (p. 352).

On the other side, several lower courts have argued that due process does require the appointment of counsel for those aspects of collateral proceedings in which a lawyer's assistance is necessary for a "fair and meaningful hearing." *Dillon v. U. S.*, 307 F.2d 445 (9th Cir. 1962). They have required appointment at either all evidentiary hearings, *P. v. Shipman*, 397 P.2d 993 (Cal. 1965), or at least those hearings where "complex factual data must be developed in order to support the prisoner's position." *U. S. ex rel. Wissenfeld v. Wilkins*, 281 F.2d 707 (2d Cir. 1960). See also *Honore*, supra (reaching a similar conclusion on equal protection grounds).

39. WAIVER OF THE RIGHT TO COUNSEL

Introduction. The Court has frequently noted that the defendant may waive his constitutional right to assistance of counsel provided he does so "knowingly and intelligently." *Johnson v. Zerbst*, 304 U.S. 458 (1938). At the same time, it has emphasized that waiver will not be "lightly assumed." "Trial courts must indulge every reasonable presumption against waiver." Id. Thus, *Carnley v. Cochran*, 369 U.S. 506 (1962), holds that waiver will not be presumed from a "silent record"; the evidence must show that the defendant was informed specifically of his right to the assistance of appointed or retained counsel and that he clearly rejected such assistance. "No amount of circumstantial evidence that the person may have been aware of his right [and intended to silently relinquish it] will suffice" as a replacement for specific notice and rejection. *Miranda v. Ariz.*, supra.

Even though the formal prerequisites of *Carnley* are established, the rejection of counsel still may not have been made "knowingly and intelligently"—i. e., it may not have been the product of a reasoned and deliberate choice based upon adequate knowledge of what the assistance of counsel encompasses. In determining whether defendant's rejection reflects such a choice, courts rely upon an analysis of the particular facts of the case, including defendant's age, mental condition, and experience, the particular setting in which the offer of counsel was made, and the manner in which it was explained. Moreover, a valid waiver at one stage of the proceeding (e. g., preliminary examination) does not necessarily indicate an intent to waive at a later stage (e. g., trial), and the prosecution must show that the defendant was given the opportunity to exercise his right to counsel at each separate stage.

Waiver prior to the entry of a guilty plea. Very frequently the defendant at arraignment may seek to waive counsel and enter a plea of guilty. The constitutional limitation upon waiver in this circumstance is supplemented by the due process requirement that the guilty plea be voluntary. To insure that both requirements are met, the Court has insisted that the trial judge, in addition to specifically advising defendant of his right to counsel, also make a careful inquiry into the basis of defendant's waiver. In *Von Moltke v. Gillies*, 332 U.S. 708 (1948), four justices suggested that the trial court must seek to insure that waiver is made "with an apprehension of the nature of the charges, the statutory offenses included within them, the range of allowable punishments thereunder, possible defenses to the charges and circumstances in mitigation thereof, and all other facts essential to a broad understanding of the whole matter." Lower courts generally view this standard as a basic guideline, rather than a precise formula, and will not hold a waiver invalid, for example, merely because the trial court failed to inform the defendant of the specific potential maximum sentence. *Cox v. Burke*, 361 F.2d 183 (7th Cir. 1966). They do stress, however, that the defendant must be fully aware of the significance of his decision, including the general nature of the particular charge made against him. Id. *Molignaro v. Smith*, 408 F.2d 795 (5th Cir. 1969).

Waiver and the right to proceed pro se. In
Faretta v. Cal., —— U.S. —— (1975), a divided
Court held that the Sixth Amendment guarantees
to the defendant the right to proceed *pro se* (i. e.,
to represent himself without counsel). *Faretta*
relied upon the "structure of the Sixth Amendment, as well as * * * the English and colonial
jurisprudence from which the Amendment emerged."   The Court noted that, while the Sixth
Amendment does not specifically refer to the right
of self-representation, that right is "necessarily
implied" by the Amendment's provisions for the
accused's presentation of his defense.   Thus, the
Sixth Amendment provisions recognizing the
right to confrontation, compulsory process, and
notice of charges refer to those rights as guaranteed to the "accused, not counsel."   Similarly,
the counsel provision speaks only of the "assistance" of counsel, and suggests thereby that "counsel, like the other defense tools guaranteed * * *
shall be an aid to a willing defendant—not an
organ of the State interposed between an unwilling defendant and his right to defend himself personally."

Faretta also reasoned that forcing counsel upon
an unwilling accused would be contrary to "the
logic of the Amendment," as reflected by the consequences of legal representation.   Thus, when
a defendant chooses to be represented by counsel,
"law and tradition may allocate to the counsel

the power to make binding decisions of trial strategy in many areas." (See p. 380). But this "allocation can only be justified * * * by the
defendant's consent, at the outset, to accept counsel as his representative." Without such acquiescence, the defense presented is not in any
"real sense" the accused's defense and cannot be
attributed to him.

Faretta recognized that a constitutional right
to proceed *pro se* "seems to cut against the grain"
of decisions, like *Gideon*, that are based on the
premise that "the help of a lawyer is essential to
assure a fair trial." It rejected, however, the
dissent's contention that the state's interest in
providing a fair trial permitted it to insist upon
representation by counsel. An analysis of the
historical roots of the Sixth Amendment suggested that the founders had placed on a higher level
the right of "free choice." Moreover, where the
defendant opposes representation by counsel, "the
potential advantage of a lawyer * * * can be
realized, if at all, only imperfectly. To force a
lawyer on a defendant can only lead him to believe that the law contrives against him." Since
the defendant will bear the personal consequences
of his conviction, he must be "free personally to
decide whether in his particular case counsel is
to his advantage."

Faretta stressed that the defendant who pro-
ceeds *pro se* must act "knowingly and intelligent-

ly" in giving up those "traditional benefits associated with the right to counsel": "Although a defendant need not himself have the skill and experience of a lawyer in order competently and intelligently to choose self-representation, he should be made aware of the dangers and disadvantages of self-representation, so that the record will establish that 'he knows what he is doing and his choice is made with eyes open.' *Adams v. U. S. ex rel. McCann*, 317 U.S. 269 (1942)." The Court also noted that the right to self-representation "is not a license to abuse the dignity of the courtroom." Under *Ill. v. Allen* (p. 62) the judge may terminate self-representation by a defendant "who deliberately engages in serious and obstructionist misconduct." Similarly, self-representation is "not a license" for failure to comply with "relevant rules of procedural and substantive law. Thus, whatever else may or may not be open to him on appeal, a defendant who elects to represent himself cannot thereafter complain that the quality of his own defense amounted to a denial of 'effective assistance of counsel.' "

40. EFFECTIVE ASSISTANCE OF COUNSEL

The constitutional right to counsel is based on the premise that counsel will effectively assist the defendant. Accordingly, the failure of counsel to render adequate assistance constitutes a denial of the defendant's constitutional right and requires reversal of his conviction. The Supreme Court has examined the requirement of effective assistance on only a few occasions, and then not at considerable length. The lower courts, on the other hand, have dealt with it rather frequently, but have varied considerably in both their definition and application of the constitutional standard.

In examining most types of ineffective assistance claims, lower courts traditionally asked whether counsel's inadequacy had turned a trial into a "farce or mockery" or otherwise deprived defendant of "fundamental fairness." See *Beasley v. U. S.,* 491 F.2d 687 (6th Cir. 1974) (collecting cases). Many courts still adhere to this standard, but others have rejected it as too "subjective" and too reflective of a due process analysis rather than the "more stringent requirements" of the Sixth Amendment. Id. These courts apply a standard of "reasonably effective assistance," measured against the customary performance of the lawyer "with ordinary training and skill in the criminal law." Id. Consider also *C. v. Saferian,* 315 N.E. 878 (Mass.1974) ("behavior of counsel falling measurably below that which might be expected from an ordinary fallible lawyer" and thereby depriving defendant of an "otherwise available substantial ground of defense"). The Supreme Court has utilized a similar standard in determining when counsel's mis-evaluation of a constitutional claim might provide a basis for challenging a subsequent guilty plea. See *McMann v. Richardson* and *Tollett v. Henderson* (discussed at pp. 279–281).

Lower courts have also disagreed as to the application of the ineffective assistance standard to the inadequate performance of privately retained counsel. Several courts hold that retained counsel's inadequacies do not present a Fourteenth Amendment issue unless there is "state action" —a requirement met only where the state participates in the inadequacy through the failure of the court to take action to correct ineffective assistance that should have been apparent to the court. *Fitzgerald v. Estelle*, 505 F.2d 1334 (5th Cir. 1974) (collecting cases); *U. S. ex rel. Hart v. Davenport*, 478 F.2d 203 (3d Cir. 1973). Other courts contend that sufficient state action is present in the imposition of a criminal sanction upon a defendant convicted without adequate assistance of counsel and the same constitutional standard of effectiveness therefore should apply whether counsel is retained or appointed. *Wilson v. Rose,* 366 F.2d 611 (9th Cir. 1966). Compare *Fitzgerald v. Estelle* (finding different levels of state obligation and therefore applying a "fundamental unfairness" standard to most retained counsel situations and a "reasonably effective assistance" standard to appointed counsel).

Perhaps the most frequently alleged basis for challenging counsel's effectiveness is his performance at trial—e. g., his failure to object to inadmissible evidence, vigorously cross-examine witnesses, or introduce favorable evidence. Courts express concern that too rigorous application of a competency standard in judging counsel's performance at trial will (1) force the trial judge to intervene whenever possible error is being committed, (2) make lawyers more reluctant to take criminal assignments, (3) place a premium on the lawyer who performs poorly, and (4) permit a lawyer with a desperate case to assure his client a new trial by deliberately committing error. Moreover, courts note that what may look like errors in retrospective could well have reflected sound trial strategy at the time. Accordingly, many courts tend to assume that alleged trial errors or omissions reflect trial strategy, and hold that "mistakes" in "judgment" or "strategy" do not reach the level of constitutional incompetency unless totally without justification. *Frand v. U. S.*, 301 F.2d 102 (10th Cir. 1962). Other courts, applying a "reasonably effective assistance" standard, are more critical in considering alleged tactical justifications, particularly where other action "would have better protected the defendant and was reasonably foreseeable." *Beasley v.*

U. S., supra. Where counsel's own statements or action clearly indicate that alleged mistakes were the product of his ignorance of a legal rule "commonplace to any attorney engaged in criminal trials," courts generally have had much less difficulty finding constitutional incompetency. *P. v. McDowell*, 447 P.2d 97 (Cal.1968). This is true even though only a single mistake was made, provided it was substantial and related to a crucial issue in the case.

Another common ground for attacking the effectiveness of counsel is the late appointment of counsel. Competent assistance of counsel necessarily requires adequate time for preparation, including appropriate investigation, both legal and factual, of all possible defenses. *Coles v. Peyton*, 389 F.2d 224 (4th Cir. 1968). In *Chambers v. Maroney*, 399 U.S. 42 (1970), the Court refused to adopt a "per se rule requiring reversal of every conviction following tardy appointment of counsel." Instead, it emphasized examination of the totality of the circumstances surrounding the tardy appointment. The defendant in *Chambers* had been adequately represented by one legal aid attorney at his original trial, but did not consult with another legal aid attorney, who represented him on re-trial, until a few minutes before that trial began. The Supreme Court stressed that the lower court, on close examination of the record, "found ample grounds for holding that the appearance of a different attorney at the second trial had not resulted in prejudice to petitioner." The rejection of a per se rule in *Chambers* does not bar a court from recognizing a prima facie presumption of ineffective assistance upon a showing of tardy appointment. Under this position, followed by several courts, the burden is then shifted to the prosecution to show that the late appointment did not result in prejudice to the defendant. *Garland v. Cox*, 472 F.2d 875 (4th Cir. 1973).

In contrast to *Chambers*, the Court has approved a per se rule of ineffective assistance where the same attorney represents two defendants whose interests are clearly in conflict. Conflicts of interest exist where codefendants find themselves in "adversary and combative positions," such as when there are factually inconsistent alibis, exculpatory statements by one defendant tending to inculpate the other, or significant discrepancies in the weight of the evidence against the two defendants. *Sawyer v. Brough*, 358 F.2d 70 (4th Cir. 1966). Ordinarily, a reviewing court must examine the trial record to determine whether such a conflict was present, but once this is established, reversal will be required. The client's right to the undivided loyalty of his attorney is "too fundamental and absolute to allow courts to indulge in nice calculations as to the amount of prejudice arising from its denial." *Glasser v. U. S.*, 315 U.S. 60, 76 (1942). But cf. *Morgan v. U. S.*, 396 F.2d 110 (2d Cir. 1968) (suggesting that reversal is unnecessary where any conflict is "so minimal that it could not have affected the result").

41. ASSISTANCE OTHER THAN COUNSEL

Transcripts. The *Griffin-Douglas* rationale (p. 326) has been extended to require the state to furnish the indigent defendant with transcripts of various proceedings where needed to implement defendant's rights. A series of cases have found a denial of equal protection in the state's refusal to provide an indigent appellant with a transcript of various proceedings from which appeals were taken. *Lane v. Brown*, 372 U.S. 477 (1963) (coram nobis hearing); *Long v. Dist. Ct.*, 385 U.S. 192 (1966) (habeas corpus hearing); *Mayer v. Chicago* (p. 336) (misdemeanor trial). Appellate review was not necessarily conditioned on the presentation of a transcript in these cases, but the transcript was readily available and was obviously the preferable means for presenting an account of the relevant proceedings. *Long v. Dist. Ct.*, supra. Compare *Norvell v. Ill.*, 373 U.S. 420 (1963). The Court has noted that the state may satisfy its equal protection obligations by providing an alternative means of reporting trial proceedings (e. g., a stipulated statement of facts), but only if that alternative "places before the appellate court an equivalent report of the events at trial from which the appellant's contention arise." *Draper v. Wash.*, 372 U.S. 487 (1963). Where the grounds of appeal "make out a colorable need for a complete transcript [e. g., defendant contends that the evidence was insufficient for conviction], the burden is on the State to show that only a portion of the transcript or an 'alternative' will suffice for an effective appeal on those grounds." *Mayer v. Chicago* (p. 336). If the transcript is needed to support the appeal, the state cannot deny it by imposing a special prerequisite that the appeal have possible merit. Thus, *Draper v. Wash.*, supra, found unconstitutional a procedure that conditioned furnishing of a transcript upon a trial court determination that the appeal was not frivolous. The Court stressed that this procedure in turn denied the defendant a "record of sufficient completeness" to attack effectively the trial court's finding of frivolity where the issues could only be evaluated through review of a transcript.

The Court has also held that the state must furnish the indigent with transcripts for purposes other than appellate review of the transcribed proceedings. *Roberts v. LaVallee*, 389 U.S. 40 (1967), found a denial of equal protection in the rejection of an indigent defendant's pretrial request for a transcript of a preliminary hearing at which the major state witnesses had testified. A dissenting opinion stressed that both the defendant and his counsel had been present at the hearing and defendant had received a free transcript of the grand jury testimony of the witnesses in question, but the majority emphasized that the state rule providing transcripts only upon payment of a fee clearly "could not meet the 'test' of prior decisions"—"that differences in access to the instruments needed to vindicate legal rights, when based upon the financial situation of the defendant, are repugnant to the constitution." Cf. *Gardner v. Cal.*, 393 U.S. 367 (1969). But note *Britt v. N. C.*, 404 U.S. 226 (1971) (state could refuse transcript of first trial, requested in preparation for a retrial, because of alternatives available in particular case).

Assistance of experts. The Supreme Court has not yet considered whether equal protection or the right to effective assistance of counsel requires state funding of experts to assist counsel in the preparation and presentation of the indigent defendant's case. Such expert assistance might come from accountants, psychiatrists, analysts of scientific evidence, or private investigators. Several lower courts have found that the effective assistance of counsel encompasses such assistance where necessary to present an effective defense. *Bush v. McCollum*, 231 F.Supp. 560 (N.

D.Tex.1964), aff'd, 344 F.2d 672 (5th Cir. 1965).
Other decisions suggest that constitutional support for obtaining the assistance of experts expected to testify at trial also may be found in the
Sixth Amendment right to compulsory process
for obtaining defense witnesses. *P. v. Watson*,
221 N.E.2d 645 (Ill.1966) (see also p. 64). A
few lower court opinions suggest that the state
has no obligation to provide expert assistance,
but those opinions generally were responding to a
defense objection to the appointment of an expert
as a witness for the trial court rather than as an
expert serving the defense alone. *U. S. ex rel.
Smith v. Baldi*, 192 F.2d 540 (3d Cir. 1951), aff'd,
344 U.S. 561 (1951). See also *Roach v. S.*, 140
S.E.2d 919 (Ga.App.1965) (suggesting that a constitutional right to assistance of experts is satisfied by the availability of a "competent and disin-
terested" state medical examiner).

In many jurisdictions, the basic constitutional
question has been avoided through adoption of
statutes or court rules authorizing the trial court
to appoint experts where needed. See, e. g., 18 U.
S.C. § 3006(A). Experts are also appointed in
other jurisdictions without specific authorization.
Frequently, however, the defense counsel must
make a special showing as to the need for an expert's assistance. That requirement itself may be
subject to constitutional attack if it places a substantial burden upon the indigent defendant.

Greenwell v. U. S., 317 F.2d 108 (D.C.Cir. 1963).
Thus, an indigent defendant might object to a requirement of an extensive showing of need on the
ground that it forces him to reveal substantially
more information about the presentation of his
defense than would otherwise be available to the
prosecutor. Cf. *U. S. v. Brodson*, 136 F.Supp. 158
(E.D.Wis.1955), rev'd, 241 F.2d 107 (7th Cir.
1957); *Williams v. Fla.* (p. 50); *Wardius v. Ore.*
(p. 50).

CHAPTER 8

RAISING CONSTITUTIONAL CLAIMS

---

42. FEDERAL AND STATE PRO-CEDURAL REQUIREMENTS

Introduction. Both federal and state courts impose various procedural requirements that have special application to the presentation of constitutional claims. Most jurisdictions, for example, require that objections to the admission of evidence obtained by an illegal search be presented by a pretrial motion to suppress. A pretrial objection is also required in many jurisdictions in attacking the constitutional validity of a confession or a lineup identification. In many states, failure to comply with these requirements will result in automatic forfeiture of the constitutional claim unless the defendant "could not reasonably" have made the motion prior to trial. N.J.Rule Crim.Proc. 3:5–7. In others, the forfeiture will not be automatic even where a timely objection could have been made, but objections at trial will be considered only at the discretion of the trial court. Appellate courts have stressed that such discretion should be exercised liberally, but they

also have been very reluctant to overturn a trial
judge's refusal to consider an "untimely" objection. *P. v. Ferguson*, 135 N.W.2d 357 (Mich.
1965).

Those jurisdictions that do not require pretrial
objections to unconstitutionally obtained evidence
usually insist that the constitutional claim be
raised at the time the evidence is introduced at
trial. Failure to make a contemporaneous objection results in loss of the objection unless the
trial court, in its discretion, deems it appropriate
to consider a subsequent claim.

Procedural restrictions relating to the timing
and form of objections also are imposed on other
motions that may encompass constitutional
claims—e. g., objections to the composition of
grand or petit juries, and requests for change of
venue. Failure to comply with these requirements will result in either an automatic forfeiture
of the objection or a restriction on consideration
of delayed objections within the discretion of the
trial court.

Constitutional limitations. If the state or federal procedural requirement is so arbitrary as to
deny the defendant a fair opportunity to raise his
claim, application of that requirement may itself
constitute an independent violation of due process. *Reece v. Ga.*, 350 U.S. 85 (1955). Similarly,
a procedural regulation tied to a particular con-

stitutional objection and imposing a substantial
burden upon anyone raising that objection may
be viewed as violating the constitutional guarantee that serves as the basis for the objection. Cf.
Simmons v. U. S. (p. 304). The Supreme Court
has rarely found it necessary, however, to examine the constitutionality of procedural requirements that arguably are invalid under these
standards. In federal cases, the procedural requirements are promulgated by the Court itself
and can appropriately be interpreted so as to
avoid constitutional difficulties. In state cases,
the questionable state procedural rules ordinarily
fail under the "adequate state ground" doctrine
(§ 43), and the Court can then proceed to review
directly the basic constitutional claim that the
state court had refused to consider as inappro-
priately raised.

43. APPELLATE REVIEW

**Procedural forfeitures and the "plain error" ex-
ception.** As a general practice, appellate courts
will review only those claims that properly were
presented at trial. However, appellate courts also
have the authority to consider "plain errors affecting substantial rights of defendants" even
though those errors were not pressed below.
Fed.Rule Crim.Proc. 52(b). Several appellate
courts recently have shown a greater willingness

to note potential "plain errors" of a constitutional dimension, particularly since the expansion of post-conviction relief (see §§ 44–45) makes it likely that those errors will eventually be considered, in any event, on collateral attack. *Alexander v. U. S.*, 390 F.2d 101 (5th Cir. 1968). Others have expressed a willingness, for similar reasons, to consider constitutional issues not raised below even when the likelihood of error is not so obvious. *S. v. Knoblock*, 170 N.W.2d 781 (Wis. 1969). Appellate courts remain reluctant, however, to consider constitutional claims not raised below where the factual record on the claim has not been fully developed. This is frequently the case with search and seizure claims; even when the testimony suggesting an illegal search came from one of the prosecution's own witnesses, it is often possible that, if defense counsel had objected, other witnesses might have been questioned on the same point and might have given contradictory testimony. *Sykes v. U. S.*, 373 F.2d 607 (5th Cir. 1966).

Supreme Court review of state decisions: the adequate state ground limitation. Supreme Court review of state court decisions is limited to consideration of federal questions, including, most notably, constitutional questions. A constitutional claim will not be considered, however, if the state court ruling is based on a legitimate state ground apart from the constitutional claim, since that ground would necessarily control the outcome of the case even if the Court were to find a constitutional violation. Accordingly, if a state court refuses to consider a constitutional claim because the defendant failed to comply with a state procedural requirement, the Supreme Court will not review that claim if the procedural forfeiture constitutes an "adequate state ground." To be viewed as an adequate state ground, both the state procedural requirement and the forfeiture sanction must serve a "legitimate state interest." *Henry v. Miss.*, 379 U.S. 443 (1965).

Most of the state procedural rulings that have been rejected as not based on an adequate state ground have involved either a clear attempt to manipulate state rules to deprive the defendant of his federal rights, or the application of a state rule in such an arbitrary manner as "to force resort to arid ritual of meaningless form." *Staub v. City of Baxley*, 355 U.S. 313 (1958). However, *Henry v. Miss.*, supra, perhaps suggests a somewhat broader view. The majority there suggested, but did not decide, that petitioner's failure to comply with a contemporaneous objection requirement (see p. 372) would not constitute an adequate state ground in a particular case if petitioner's subsequent objection, though untimely, appropriately served the same interests in judicial efficiency as a contemporaneous objection.

44. POST–CONVICTION REMEDIES:
FEDERAL HABEAS CORPUS FOR
STATE PRISONERS

Introduction. The writ of *habeas corpus ad subjiciendum* is a judicial order directing a government official (e. g., a warden) to bring a person within his custody before the court so that it can inquire into the legality of that custody and discharge that person if the custody is deemed invalid. The writ is given constitutional recognition in Article I, § 9, which prohibits suspension of the writ "unless when in cases of rebellion or invasion, the public safety may require it." The constitutional mandate does not define the precise scope of the writ, and the first judiciary act authorized federal courts to issue the writ only on behalf of prisoners "in custody under the authority of the United States." In 1867 the writ was made applicable to any person "restrained of his * * * liberty in violation of the Constitution," including state prisoners.

Initially, the writ only permitted a prisoner to challenge a state conviction on constitutional grounds that related to the jurisdiction of the state court. But the scope of the inquiry was gradually expanded over the years, and *Fay v. Noia*, 372 U.S. 391 (1963), concluded that the writ now extends to all constitutional challenges. A subsequent concurring opinion in *Schneckloth v. Bustamonte*, 412 U.S. 218 (1973), suggests, however, that the scope of the writ may be subject to reconsideration. The concurring opinion, having the substantial support of four justices, urged that the Court reconsider prior decisions and hold that prisoners cannot collaterally challenge their convictions on the ground that the state court admitted evidence obtained by an unconstitutional search. The concurring opinion argued that unconstitutional search claims do not concern the reliability of the adjudication of guilt, and the deterrent function of the exclusionary rule is not served by permitting collateral attacks based on that rule. The majority in *Schneckloth* did not reach the issue posed in the concurring opinion. See also *Parker v. N. C.*, 397 U.S. 790 (1970) (raising the question as to whether racial exclusion in grand jury selection "is open [for consideration] in a federal habeas corpus action").

Impact of prior adjudication. In *Brown v. Allen,* 344 U.S. 443 (1953), and *Townsend v. Sain,* 372 U.S. 293 (1963), the Supreme Court emphasized that federal constitutional claims of state prisoners were cognizable in federal habeas corpus proceedings even though those claims had been fully adjudicated by the state court. The prisoner is entitled to an independent, federal court determination of his federal claim, and the state court rulings therefore cannot be binding upon the fed-

eral habeas court.   Both *Brown* and *Townsend*
noted, however, that the state court's findings of
fact ordinarily can be accepted by the federal habeas court.   Following *Townsend,* the federal habeas corpus act was amended to establish a presumption of correctness for state factual findings
unless certain specified deficiencies existed in the
state proceedings.   See 28 U.S.C. § 2254(d);
Townsend v. Sain, supra; *LaVallee v. Delle Rose,*
410 U.S. 690 (1973).

Impact of procedural "forfeitures."   Prior to
Fay v. Noia, 372 U.S. 391 (1963), a defendant's
forfeiture of his constitutional claim in a state
court through failure to comply with valid state
procedural requirements was viewed as preclud-
ing consideration of that claim on application for
habeas corpus.   *Fay* rejected this position in
holding that the "adequate state ground" limitation, which bars Supreme Court appellate review
following a valid procedural forfeiture [see § 43],
does not apply to federal habeas corpus.   The
Court stressed that the "jurisdictional prerequisite [for issuance of the writ] is not the judgment of the state court, but detention *simplici-
ter*," and therefore the exercise of habeas jurisdiction should not be controlled by the scope of
the state court's ruling.   *Fay,* nevertheless, did
recognize a "limited discretion" in the habeas
court to deny relief to an applicant whose procedural default in the state proceedings reflected a

decision to "deliberately bypass the orderly procedure of the state court." In such a case, denial
of federal habeas relief is justified under the "equitable principles" that traditionally govern the
exercise of habeas jurisdiction. That justification is lost, however, if the state courts have subsequently considered the constitutional claim on
the merits notwithstanding the deliberate bypass.
Warden v. Hayden, 387 U.S. 294 (1967).

The *Fay* opinion did not explore at length what
constitutes a "deliberate bypass", but it did stress
that the determination of that issue should be in
accord with the "classic definition of waiver—'an
intentional relinquishment or abandonment of a
known right or privilege.'" It also noted that
the bypass must reflect the "considered choice of
the petitioner. * * * A choice made by counsel
not participated in by the petitioner does not automatically bar relief." In *Henry v. Miss.*, supra,
however, the Court stated that counsel's strategic
decision not to object to the admission of illegally
seized evidence could constitute a deliberate bypass even though there had been no consultation
with the defendant on that strategy.

Lower courts have divided as to when a deliberate bypass or "waiver" may exist notwithstanding defendant's lack of participation in counsel's decision not to exercise one of defendant's
constitutional rights. Several variables have been
viewed as relevant, including (1) the techni-

cal or strategic use of the right, (2) the fundamental nature of the right, and (3) the opportunity for meaningful consultation prior to the point at which the right should have been exercised. *U. S. ex rel. Bruno v. Herold*, 408 F.2d 125 (2d Cir. 1969). Decisions such as the waiver of a jury are generally viewed as requiring defendant's personal participation, while the decision not to object to the introduction of evidence on Fourth Amendment grounds is generally treated as not requiring that participation. *Nelson v. Cal.*, 346 F.2d 73 (9th Cir. 1965). Compare, however, *Lanier v. S.*, 486 P.2d 981 (Alaska 1971); *Tollet v. Henderson*, 411 U.S. 258, 271 (1973) (Marshall, J., dis.).

Exhaustion of state remedies. Federal courts traditionally have refused to consider habeas applications of state prisoners who have failed to exhaust currently available state remedies. This qualification, now codified in the federal habeas statute [28 U.S.C. § 2254(b)], stems from considerations of federal-state comity rather than any inherent limitation upon the power of the federal courts. *Fay*, supra at 420. In its most common application, the exhaustion requirement precludes consideration of a habeas application by a prisoner whose claim was raised at trial and is still subject to state appellate review. It also precludes consideration of claims that were not properly raised in the original state proceedings, but are still open to consideration by the state courts in post-conviction proceedings. *Ex parte Hawk*, 321 U.S. 114 (1944). However, "exhaustion of one of several alternative [state] remedies is all that is necessary." *Brown v. Allen*, 344 U.S. 443 (1953). If the applicant's claim was considered by the state courts on direct appeal, he is not required to initiate a state collateral attack even if the state post-conviction remedy would permit reconsideration of his claim.

Custody. The federal habeas corpus statute provides that the writ "shall not extend to a prisoner unless he is in custody * * *." The "custody-requirement" is derived from the procedural function of the writ as an order directing the jailer to bring his prisoner before the court, but it no longer is interpreted as requiring such immediate physical control over the applicant as the form of the writ might suggest. In *Jones v. Cunningham*, 371 U.S. 236 (1963), for example, the Court held that an applicant on parole was subject to sufficient "restraints" to "invoke the help of the Great Writ." These restraints included restrictions upon movement, employment, and association imposed by typical parole conditions, and the "constant fear that a single deviation, however slight, might be enough to result in his being returned to prison * * * with few, if any, of the procedural safeguards that normally must be and are provided to those charged with crime." The

Jones rationale has been applied to prisoners on probation, where similar restraints are imposed. *Benson v. Cal.*, 328 F.2d 159 (9th Cir. 1964). See also *Hensley v. Municipal Court*, 411 U.S. 345 (1973) (*Jones* applicable to petitioner released on his own recognizance in conjunction with a stay of sentence execution pending final disposition of his habeas application).

In *Peyton v. Rowe*, 391 U.S. 54 (1968), the Court held that a defendant serving the first of two consecutive sentences was "in custody" for the aggregate term of both sentences and therefore could immediately challenge the second sentence. Postponing adjudication of his claim against the second sentence until he started to serve that sentence would undermine the effectiveness of the habeas remedy. The delay might, for example, make it far more difficult for the state and the applicant to present factual material relevant to the claim when the petition was finally considered. Also, if delay were permitted, the defendant would probably serve part of the second sentence before his challenge was decided, and thus he might be unnecessarily incarcerated under a conviction eventually held unconstitutional. *Braden v. 30th Judicial Dist.*, 410 U.S. 484 (1973), relying upon *Peyton*, noted that a defendant serving a sentence in one jurisdiction, but subject to a detainer from a second jurisdiction on a pending sentence to be served there, can currently utilize habeas corpus to challenge the conviction in the second jurisdiction.

45. POST–CONVICTION REMEDIES—FEDERAL PRISONER (28 U.S.C. § 2255)

Relation to habeas corpus. In 1948, Congress adopted a statutory post-conviction remedy for federal prisoners, 28 U.S.C. § 2255, that was designed to serve as a substitute for habeas corpus. The primary objective of section 2255 was to shift the burden of post-conviction review from courts in the district of incarceration, where habeas petitions were filed, to the court that originally imposed sentence. The section was not intended to alter the scope of the remedy available to federal prisoners, and the Supreme Court has held that section 2255 will be viewed as providing "a remedy exactly commensurate with that which had been available by habeas corpus." *Hill v. U. S.*, 368 U.S. 424 (1962); *U. S. v. Hayman*, 342 U. S. 205 (1952). With respect to constitutional claims, the section 2255 remedy is similar in many respects to the habeas corpus remedy for state prisoners, but there are certain significant distinctions.

Scope. Section 2255, like habeas corpus, extends to all constitutional claims, see, e. g., *Kaufman v. U. S.*, 394 U.S. 217 (1969), but this breadth of coverage also may be subject to reconsideration in light of *Schneckloth v. Bustamonte,* discussed at p. 377.

Where the applicant's constitutional claim was previously decided on the merits, the court considering the section 2255 application ordinarily need not review that claim. *Castellana v. U. S.,* 378 F.2d 231 (2d Cir. 1967); *Sanders v. U. S.,* 373 U.S. 1 (1963). The principle of *Brown v. Allen* and *Townsend v. Sain* (p. 377), requiring independent federal determination of constitutional claims resolved in state courts, obviously has no bearing upon a section 2255 proceeding. Since the trial ruling in a section 2255 proceeding also was rendered by a federal court, that ruling need not be reconsidered unless it was based on a "deficient" factual adjudication or on legal principles that subsequently have been modified so as to possibly produce a different result. In determining whether a new factual adjudication is required, the section 2255 court applies standards largely similar to those established in *Townsend,* supra.

Where the constitutional claim could have been, but was not raised properly in the prior federal proceedings (either at trial or on direct appeal), the deliberate bypass standard of *Fay v. Noia* apparently applies unless a specific statutory provision or Federal Rule of Criminal Procedure provides otherwise. Thus, in *Kaufman v. U. S.*, supra, the Court held that the district court could not refuse to consider a Fourth Amendment claim presented in a section 2255 application simply because that claim had not been presented on direct appeal. As under *Fay*, the failure to comply with a procedural requirement relating to direct review may only preclude collateral attack if the failure was a product of a deliberate bypass decision, and, even then, the section 2255 court may disregard the bypass if the "ends of justice" would be served by such action. *Sanders v. U. S.*, supra. Although the *Fay* standard initially appeared to apply to all constitutional claims not properly presented in earlier proceedings, *Davis v. U. S.*, 411 U.S. 233 (1973), noted that a specific forfeiture requirement approved by Congress would prevail in a section 2255 proceeding even though that requirement was more restrictive than the deliberate bypass rule. In *Davis*, a divided Court held that a claim of grand jury discrimination, not raised before trial as required by Fed.R.Crim.P. 12(b), could not subsequently be presented in a § 2255 proceeding even if the failure to comply with Fed.R.Crim.P. 12(b) was not a deliberate bypass. Rule 12(b) provides that all claims based on defects in the institution of the prosecution that are not raised before trial are deemed to be "waived" unless the trial judge for "good cause" grants relief from the waiver. The

Davis opinion stressed the express waiver clause in Rule 12(b) and the acceptance of the Rule by Congress. Although the Rule does not refer to § 2255 proceedings, the majority found it "inconceivable" that Congress could have "intended to perversely negate the Rule's purpose by permitting * * * [a] much more liberal requirement of waiver in federal habeas proceedings."

Section 2255 proceedings are roughly similar to state prisoner habeas proceedings in the significance attached to the availability of other procedures for raising constitutional claims. A policy comparable to that reflected in the exhaustion-of-state-remedies requirement (p. 380) is applied to section 2255 proceedings in the interests of "the orderly administration of the criminal law." *Bowen v. Johnston*, 306 U.S. 19 (1939). Thus, section 2255 motions will not be entertained during the pendency of a direct appeal.

Section 2255, like habeas corpus, also is limited by a "custody requirement," and the rulings expanding the concept of custody as applied to habeas corpus generally are also applicable under section 2255. It should be noted, moreover, that when the petitioner is no longer within federal custody, another post-conviction remedy, the writ of coram nobis, may be utilized to raise certain types of constitutional issues. See *U. S. v. Morgan*, 346 U.S. 502 (1954).

46. STATE POST–CONVICTION REMEDIES

Introduction. Almost every state has one or more post-conviction procedures that permit prisoners to challenge at least some constitutional violations. A substantial group of states have adopted special post-conviction statutes or court rules, roughly similar to section 2255, that encompass all constitutional claims. *Case v. Neb.*, 381 U.S. 336, 338 (1965) (Brennan, J., con.). Others, following the federal habeas corpus statute, have held that at least some constitutional violations are jurisdictional defects cognizable under a common law or statutory writ of habeas corpus. *Ex Parte Story*, 203 P.2d 474 (Okla. Crim.1949). The writ of coram nobis is also viewed in several states as an appropriate remedy for presenting certain types of constitutional claims. *P. v. Cooper*, 120 N.E.2d 813 (N.Y.1954).

The failure of a state to provide any of the remedies noted above, or a similar remedy in a different form (e. g., a broadly fashioned "delayed motion for new trial"), may create constitutional difficulties. Several commentators have contended that the state's duty to recognize constitutional claims at trial carries with it a correlative duty to create a post-conviction procedure permitting consideration of at least those constitutional claims that could not readily be raised at

[*387*]

trial (e. g., ineffective assistance of counsel). The Supreme Court has had no occasion to rule on this issue, and the widespread state adoption of various post-conviction remedies may have rendered the issue moot. *Case v. Neb.*, supra.

Scope. State courts generally will not reconsider on collateral attack constitutional issues that were raised and decided on the merits at trial and on appeal. Otherwise, many of the currently available state remedies are as extensive in scope as federal habeas corpus for state prisoners. Those remedies frequently permit consideration of claims that were not raised in prior proceedings due to inadvertence. They also follow the lead of *Jones v. Cunningham*, supra, and have extended custody requirements to include persons not within the immediate physical control of the respondent. *In re Cawley*, 120 N.W.2d 816 (Mich.1963). Other states, however, provide much narrower remedies. They apply only to prisoners and permit consideration only of constitutional claims that could not reasonably have been raised at trial.

INDEX

References are to Pages

INDEX

References are to Pages

INDEX

INDEX

INDEX

INDEX

References are to Pages

INDEX

INDEX

INDEX

INDEX

References are to Pages